국제토셀위원회

# TOSEL
# 실전문제집 ②

# HIGH
# JUNIOR

최신 기출 경향반영 실전모의고사 수록
국제토셀위원회 공식교재

# CONTENTS



OMR 카드

정답과 해설  별책

# About this book

## ① Actual Test

토셀 최신 유형을 반영하여
실전 모의고사를 4회 실었습니다.
수험자들의 토셀 시험 대비 및
적응력 향상에 도움이 됩니다.

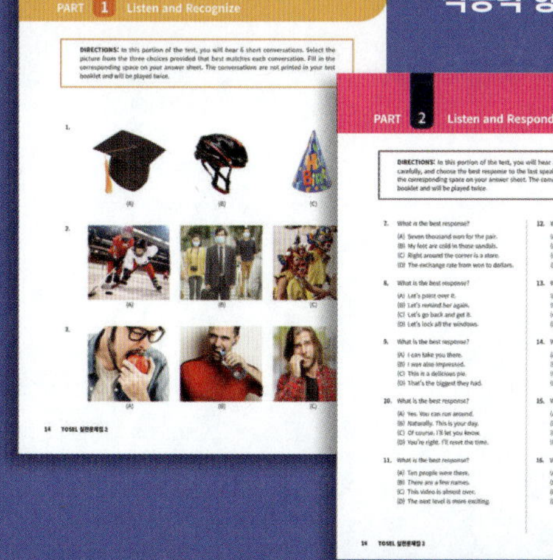

## ② Appendix

## ③ Answer

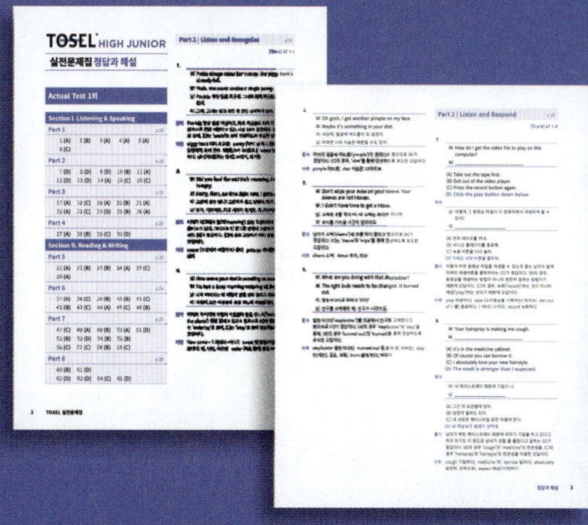

필수 어휘를 포함해 모의고사
빈출 어휘 목록을 수록했습니다.
평소 어휘 정리뿐만 아니라
시험 직전 대비용으로 활용 가능합니다.

자세한 해설과 문제 풀이로
오답 확인 및 시험 대비를 위한 정리가 가능합니다.

1
영어를 시작하는 단계

2
영어의 밑바탕을
다지는 단계

3
영어의 도약단계

TOSEL

TOSEL
Cocoon

유치원생

TOSEL

TOSEL
Pre Starter

초등 1,2학년

TOSEL

TOSEL
Starter

초등 3,4학년

TOSEL

TOSEL
Basic

초등 5,6학년

4
영어의 실전단계

5
영어의 고급화 단계

6
영어의 완성단계

TOSEL

TOSEL

TOSEL

TOSEL
Junior
중학생

TOSEL
High Junior
고등학생

TOSEL
Advanced
대학생, 직장인

# About TOSEL<sup>®</sup>



**TOSEL**은 각급 학교 교과과정과 연령별 인지단계를 고려하여 단계별 난이도와 문항으로
영어 숙달 정도를 측정하는 영어 사용자 중심의 맞춤식 영어능력인증 시험제도입니다.
평가유형에 따른 개인별 장점과 단점을 파악하고, 개인별 영어학습 방향을 제시하는 성적분석자료를 제공하여
영어능력 종합검진 서비스를 제공함으로써 영어 사용자인 소비자와
영어능력 평가를 토대로 영어교육을 담당하는 교사 및 기관 인사관리자인 공급자를
모두 만족시키는 영어능력인증 평가입니다.

**TOSEL**은 인지적-학문적 언어 사용의 유창성 (Cognitive-Academic Language Proficiency, CALP)과
기본적-개인적 의사소통능력 (Basic Interpersonal Communication Skill, BICS)을
엄밀히 구분하여 수험자의 언어능력을 가장 친밀하게 평가하는 시험입니다.

## 대상

유아, 초, 중, 고등학생,
대학생 및 직장인 등 성인

## 목적

한국인의 영어구사능력 증진과
비영어권 국가의 영어 사용자의
영어구사능력 증진

## 용도

실질적인 영어구사능력 평가 +
입학전형 및 인재선발 등에 활용
및 직무역량별 인재 배치

## 연혁

| | |
|---|---|
| 2002.02 | 국제토셀위원회 창설 (수능출제위원역임 전국대학 영어전공교수진 중심) |
| 2004.09 | TOSEL 고려대학교 국제어학원 공동인증시험 실시 |
| 2006.04 | EBS 한국교육방송공사 주관기관 참여 |
| 2006.05 | 민족사관고등학교 입학전형에 반영 |
| 2008.12 | 고려대학교 편입학시험 TOSEL 유형으로 대체 |
| 2009.01 | 서울시 공무원 근무평정에 TOSEL 점수 가산점 부여 |
| 2009.01 | 전국 대부분 외고, 자사고 입학전형에 TOSEL 반영 |
| | (한영외국어고등학교, 한일고등학교, 고양외국어고등학교, 과천외국어고등학교, 김포외국어고등학교, |
| | 명지외국어고등학교, 부산국제외국어고등학교, 부일외국어 고등학교, 성남외국어고등학교, 인천외국어고등학교, |
| | 전북외국어고등학교, 대전외국어고등학교, 청주외국어고등학교, 강원외국어고등학교, 전남외국어고등학교) |
| 2009.12 | 청심국제중·고등학교 입학전형 TOSEL 반영 |
| 2009.12 | 한국외국어교육학회, 팬코리아영어교육학회, 한국음성학회, 한국응용언어학회 TOSEL 인증 |
| 2010.03 | 고려대학교, TOSEL 출제기관 및 공동 인증기관으로 참여 |
| 2010.07 | 경찰청 공무원 임용 TOSEL 성적 가산점 부여 |
| 2014.04 | 전국 200개 초등학교 단체 응시 실시 |
| 2017.03 | 중앙일보 주관기관 참여 |
| 2018.11 | 관공서, 대기업 등 100여 개 기관에서 TOSEL 반영 |
| 2019.06 | 미얀마 TOSEL 도입 발족식 |
| | 베트남 TOSEL 도입 협약식 |
| 2019.11 | 2020학년도 고려대학교 편입학전형 반영 |
| 2020.04 | 국토교통부 국가자격시험 TOSEL 반영 |
| 2021.07 | 소방청 간부후보생 선발시험 TOSEL 반영 |

# About TOSEL®  —————  TOSEL에 대하여

## What's TOSEL?

"Test of Skills in the English Language"

TOSEL은 비영어권 국가의 영어 사용자를 대상으로 영어구사능력을 측정하여
그 결과를 공식 인증하는 영어능력인증 시험제도입니다.

## 영어 사용자 중심의 맞춤식 영어능력 인증 시험제도

### 맞춤식 평가

**획일적인 평가에서
세분화된 평가로의 전환**

TOSEL은 응시자의 연령별 인지단계에
따라 별도의 문항과 난이도를 적용하여
평가함으로써 평가의 목적과 용도에
적합한 평가 시스템을
구축하였습니다.

### 공정성과 신뢰성 확보

**국제토셀위원회의 역할**

TOSEL은 고려대학교가 출제
및 인증기관으로 참여하였고
대학입학수학능력시험
출제위원 교수들이 중심이 된
국제토셀위원회가 주관하여
사회적 공정성과 신뢰성을 확보한
평가 제도입니다.

### 수입대체 효과

**외화유출 차단 및 국위선양**

TOSEL은 해외시험응시로 인한
외화의 유출을 막는 수입대체의 효과를
기대할 수 있습니다. TOSEL의 문항과
시험제도는 비영어권 국가에 수출하여
국위선양에 기여하고 있습니다.

# Why TOSEL 왜 TOSEL인가

### 01 학교 시험 폐지

일선 학교에서 중간, 기말고사 폐지로 인해 객관적인 영어 평가 제도의 부재가 우려됩니다. 그러나 전국단위로 연간 4번 시행되는 TOSEL 평가시험을 통해 학생들은 정확한 역량과 체계적인 학습방향을 꾸준히 진단받을 수 있습니다.

### 02 연령별/단계별 대비로 영어학습 점검

TOSEL은 응시자의 연령별 인지단계 및 영어 학습 단계에 따라 총 7단계로 구성되었습니다. 각 단계에 알맞은 문항유형과 난이도를 적용해 모든 연령 및 학습 과정에 맞추어 가장 효율적으로 영어실력을 평가할 수 있도록 개발된 영어시험입니다.

### 03 학교내신성적 향상

TOSEL은 학년별 교과과정과 연계하여 학교에서 배우는 내용을 학습하고 평가할 수 있도록 문항 및 주제를 구성하여 내신영어 향상을 위한 최적의 솔루션을 제공합니다.

### 04 수능대비 직결

유아, 초, 중등시절 어렵지 않고 즐겁게 학습해 온 영어이지만, 수능시험준비를 위해 접하는 영어의 문항 및 유형 난이도에 주춤하게 됩니다. 이를 대비하기 위해 TOSEL은 유아부터 성인까지 점진적인 학습을 통해 수능대비를 자연적으로 해나갈 수 있습니다.

### 05 진학과 취업에 대비한 필수 스펙관리

개인별 '학업성취기록부' 발급을 통해 영어학업성취이력을 꾸준히 기록한 영어학습 포트폴리오를 제공하여 영어학습 이력을 관리할 수 있습니다.

### 06 자기소개서에 토셀 기재

개별적인 진로 적성 Report를 제공하여 진로를 파악하고 자기소개서 작성시 적극적으로 활용할 수 있는 객관적인 자료를 제공합니다.

### 07 영어학습 동기부여

시험실시 후 응시자 모두에게 수여되는 인증서는 영어학습에 대한 자신감과 성취감을 고취시키고 동기를 부여합니다.

### 08 AI 분석 영어학습 솔루션

200만 명의 응시데이터를 기반으로 영어인증시험 제도 중 세계 최초로 인공지능이 분석한 개인별 AI 정밀진단 성적표를 제공합니다. 최첨단 AI 정밀진단 성적표는 최적의 영어학습 솔루션을 제시하여 영어 학습에 소요되는 시간과 노력을 획기적으로 절감해줍니다.

### 09 명예의 전당, 우수협력기관 지정

우수교육기관은 'TOSEL 우수 협력 기관'에 지정되고, 각 시/도별, 최고득점자를 명예의 전당에 등재합니다.

# Evaluation —— 평가



## 평가의 기본원칙

TOSEL은 PBT(Paper Based Test)를 통하여 간접평가와 직접평가를 모두 시행합니다.

**TOSEL**은 언어의 네 가지 요소인 **읽기, 듣기, 말하기, 쓰기 영역을 모두 평가합니다.**

문자언어
음성언어

읽기능력
쓰기능력

듣기능력
말하기능력

대한민국 대표 영어능력 인증 시험제도

**TOSEL**®

| | |
|---|---|
| **Reading 읽기** | 모든 레벨의 읽기 영역은 직접 평가 방식으로 측정합니다. |
| **Listening 듣기** | 모든 레벨의 듣기 영역은 직접 평가 방식으로 측정합니다. |
| **Writing 쓰기** | 모든 레벨의 쓰기 영역은 간접 평가 방식으로 측정합니다. |
| **Speaking 말하기** | 모든 레벨의 말하기 영역은 간접 평가 방식으로 측정합니다. |

**TOSEL**은 연령별 인지단계를 고려하여 **아래와 같이 7단계로 나누어 평가합니다.**

|  | | |
|---|---|---|
| **1** 단계 | TOSEL® COCOON | 5~7세의 미취학 아동 |
| **2** 단계 | TOSEL® Pre-STARTER | 초등학교 1~2학년 |
| **3** 단계 | TOSEL® STARTER | 초등학교 3~4학년 |
| **4** 단계 | TOSEL® BASIC | 초등학교 5~6학년 |
| **5** 단계 | TOSEL® JUNIOR | 중학생 |
| **6** 단계 | TOSEL® HIGH JUNIOR | 고등학생 |
| **7** 단계 | TOSEL® ADVANCED | 대학생 및 성인 |

# Grade Report 성적표 및 인증서

## 개인 AI 정밀진단 성적표

**십 수년간 전국단위 정기시험으로 축적된 빅데이터를 교육공학적으로 분석 · 활용하여 산출한 개인별 성적자료**

정확한 영어능력진단 / 섹션별 · 파트별 영어능력 및 균형 진단 / 명예의 전당 등재 여부 / 온라인 최적화된 개인별 상세 성적자료를 위한 QR코드 / 응시지역, 동일학년, 전국에서의 학생의 위치

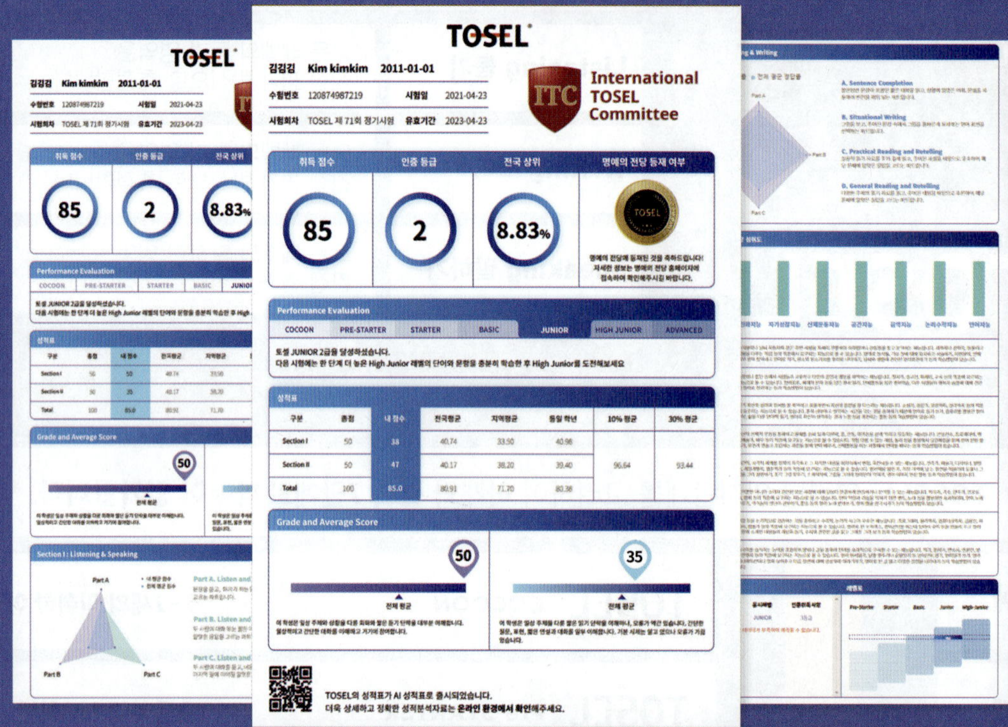

## 단체 및 기관 응시자 AI 통계 분석 자료

십 수년간 전국단위 정기시험으로 **축적된 빅데이터를 교육공학적으로 분석 · 활용**하여 산출한 응시자 통계 분석 자료

- 단체 내 레벨별 평균성적추이, LR평균 점수, 표준편차 파악
- 타 지역 내 다른 단체와의 점수 종합 비교 / 단체 내 레벨별 학생분포 파악
- 동일 지역 내 다른 단체 레벨별 응시자의 평균 나이 비교
- 동일 지역 내 다른 단체 명예의 전당 등재 인원 수 비교
- 동일 지역 내 다른 단체 최고점자의 최고 점수 비교
- 동일 지역 내 다른 응시자들의 수 비교

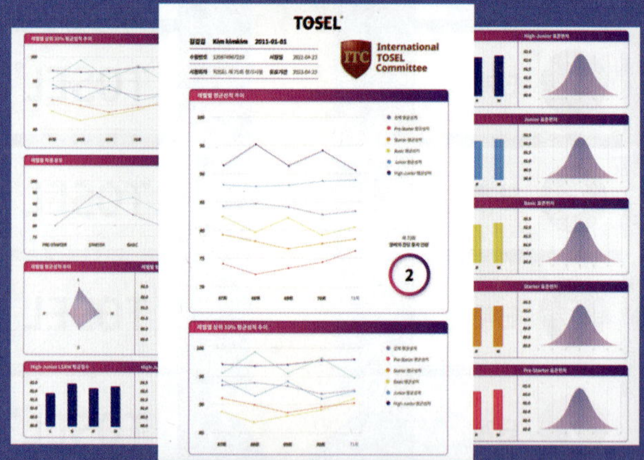

## '토셀 명예의 전당' 등재

특별시, 광역시, 도 별 **1등 선발**
(7개시 9개도 **1등 선발**)

*홈페이지 로그인 - 시험결과 - 명예의 전당에서
 해당자 등재 증명서 출력 가능

## '학업성취기록부'에 토셀 인증등급 기재

개인별 **'학업성취기록부'** 평생 발급
진학과 취업을 대비한 **필수 스펙관리**

## 인증서

**대한민국 초,중,고등학생의 영어숙달능력 평가 결과 공식인증**

고려대학교 인증획득 (2010. 03)   팬코리아영어교육학회 인증획득 (2009. 10)   한국응용언어학회 인증획득 (2009. 11)

한국외국어교육학회 인증획득 (2009. 12)   한국음성학회 인증획득 (2009. 12)

# Actual Test 1

# Section I

## Listening and Speaking

In SECTION I, you will be asked to demonstrate how well you understand spoken English. You will have approximately 25 minutes to complete this section. There are 30 questions separated into four parts, and directions are given for each part. You must mark your answers on the answer sheet provided.

**Part** **1** Listen and Recognize

6 Questions

**Part** **2** Listen and Respond

10 Questions

**Part** **3** Short Conversations

10 Questions

**Part** **4** Talks

4 Questions

**DIRECTIONS:** In this portion of the test, you will hear 6 short conversations. Select the picture from the three choices provided that best matches each conversation. Fill in the corresponding space on your answer sheet. The conversations are not printed in your test booklet and will be played twice.

1.

(A)      (B)      (C)

2.

(A)      (B)      (C)

3.

 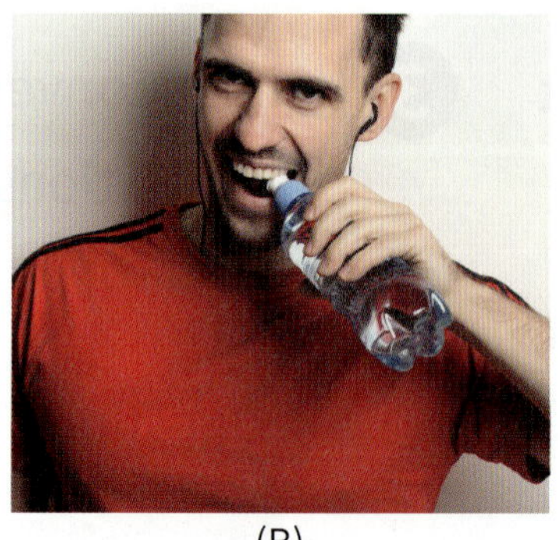 

(A)      (B)      (C)

4.

(A)   (B)   (C)

5.

(A)   (B)   (C)

6.

(A)   (B)   (C)

**DIRECTIONS:** In this portion of the test, you will hear 10 incomplete conversations. Listen carefully, and choose the best response to the last speaker from the choices provided. Fill in the corresponding space on your answer sheet. The conversations are not printed in your test booklet and will be played twice.

7.  What is the best response?

(A) Seven thousand won for the pair.
(B) My feet are cold in those sandals.
(C) Right around the corner is a store.
(D) The exchange rate from won to dollars.

8.  What is the best response?

(A) Let's paint over it.
(B) Let's remind her again.
(C) Let's go back and get it.
(D) Let's lock all the windows.

9.  What is the best response?

(A) I can take you there.
(B) I was also impressed.
(C) This is a delicious pie.
(D) That's the biggest they had.

10.  What is the best response?

(A) Yes. You can run around.
(B) Naturally. This is your day.
(C) Of course. I'll let you know.
(D) You're right. I'll reset the time.

11.  What is the best response?

(A) Ten people were there.
(B) There are a few names.
(C) This video is almost over.
(D) The next level is more exciting.

12.  What is the best response?

(A) They're the same price.
(B) But I'm sleepy right now.
(C) Your sleeping bag is here.
(D) I can reach the light for you.

13.  What is the best response?

(A) I'm not sure of its name.
(B) It is absolutely stunning.
(C) That's as far as I can walk.
(D) Let's wait until the sun rises.

14.  What is the best response?

(A) About five years old.
(B) We got him a week ago.
(C) She's a great little puppy.
(D) He was always quite heavy.

15.  What is the best response?

(A) Why not join a gym?
(B) How about a little pie?
(C) Is math really that hard?
(D) Would art class help me?

16.  What is the best response?

(A) Weren't his legs tired?
(B) Do they hunt for deer?
(C) So it supposedly has ghosts?
(D) Don't you dance better than her?

# PART 3 — Short Conversations



**DIRECTIONS:** In this portion of the test, you will hear a series of 10 short conversations. Choose the correct answer for each question from the choices provided and fill in the corresponding space on your answer sheet. The conversations are not printed in your test booklet and will be played twice.

17. Where does this conversation most likely take place?

   (A) bakery
   (B) butcher's
   (C) barber shop
   (D) beauty shop

18. What does the man ask the woman to do?

   (A) turn down a TV
   (B) fix a broken TV set
   (C) take out a barking dog
   (D) finish her music homework

19. What profession does the boy want to have?

   (A) artist
   (B) doctor
   (C) lawyer
   (D) engineer

20. Why does the woman call the man?

   (A) to reserve a tennis court
   (B) to ask about bowling rates
   (C) to inquire about a driver's license.
   (D) to learn the dates of a shopping sale

21. What is the main topic of the conversation?

   (A) gift wrapping
   (B) a clothing choice
   (C) a dinner guest list
   (D) transportation options

22. What is the man's problem?

   (A) He woke up late for work.
   (B) He does not know the password.
   (C) The internet connection is not working.
   (D) There is nowhere to plug in his computer.

23. What is the likely relationship between the speakers?

   (A) car sales clerk - customer
   (B) freezer sales clerk - customer
   (C) barbecue sales clerk - colleague
   (D) telephone sales clerk - colleague

24. What does the woman mean by "that way"?

   (A) via mobile app
   (B) in person at a bank
   (C) through a cryptocurrency
   (D) at an automatic teller machine

25. How did the man hurt his thumb?

   (A) moving glass
   (B) falling at work
   (C) opening a window
   (D) picking up a broken cup

26. What is the woman's plan?

   (A) going into town
   (B) organizing a winter trip
   (C) delaying a trip up a hill
   (D) waiting to hike down a slope

**DIRECTIONS:** In this portion of the test, you will hear 2 talks. Listen carefully to each talk and answer the questions in your test booklet by choosing the best answer from the choices provided. Fill in the corresponding space on your answer sheet. The talks are not printed and will be played twice.

[27-28]

27.  What is Brain 3000?

(A) a self-help online course
(B) a teaching and learning robot
(C) a professional tutoring organization
(D) a student-to-student tutoring program

28.  How can students apply to use Brain 3000?

(A) by visiting Mrs. Travali
(B) by paying a senior student
(C) by completing an online form
(D) by purchasing a corporate product

[29-30]

29.  How long is the ferry ride to Harper Island?

(A) half an hour
(B) one hour
(C) an hour and a half
(D) two hours

30.  What will the class do on Harper Island?

(A) have lunch
(B) tour an old prison
(C) walk through fields
(D) talk to asylum inmates

# Section II

## Reading and Writing

In SECTION II, you will be asked to demonstrate how well you understand written English. You will have approximately 35 minutes to complete this section. There are 35 questions separated into four parts, and directions are given for each part. You must mark your answers on the answer sheet provided.

**Part** **5** **Picture Description**
6 Questions

**Part** **6** **Sentence Completion**
10 Questions

**Part** **7** **Practical Reading Comprehension**
13 Questions

**Part** **8** **General Reading Comprehension**
6 Questions

**DIRECTIONS:** In this portion of the test, you will be shown 6 pictures and corresponding incomplete sentences. From the choices provided, choose the word or words that match each picture and complete the sentence. Then, fill in the corresponding space on your answer sheet.

**31.**

This milk has already gone bad, and it's not even past its __________ !

(A) expiry date
(B) food period
(C) rotten hours
(D) eating deadline

**32.**

Jimmy got on the wrong train __________ and ended up miles away from his destination.

(A) for sale
(B) by heart
(C) for good
(D) by accident

**33.**

The preschool teacher teaches kids to __________ the room themselves after playtime.

(A) put on
(B) tidy up
(C) build in
(D) throw out

**34.** 

Ironically, the summer water sports competition will take _________ in late autumn this year.

(A) spot
(B) place
(C) venue
(D) location

**35.** 

I held a bucket until the plumber came to fix water _________ from the ceiling.

(A) reveal
(B) handle
(C) leakage
(D) discovery

**36.** 

Our plane made it through the turbulence, and we're all safe and _________ on the ground now.

(A) solid
(B) sound
(C) strong
(D) sincere

# PART 6 Sentence Completion

> **DIRECTIONS:** In this portion of the test, you will be given 10 incomplete sentences. From the choices provided, choose the word or words that correctly complete the sentence. Then, fill in the corresponding space on your answer sheet.

**37.** One of Jen's best friends __________ nominated for a prize.

(A) be
(B) was
(C) may
(D) were

**38.** You will be __________ sorry if you don't stop teasing your sister right now!

(A) very
(B) such
(C) extreme
(D) absolute

**39.** If you look __________ your right, you'll see the famous Tokyo Tower.

(A) in
(B) to
(C) for
(D) from

**40.** This elderly gentleman may __________ some help with his bags.

(A) need
(B) needing
(C) be need
(D) be have need

**41.** If you cheat on your assignments, your punishment will be __________.

(A) swift
(B) swifts
(C) swiftly
(D) swifting

**42.** I discovered I __________ old smelly cheese in my locker. I threw the cheese out, and my locker smells better.

(A) had left
(B) have left
(C) had to leave
(D) have to leave

**43.** The wooden chest, __________ to Maria by her grandmother, sat in the dining room.

(A) give
(B) gave
(C) given
(D) giving

**44.** There's the guy __________ was telling you about.

(A) I
(B) that
(C) who
(D) what

**45.** Don't forget __________ your seat belt. The roads are icy, and wearing a seat belt is the law.

(A) buckled
(B) buckling
(C) to buckle
(D) that buckled

**46.** __________ simply asked someone for directions, we would not be lost now.

(A) We had
(B) Had we
(C) If had we
(D) If we would

**DIRECTIONS:** In this portion of the test, you will be provided with two longer reading passages. For the first passage, complete the blanks in the passage summary using the words provided. Fill in your choices in the corresponding spaces on your answer sheet. The second passage will be followed by four questions. For each question, choose the best answer according to the passage.

Questions 60-61. Read the passage and answer the questions.

Bobcats are meat-eating wildcats that are quite common in North America. However, despite their large population numbers, they are rarely seen by humans, perhaps because they are nocturnal. These elusive animals are approximately twice the size of domestic house cats. Their furry coats are usually brown or a brownish red color. Bobcats are extremely powerful hunters, and are capable of capturing prey much larger than themselves. They sneak up on prey and jump on their victims at the last minute, with leaps of up to 3 meters. Bobcats are solitary animals. Unlike dogs or wolves, who travel in packs, bobcats travel and hunt alone.

Summary:

Bobcats are _____[A]_____, undomesticated cats that are populous in North America. They do not often get spotted by people. Most bobcats have brown or brownish fur. They are good at hunting and can catch prey that are bigger than their body size. They _____[B]_____ approach their prey. They also travel alone.

60. Choose the most suitable word for blank [A], connecting the summary to the passage.

(A) hairless
(B) miniature
(C) carnivorous
(D) endangered

61. Choose the most suitable word for blank [B], connecting the summary to the passage.

(A) rarely
(B) noisily
(C) foolishly
(D) stealthily

**Questions 62-65.** Read the passage and answer the questions.

[1] The famous Sistine Chapel, in the Vatican, Italy, was built in 1481. It was immediately filled with beautiful artwork by master artists. By 1512, the Michelangelo had painted the famous ceiling. In 1541, the last artwork by the artist Rafael was finished. These precious artworks lasted centuries. However, by the 1980s, a problem was clear. The artworks had probably lost a lot of their original colors. The decision was made to clean and restore the art.

[2] <u>This</u> was extremely controversial. Supporters of the restoration noted that there were centuries of water damage to the ceiling. The water damage had created cracks. The cracks had let salt through, which had whitened the paintings.  However, art historians noted that the restoration may have altered the paintings significantly from their original state. It is not always clear what techniques a master painter like Michelangelo was using. Modern restorers must make guesses about the intention of the original artists. Critics of the decision to restore the paintings worried that some of those guesses were wrong.

[3] In short, art restoration in general is often controversial. However, when it comes to paintings as important as those in the Sistine Chapel, the controversies have been endless.

62. Which of the following would be the best title for the passage?

    (A) The Art and Style of Michelangelo
    (B) The Man Who Painted the Sistine Chapel
    (C) The Sistine Chapel Restoration Controversy
    (D) The People Who Restored the Sistine Chapel

63. According to the passage, what did salt do?

    (A) create the paintings
    (B) lighten the artworks
    (C) darken the artworks
    (D) preserve the paintings

64. What does the underlined "This" mean?

    (A) the decision to restore the art
    (B) the mistakes made by Michelangelo
    (C) the company hired to work on the art
    (D) the cost to fix the art in the Sistine Chapel

65. According to the passage, what is most likely true about restoring the Sistine Chapel?

    (A) It is overly expensive.
    (B) It has all been finished.
    (C) It will always be controversial.
    (D) It is what the original artist wants.

# This is the end of
# the **TOSEL** Actual Test.
# Thank you.

# Actual Test 2

# Section I

---

# Listening and Speaking

In SECTION I, you will be asked to demonstrate how well you understand spoken English. You will have approximately 25 minutes to complete this section. There are 30 questions separated into four parts, and directions are given for each part. You must mark your answers on the answer sheet provided.

**Part** ❶ Listen and Recognize

6 Questions

**Part** ❷ Listen and Respond

10 Questions

**Part** ❸ Short Conversations

10 Questions

**Part** ❹ Talks

4 Questions

# PART 1 Listen and Recognize

**DIRECTIONS:** In this portion of the test, you will hear 6 short conversations. Select the picture from the three choices provided that best matches each conversation. Fill in the corresponding space on your answer sheet. The conversations are not printed in your test booklet and will be played twice.

1.

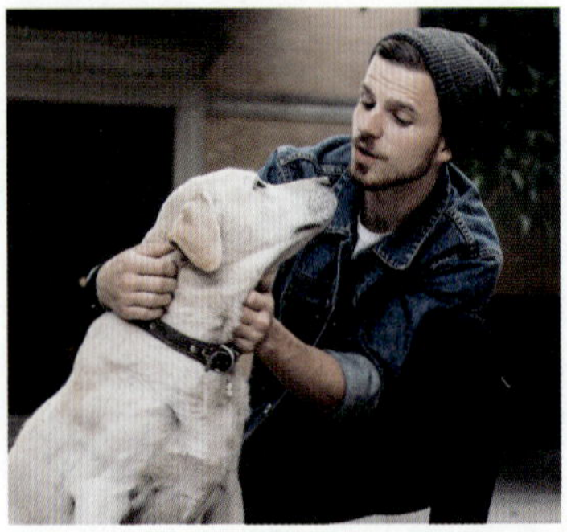
(A)

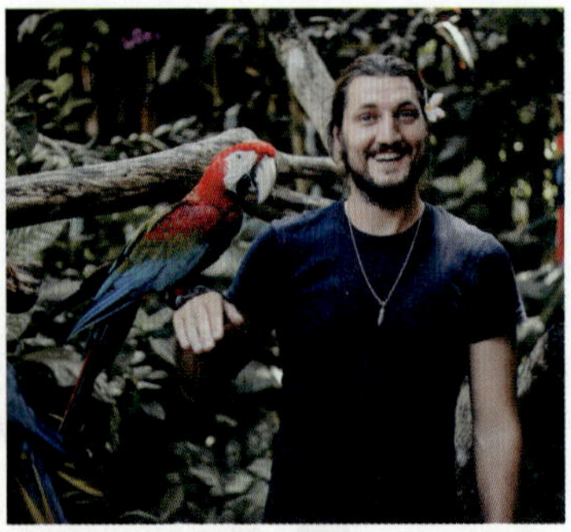
(B)

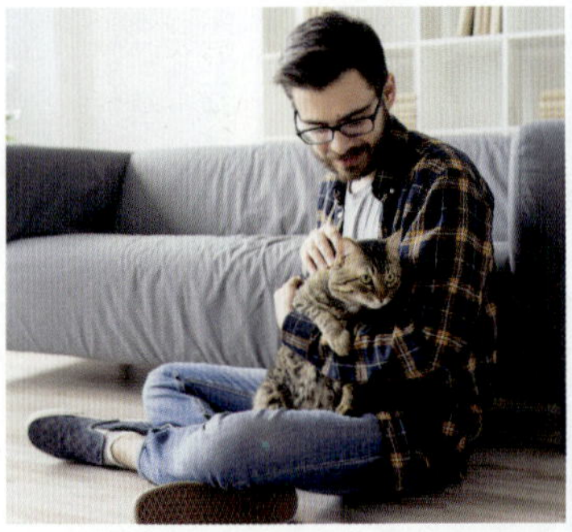
(C)

2.

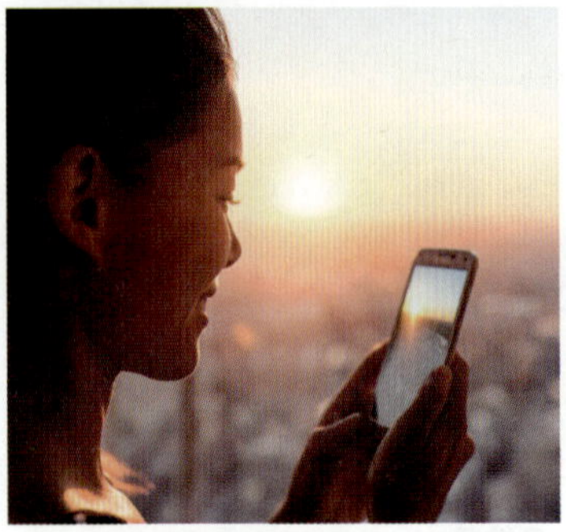
(A)

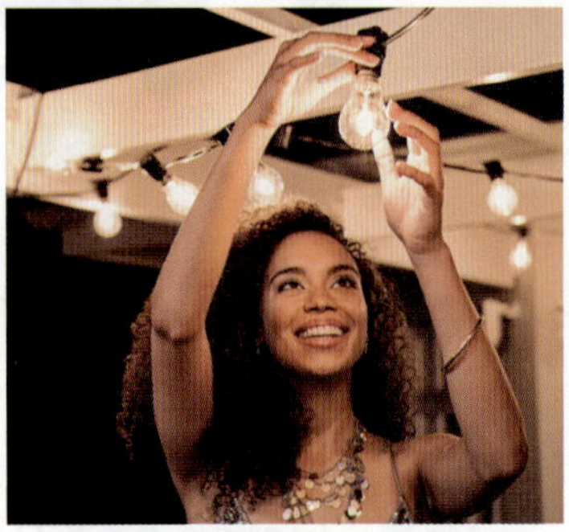
(B)

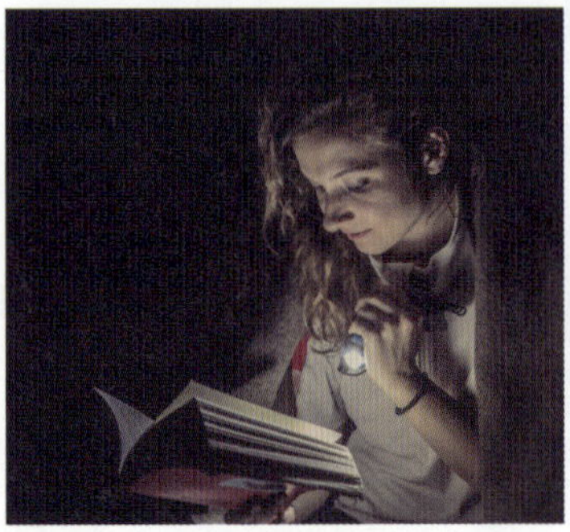
(C)

3.

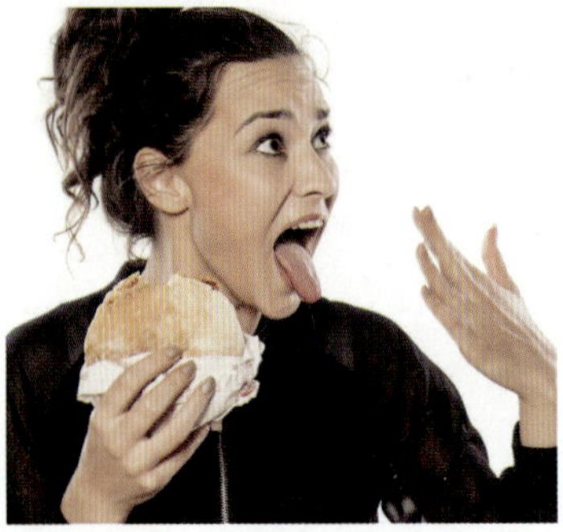
(A)

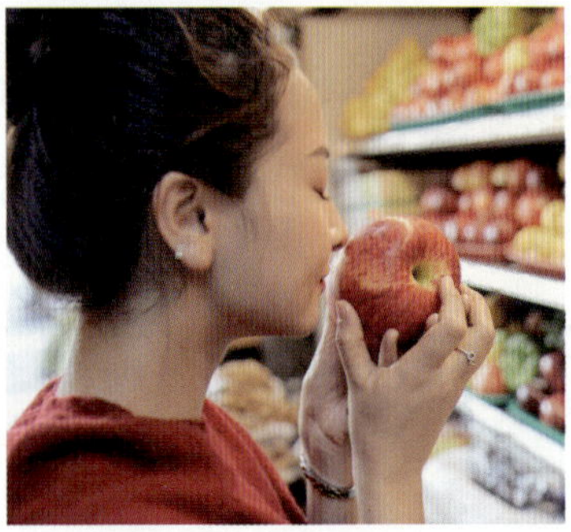
(B)

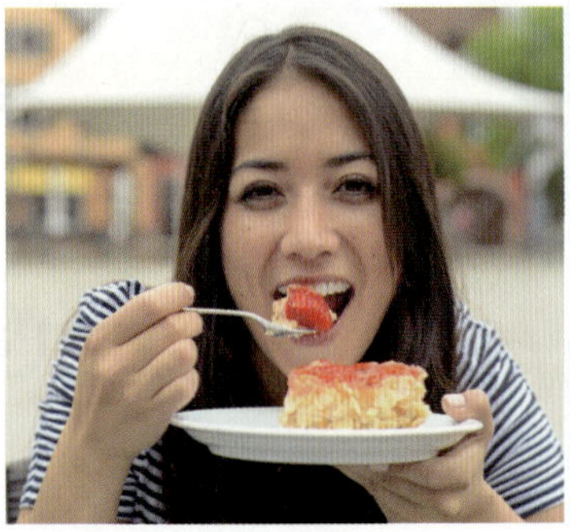
(C)

4.

(A)　　　　　　(B)　　　　　　(C)

5.

(A)　　　　　　(B)　　　　　　(C)

6.

(A)　　　　　　(B)　　　　　　(C)

**DIRECTIONS:** In this portion of the test, you will hear 10 incomplete conversations. Listen carefully, and choose the best response to the last speaker from the choices provided. Fill in the corresponding space on your answer sheet. The conversations are not printed in your test booklet and will be played twice.

7.  What is the best response?

(A) Voting is in the gym.
(B) Absolutely. She loves it.
(C) I'm not running this year.
(D) No, I can't. I was last year.

8.  What is the best response?

(A) It's on the living room table.
(B) The waterfront is foggy today.
(C) There's some soup in the fridge.
(D) They're the second door on the left.

9.  What is the best response?

(A) Give it to me.
(B) Lie down for a while.
(C) Show me your locker.
(D) Turn off the light then.

10.  What is the best response?

(A) One way to go about it.
(B) I'm ready when you're ready.
(C) By six-thirty at the very latest.
(D) I changed the battery in the clock.

11.  What is the best response?

(A) I miss mine, too.
(B) Yes, I'm on holiday.
(C) No, she cannot come.
(D) My grandpa told you, too.

12.  What is the best response?

(A) It's an old family recipe.
(B) That's not where we sit.
(C) These bananas are rotten.
(D) He cooked the soup too long.

13.  What is the best response?

(A) She called her friend.
(B) We'll deny all charges.
(C) You can always get a refill.
(D) I'm just hammering some boards.

14.  What is the best response?

(A) Never! It's not right to.
(B) Hardly! I laughed so much.
(C) I know! I loved the last joke.
(D) Exactly! I was upset about it.

15.  What is the best response?

(A) What would you like to drink?
(B) Did it ruin the stuff you bought?
(C) Are they from a supplier in Spain?
(D) Should we put these tables together?

16.  What is the best response?

(A) Two scoops are three dollars.
(B) That one does contain walnuts.
(C) We're sorry he couldn't enjoy it.
(D) Vanilla is also my favorite flavor.

**DIRECTIONS:** In this portion of the test, you will hear a series of 10 short conversations. Choose the correct answer for each question from the choices provided and fill in the corresponding space on your answer sheet. The conversations are not printed in your test booklet and will be played twice.

17. What does the man play in the band?

    (A) drums
    (B) recorder
    (C) accordion
    (D) tambourine

18. What does the man ask the woman to do?

    (A) buy a medical kit
    (B) pick up cold medicine
    (C) get a shoulder bandage
    (D) ask the doctor a question

19. Where most likely are the speakers?

    (A) a cafe
    (B) a garden
    (C) a supermarket
    (D) a wedding hall

20. What is the main topic of the conversation?

    (A) deals on spring jackets
    (B) where to buy textbooks
    (C) shopping at used goods stores
    (D) problems with shopping online

21. What does the woman want?

    (A) a new spray bottle
    (B) a glass display case
    (C) a set of stickers for her son
    (D) a way to remove sticker glue

22. Who are the man and woman, most likely?

    (A) readers in a library
    (B) teachers at a school
    (C) parents of a student
    (D) students at a ceremony

23. What does the man say he will do?

    (A) offer interviewing tips
    (B) practice interview skills
    (C) make dinner for the woman
    (D) drive the woman to an interview

24. What does the man mean by "off the hook"?

    (A) receiving a top grade
    (B) failing an important class
    (C) top of the class in physics
    (D) allowed not to do something

25. What does the woman need for try-outs?

    (A) her own bat and glove
    (B) gym clothes and runners
    (C) filled-out application forms
    (D) permission from her parents

26. What is the woman having trouble with?

    (A) updating her profile
    (B) cropping photographs
    (C) understanding a user contract
    (D) logging into her email account

**DIRECTIONS:** In this portion of the test, you will hear 2 talks. Listen carefully to each talk and answer the questions in your test booklet by choosing the best answer from the choices provided. Fill in the corresponding space on your answer sheet. The talks are not printed and will be played twice.

[27-28]

27. What does the tour show?

(A) an old coal mine
(B) a weapons factory
(C) an ancient art museum
(D) a nuclear power exhibit

28. What can listeners do right after the tour?

(A) talk to an engineer
(B) see a fencing display
(C) buy things at a gift shop
(D) try mud-pack facial creams

[29-30]

29. Why is the man disappointed in the students?

(A) They stole another student's lunch.
(B) They pulled the fire alarm at school.
(C) They used their phones during a test.
(D) They misbehaved during a presentation.

30. What punishment will the students receive?

(A) a lower grade
(B) no class party
(C) clean-up work
(D) detention after school

# Section II

# Reading and Writing

In SECTION II, you will be asked to demonstrate how well you understand written English. You will have approximately 35 minutes to complete this section. There are 35 questions separated into four parts, and directions are given for each part. You must mark your answers on the answer sheet provided.

**Part** **5** Picture Description

6 Questions

**Part** **6** Sentence Completion

10 Questions

**Part** **7** Practical Reading Comprehension

13 Questions

**Part** **8** General Reading Comprehension

6 Questions

**31.**

The traveler couldn't afford a vehicle. She had to explore the desert _________.

(A) in step
(B) in shoe
(C) on foot
(D) on walk

**32.**

I'll miss you while you're gone. Please _________ in touch.

(A) do
(B) keep
(C) bring
(D) make

**33.**

Jackson got bad grades on a test. He _________ his mind to study harder.

(A) fixed up
(B) took out
(C) tried out
(D) made up

34.

Please _________ your card in the reader here and enter your 4-digit password.

(A) tip
(B) link
(C) swipe
(D) check

35.

For some, boarding a cruise ship may not be pleasant due to severe motion _________.

(A) shake
(B) illusion
(C) disease
(D) sickness

36.

Liam built his own unique drone within just a few hours. He's such a _________!

(A) fine dust
(B) good deal
(C) fat chance
(D) smart cookie

**DIRECTIONS:** In this portion of the test, you will be given 10 incomplete sentences. From the choices provided, choose the word or words that correctly complete the sentence. Then, fill in the corresponding space on your answer sheet.

37. Do you know that girl in Grade 7 ________ gave a speech about racism?

    (A) she
    (B) who
    (C) when
    (D) where

38. The typhoon victims were each provided ________ a box of essential items.

    (A) at
    (B) to
    (C) with
    (D) from

39. We asked Robin if he ________ any help with preparations, but he told us not to worry.

    (A) need
    (B) needed
    (C) will have a need
    (D) would have need

40. Stop doing those push-ups. You ________ exercise so soon after eating. You'll get sick.

    (A) will
    (B) might
    (C) wouldn't
    (D) shouldn't

41. Every student at our school ________ aware of the rules regarding skateboards on school grounds.

    (A) is
    (B) do
    (C) are
    (D) does

42. Don't you find it ________ when people keep sniffing instead of just blowing their nose?

    (A) annoy
    (B) is annoy
    (C) annoyed
    (D) annoying

43. Kelly and I introduced ________ to our new neighbors yesterday.

    (A) us
    (B) ourself
    (C) ourselves
    (D) themselves

44. ________ the heat, we played basketball outside.

    (A) In spite
    (B) In spite of
    (C) Despite of
    (D) Despite there was

45. Abdul's teachers urged him ________ his artwork in the contest.

    (A) enter
    (B) to enter
    (C) entering
    (D) he should enter

46. It's entirely your choice whether ________ go on the trip with us.

    (A) if you
    (B) you or if
    (C) or not you
    (D) you or not

**DIRECTIONS:** In this portion of the test, you will be given 4 practical reading passages. Each passage will be followed by two, three, or four questions. For each question, choose the best answer according to the passage and fill in the corresponding space on your answer sheet.

Questions 47-48. Refer to the following poster.

47. What is the purpose of the poster?

   (A) to announce a clothing sale
   (B) to advertise a performance festival
   (C) to find applicants for an arts school
   (D) to notify the public of arts scholarships

48. What is true?

   (A) Acts come from ten countries.
   (B) Outdoor performances are free.
   (C) Indoor acts cost less for students.
   (D) Costume discounts are available for entrants.

49. What is the most likely relationship between Derek and Taylor?

(A) co-volunteers
(B) band musicians
(C) student - teacher
(D) basketball teammates

50. What will Derek do on Thursday?

(A) receive training
(B) teach a volunteer
(C) attend a sports match
(D) sing for senior citizens

51. What does the underlined "there" refer to?

(A) at home
(B) on a bus
(C) outside a school
(D) at a seniors' home

**Questions 52-55.** Refer to the following social media post.

Posted by Kelida: June 3, 2017
Subscribe to: www.kelidashcam.wetube.com
for more great videos!

**76 Comments**

Add a comment...

**Willis:**
People can be so awful. What kind of person yells at an old lady because she's driving slowly?

> **Alexira:**
> Maybe it's not cool to yell at an old person, but that lady was driving WAY under the speed limit.

**Jaygirl:**
Check out 5:34. You can totally see that the guy in the blue car is at fault. The yellow taxi had the right of way. No wonder the taxi driver is mad.

**Heronutter:**
Why can't people be patient when they are driving? Drivers should avoid underline confrontations.

---

52. What does the video show?

(A) travel advice
(B) bicycle races
(C) angry motorists
(D) people opening toys

53. Which of the following is true?

(A) The video was posted in 2017.
(B) Viewers must be over 12 years old.
(C) There are 80 comments below the video.
(D) Watching the video requires a subscription.

54. What does Jaygirl claim?

(A) Someone moves too slowly.
(B) A taxi driver is mad for no reason.
(C) The video does not load properly.
(D) Someone in a blue car makes a mistake.

55. The underlined word "confrontations" is closest in meaning to:

(A) fights
(B) officers
(C) cameras
(D) permissions

Questions 56-59. Refer to the following article.

<table>
<tr><td>Page 5</td><td>Masonville Herald</td><td>Masonville<br>February 3, 2019</td></tr>
</table>

Local woman Gina Lee (42) has won her long-running negotiations with authorities to keep Drago, her 8-foot, 507-pound alligator. Said Lee of Drago, "He's such a sweetheart, and there have been no complaints from any neighbors."

Lee's attorney, Parma Denzig, said "We are fairly satisfied with the outcome of the case." City Hall employee Ken Harley said, "This case differed from many pet licensing cases in that Ms. Lee's original permit for Drago was granted when Drago was a little alligator. Once he passed the 5.5-foot mark, though, he no longer fit in the size restrictions for pets according to Masonville <u>bylaws</u>. We feel that the case's conclusion balances public safety and pet owners' rights.

56. Who most likely went to law school?

(A) Drago
(B) Gina Lee
(C) Ken Harley
(D) Parma Denzig

57. How long was Drago at the time the story was published?

(A) 5 feet
(B) 5.5 feet
(C) 8 feet
(D) 8.5 feet

58. What does Lee say about Drago?

(A) He needs a mate.
(B) He is getting too fat.
(C) He has a nice temperament.
(D) He eats more than she expected.

59. The underlined word "bylaws" is closest in meaning to:

(A) federal rules
(B) permit holders
(C) local regulations
(D) married relatives

**DIRECTIONS:** In this portion of the test, you will be provided with two longer reading passages. For the first passage, complete the blanks in the passage summary using the words provided. Fill in your choices in the corresponding spaces on your answer sheet. The second passage will be followed by four questions. For each question, choose the best answer according to the passage.

**Questions 60-61.** Read the passage and answer the questions.

The world today is divided into six to seven continents: Africa, Antarctica, Australia, North America, South America, Asia, and Europe. (Some people put the last two together as "Eurasia".) One German researcher, Alfred Wegener, looked at their shapes, and thought that some of the continents maybe used to be connected. Particularly, South America and Africa looked like two puzzle pieces that fit together. In 1912, he proposed the theory of continental drift, meaning that the continents used to be joined together, had then separated, and were slowly moving around the globe. At the time, the theory was not accepted by many scientists. However, by the 1950s, scientists generally agreed that continental drift was a real phenomenon.

Summary:

Currently, the world's continents are divided. However, as Alfred Wegener noted in 1912, different continents have shapes like puzzle pieces. He hypothesized that the continents had once been connected and that they were now in a state of_____ [A] _____. His theory of "continental drift" was _____ [B] _____ controversial, but is now widely accepted.

60. Choose the most suitable word for blank [A], connecting the summary to the passage.

(A) shock
(B) union
(C) danger
(D) motion

61. Choose the most suitable word for blank [B], connecting the summary to the passage.

(A) hardly
(B) initially
(C) particularly
(D) surprisingly

**Questions 62-65.** Read the passage and answer the questions.

[1] First grown in Afghanistan in around 900 AD and now found in most countries, carrots are an incredibly versatile vegetable. There are many kinds of carrots. While many people may think of the color orange when they think of carrots, in fact there are at least twenty species of carrots, and these come in all kinds of shades from white, to yellow, to red, to purple.

[2] Carrots contain many substances that make them versatile for cooking. Fans of carrot cake and carrot muffins know that carrots are a very sugary vegetable. What they may not also know is how much water is in a carrot. Each carrot consists of approximately 88 percent water. Moreover, carrots are very high in beta-carotene, a chemical that is <u>converted</u> into vitamin A in the human body. However, healthy eaters should note that it is important to cook these vegetables to maximize the amount of beta-carotene each carrot releases.

[3] In conclusion, carrots are diverse and are found all over. Anyone with an interest in cooking and in health should consider carrots as a key part of their diet.

62. What is the main idea of the passage?

   (A) Carrots are disappearing.
   (B) Carrots are very versatile.
   (C) Carrots are extremely sugary.
   (D) Carrots are originally from Afghanistan.

63. Which of the following is mentioned about carrots?

   (A) their price
   (B) their diseases
   (C) their water content
   (D) their least popular color

64. The underlined word "converted" is closest in meaning to:

   (A) hired
   (B) stuffed
   (C) transformed
   (D) marginalized

65. According to the passage, what can be inferred about carrots?

   (A) They are used in desserts.
   (B) Most people eat them raw.
   (C) They are bad for our health.
   (D) Purple is their most popular color.

# This is the end of the **TOSEL** Actual Test.
# Thank you.

# Actual Test 3

# Section I

---

# Listening and Speaking

In SECTION I, you will be asked to demonstrate how well you understand spoken English. You will have approximately 25 minutes to complete this section. There are 30 questions separated into four parts, and directions are given for each part. You must mark your answers on the answer sheet provided.

**Part** ❶ Listen and Recognize

6 Questions

**Part** ❷ Listen and Respond

10 Questions

**Part** ❸ Short Conversations

10 Questions

**Part** ❹ Talks

4 Questions

**DIRECTIONS:** In this portion of the test, you will hear 6 short conversations. Select the picture from the three choices provided that best matches each conversation. Fill in the corresponding space on your answer sheet. The conversations are not printed in your test booklet and will be played twice.

1.

(A)　　　　　　　　　　　(B)　　　　　　　　　　　(C)

2.

(A)　　　　　　　　　　　(B)　　　　　　　　　　　(C)

3.

(A)　　　　　　　　　　　(B)　　　　　　　　　　　(C)

4.

(A)          (B)          (C)

5.

(A)          (B)          (C)

6.

(A)          (B)          (C)

**DIRECTIONS:** In this portion of the test, you will hear 10 incomplete conversations. Listen carefully, and choose the best response to the last speaker from the choices provided. Fill in the corresponding space on your answer sheet. The conversations are not printed in your test booklet and will be played twice.

7.   What is the best response?

(A)  Yes, the weather is great.
(B)  No, they will meet us later.
(C)  No, the wallpaper is still good.
(D)  Yes, I can help you with the dishes.

8.   What is the best response?

(A)  When are you getting me a dog?
(B)  What size of turtle do you mean?
(C)  Why is my cat eating so little food?
(D)  Where are you keeping your snake?

9.   What is the best response?

(A)  Is your screen the issue?
(B)  What kind of blog was it?
(C)  Who helps you with that blog?
(D)  Do you need to fix your mouse?

10.   What is the best response?

(A)  This alarm clock has a nice ring.
(B)  We need to be up before sunrise.
(C)  I have an extra pair of boots for you.
(D)  They have to be in bed by ten tonight.

11.   What is the best response?

(A)  The hall was so beautiful.
(B)  I'm not sure of the guest list.
(C)  I'll be there as soon as I can.
(D)  They are serving hamburgers.

12.   What is the best response?

(A)  Just leave yours on the corner.
(B)  Just wash the fruit you'll eat today.
(C)  Just some old clothes I don't need.
(D)  Just a bit of room is left in each one.

13.   What is the best response?

(A)  That's the team I cheer for.
(B)  It will be in Wisley Stadium.
(C)  He was injured halfway through.
(D)  The last inning was really exciting.

14.   What is the best response?

(A)  He is still living overseas.
(B)  You were going to be out all day.
(C)  She and I have never been close.
(D)  They are visiting us next summer.

15.   What is the best response?

(A)  Barely, but at least it is all done.
(B)  The more that come, the merrier.
(C)  Sure, I can add a few words to it.
(D)  Great content, weak writing style.

16.   What is the best response?

(A)  Me, too. Let's walk it off.
(B)  Me, neither. I'm so tired.
(C)  I can, too. I'll get dessert.
(D)  I can't, either. Let's sit down.

> **DIRECTIONS:** In this portion of the test, you will hear a series of 10 short conversations. Choose the correct answer for each question from the choices provided and fill in the corresponding space on your answer sheet. The conversations are not printed in your test booklet and will be played twice.

17. What is the main topic of the conversation?

    (A) dirty hands
    (B) interior design
    (C) a beaded bracelet
    (D) a temporary tattoo

18. What is the man's problem?

    (A) He lost a key.
    (B) He left a gate open.
    (C) He killed some plants.
    (D) He slipped in a garden.

19. According to the man, how can the woman feel better?

    (A) by icing her foot
    (B) by soaking her heels
    (C) by painting her toenails
    (D) by rubbing cream on her leg

20. What does the woman think about the man's cereal?

    (A) It is her favorite.
    (B) It is very high in fat.
    (C) It has too much sugar.
    (D) It has an appropriate name.

21. What is the most likely relationship between the speakers?

    (A) surgeon - patient
    (B) office worker - office worker
    (C) fitness instructor - gym user
    (D) waterslide employee - waterslide manager

22. What will the man do next?

    (A) dry towels
    (B) wash towels
    (C) dry work clothes
    (D) wash work clothes

23. What is the man's purpose in the conversation?

    (A) to select a new test date
    (B) to cancel a visit to his dentist
    (C) to check the spelling on a form
    (D) to change an appointment time

24. What does the man ask the woman to do?

    (A) press a button on the TV
    (B) find a lost remote control
    (C) remove a remote control button
    (D) change the colors on a remote control

25. Where does this conversation most likely take place?

    (A) at a political rally
    (B) at a weather station
    (C) in a zookeeper's office
    (D) in a news writers' room

26. What does "there" mean when the man says, "You won't be there long"?

    (A) on the grass
    (B) on the blanket
    (C) on the doorstep
    (D) on the pavement

**DIRECTIONS:** In this portion of the test, you will hear 2 talks. Listen carefully to each talk and answer the questions in your test booklet by choosing the best answer from the choices provided. Fill in the corresponding space on your answer sheet. The talks are not printed and will be played twice.

[27-28]

27. Whom is the speaker most likely introducing?

(A) a producer
(B) a comedian
(C) a film director
(D) a dramatic actor

28. What does the speaker mention about Mariana Sanchez?

(A) She has attended clown school.
(B) She has written for other people.
(C) She has worked in postal delivery.
(D) She has performed on thirty stages.

[29-30]

29. According to the speaker, what will the weather be like in the morning?

(A) mainly rainy, with a chance of hail
(B) mostly cloudy, with patches of rain
(C) generally clear, with occasional clouds
(D) sunny overall, with one thundershower

30. According to the speaker, what time will the sun set?

(A) 8:00 PM
(B) 8:09 PM
(C) 9:10 PM
(D) 10:09 PM

# Section II

## Reading and Writing

In SECTION II, you will be asked to demonstrate how well you understand written English. You will have approximately 35 minutes to complete this section. There are 35 questions separated into four parts, and directions are given for each part. You must mark your answers on the answer sheet provided.

**Part** (5) **Picture Description**

6 Questions

**Part** (6) **Sentence Completion**

10 Questions

**Part** (7) **Practical Reading Comprehension**

13 Questions

**Part** (8) **General Reading Comprehension**

6 Questions

> **DIRECTIONS:** In this portion of the test, you will be shown 6 pictures and corresponding incomplete sentences. From the choices provided, choose the word or words that match each picture and complete the sentence. Then, fill in the corresponding space on your answer sheet.

**31.**

Carrie and Ben played a prank on their dad, and now they're in __________.

(A) case
(B) matter
(C) trouble
(D) question

**32.**

Why does everybody only mess up the house all the time and never help __________?

(A) tidy up
(B) throw up
(C) hang out
(D) weed out

**33.**

Don't bother going to that town. It's not __________ the trip.

(A) price
(B) merit
(C) value
(D) worth

34.

I only see my _________ family, including my aunts and uncles, on special occasions.

(A) passed
(B) nuclear
(C) extended
(D) magnified

35.

We're going to _______ bowling this weekend. Do you want to come?

(A) go
(B) ride
(C) take
(D) throw

36.

Alexei usually hides his emotions, but then he'll suddenly _______ angry.

(A) get
(B) roll
(C) pick
(D) bear

DIRECTIONS: In this portion of the test, you will be given 10 incomplete sentences. From the choices provided, choose the word or words that correctly complete the sentence. Then, fill in the corresponding space on your answer sheet.

37. This is without a doubt _______ cutting-edge application of our company's technology.

(A) most
(B) most of
(C) the most
(D) more than

38. Ray and Judy, _______ met at a party, have been married fifty years.

(A) who
(B) which
(C) whom
(D) of whom

39. Your glasses are somewhere _______ that pile of papers.

(A) lower
(B) of lower
(C) beneath
(D) of beneath

40. Don't blame _______ for one small mistake. You'll know better for next time.

(A) you
(B) your
(C) you're
(D) yourself

41. I found the art show _______ from beginning to end. I highly recommend it.

(A) fascinate
(B) fascinating
(C) be fascinating
(D) to be fascinated

42. The turnout for the events last weekend _______ quite low, so the organizers are rethinking next year's plans.

(A) is
(B) are
(C) was
(D) were

43. I don't know whether _______ or not, but I've decided to go to South America.

(A) approve
(B) you approve
(C) approve you
(D) do you approve

44. Once she sets her mind to something, there's no stopping her _______ her goal.

(A) achieve
(B) to achieve
(C) from achieving
(D) that she achieves

45. Ten years ago, he _______ as a cook in the biggest hotel in town.

(A) works
(B) was working
(C) has been working
(D) was started his work

46. While _______ up the mountain, some rocks broke loose.

(A) climbing
(B) was climbing
(C) it was a climb
(D) I was climbing

**DIRECTIONS:** In this portion of the test, you will be given 4 practical reading passages. Each passage will be followed by two, three, or four questions. For each question, choose the best answer according to the passage and fill in the corresponding space on your answer sheet.

**Questions 47-48.** Refer to the following text chain.

**47.** Why does Alicia write to Mario?

(A) to ask where Kevin bought something
(B) to find out why Kevin is quitting music
(C) to find out why Mario has Kevin's music
(D) to ask whether Kevin is selling something

**48.** Which of the following can be inferred about Alicia?

(A) She is going to Kevin's house tonight.
(B) She refuses to see Helga after a fight.
(C) She does not like Kevin's violin playing.
(D) She has not been invited to Helga's party.

Questions 49-51. Refer to the following advertisement.

# Crazy Chem Chemistry Set

· Fun, safe educational product for young chemists
· 110 different experiments to do at home
· Appropriate for teenagers aged 13 and up (adult supervision required at all times)

8 new available for as low as $35.99 (free shipping for Yangtze Optimum members)
15 used available for as low as $24.25 (plus $6.00 shipping)

**Customer reviews**

**Sandra:**
Be aware: Not everything to conduct all the experiments is included. You still need stuff like filter papers.

**Maiko:**
This is 400 times better than those silly cheap sets that just contain colored water. It's hardcore: the chemicals here are real and some are toxic.

49. What is the minimum price of a new set for Yangtze Optimum members?

(A) $24.25
(B) $30.25
(C) $35.99
(D) $41.99

50. What is true about the set?

(A) Users must be legally adults.
(B) Filter papers are sold separately.
(C) It is designed to be used in schools.
(D) It allows users to do up to 100 experiments.

51. What does Maiko mean by "It's hardcore"?

(A) The set comes in a hard case.
(B) The set contains toxic chemicals.
(C) The set lacks the 400 promised chemicals.
(D) The set's chemicals are only colored water.

Questions 52-55. Refer to the following instructions.

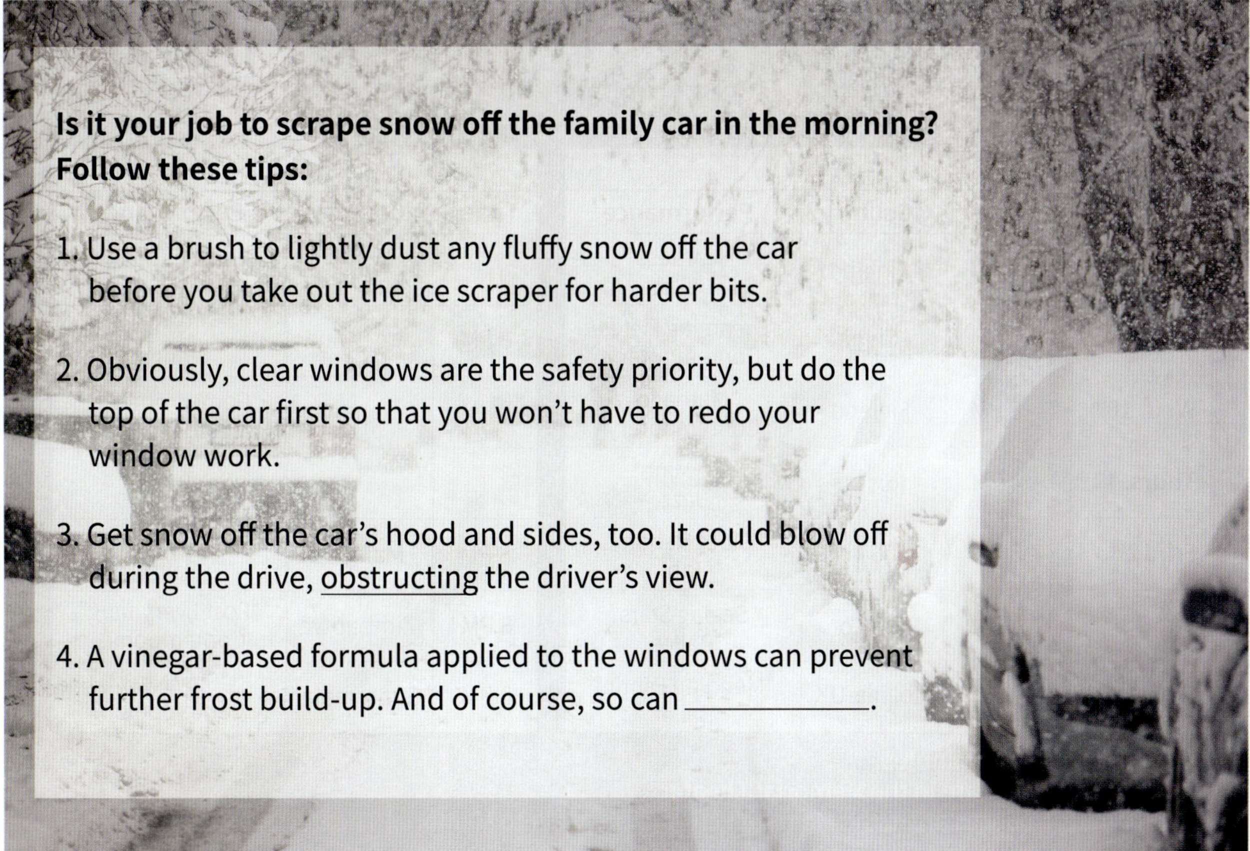


**52.** What are these instructions mainly for?

(A) removing snow from a car
(B) driving in snowy conditions
(C) cleaning a dirty vehicle in winter
(D) preparing a car for winter storage

**53.** Which instruction is mentioned?

(A) Stand on the vehicle's roof.
(B) Use a scraper for hard parts.
(C) Lift up the windshield wipers.
(D) Wash the car's undercarriage.

**54.** Which of the following would most likely go in the blank?

(A) a large pile of snow
(B) a stiff sweeping brush
(C) a plastic ice-scraping tool
(D) a blanket covering the car

**55.** The underlined "obstructing" is closest in meaning to:

(A) showing
(B) blocking
(C) legalizing
(D) facilitating

Questions 56-59. Refer to the following schedule.

## Program October 8-14

| | Show 1 | | | Show 2 | | |
|---|---|---|---|---|---|---|
| | Time | Country | Performance | Time | Country | Performance |
| Mon, 8th | 8 PM | Finland | "Heartless" Ballet | | | |
| Tues, 9th | 4 PM | China | "Dreaming Fields" Contemporary | 8 PM | Argentina | "Nowhere" Tango |
| Wed, 10th | 8 PM | Finland | "Marriage" Contemporary | 8 PM | Japan | "Come from Afar" Ballet |
| Thurs, 11th | 4 PM | Russia | "Be Mine" Jazz | | | |
| Fri, 12th | 8 PM | USA | "Cities Reborn" Tap | 8 PM | Malaysia | "Seeing Waves" Ballet |
| Sat, 13th | 5 PM/ 8 PM | Mexico | "Seeing Stars" Ballet | 8 PM | Zimbabwe | "Post Everything" Contemporary |
| Sun, 14th | 5 PM/ 8 PM | Albania-UK | "Mending Fabric" Ballet | 8 PM | Guatemala | "Stay Near" Contemporary |

Performances are 90 minutes.
Ballet performances are in the Memorial Theater.
All other performances are in the Main Hall (10-minute walk to Memorial Theater).

56. Where would this schedule most likely be published?

(A) on an advertisement for tap shoes

(B) on an international dance festival's website

(C) on a subway platform highlighting train times

(D) on a poster board for a theater's summer workshops

57. What is mentioned about Finland?

(A) It performs on a weekend.

(B) It performs both jazz and ballet.

(C) It has two different performances.

(D) It performs before Japan on Wednesday.

58. According to the schedule, what is the maximum number of different performances one viewer could see?

(A) 7

(B) 10

(C) 12

(D) 14

59. Which of the following is true?

(A) Mexico has three different shows.

(B) The USA has two tap performances.

(C) The UK's show is a collaboration with Guatemala.

(D) Russia's performance takes place in the Main Hall.

**DIRECTIONS:** In this portion of the test, you will be provided with two longer reading passages. For the first passage, complete the blanks in the passage summary using the words provided. Fill in your choices in the corresponding spaces on your answer sheet. The second passage will be followed by four questions. For each question, choose the best answer according to the passage.

**Questions 60-61.** Read the passage and answer the questions.

Rip currents are narrow yet strong water flows from the shore to the open sea. They form in shallow spots near shorelines and around human-made structures in water, such as docks. They can range from 15 meters to 90 meters long. Rip currents are surprisingly fast. Most rip currents flow at around 60 centimeters per second. However, they can flow as fast as 2 meters per second. Because of the potentially deadly strength of rip currents, swimmers should not try to swim against them. Instead, swimmers who feel they are being pulled out to sea should first swim in alignment with the shore. When they get out of the rip current, they can then swim diagonally towards the shore.

Summary:

Rip currents are powerful water flows that occur in shallow parts of the ocean near the shore or near ___[A]___ structures. Ranging in length from 15 to 90 meters, they flow at speeds of up to 2 meters per second. To escape a rip current, swimmers should swim ___[B]___ to the shore at first, and then at a diagonal towards the shore.

60. Choose the most suitable word for blank [A], connecting the summary to the passage.

(A) coral
(B) natural
(C) tropical
(D) artificial

61. Choose the most suitable word for blank [B], connecting the summary to the passage.

(A) parallel
(B) squarely
(C) diagonally
(D) perpendicularly

**Questions 62-65. Read the passage and answer the questions.**

[1] While they may not be commonly needed for residents of many modern cities, the abilities to chop wood, saw logs, and climb trees are still important for lumberjacks—that is, people who work in the logging industry.

[2] Held each year since 1960 in the state of Wisconsin, USA, the Lumberjack World Championships test competitors in traditional lumberjack skills. Contestants show their ability to saw, chop, and climb. There's even an event for logrolling in which competitors run on logs that are floating in water. In each <u>round</u>, the competitors must stay on a log for a certain amount of time. They are then given smaller and smaller logs to stand on. In the end, the winner survives the best three out of five rounds.

[3] Meanwhile, in the 90-foot speed climb, contestants win by being the fastest person to go all the way up and down a cedar pole. In the single buck event, competitors saw through a pine log, and in the block chop event they use an ax to chop down a vertical standing log.

[4] The races are more than just entertainment for urban spectators. Rather, they are a reminder of the skills involved in the work of lumberjacks.

62. What is the passage mainly about?

    (A) a discontinued contest
    (B) lumberjack skills of the 1960s
    (C) the people in a sporting championship
    (D) proceedings in a competition for lumberjacks

63. Which of the following is mentioned about the Lumberjack World Championships?

    (A) its frequency
    (B) which town hosts it
    (C) how judges are selected
    (D) how many people compete

64. The underlined "round" is closest in meaning to:

    (A) disk
    (B) match
    (C) cylinder
    (D) inspection

65. According to the passage, what can be inferred?

    (A) The single buck event requires a saw.
    (B) The logrolling event requires rubber boots.
    (C) The 90-foot speed climb requires teamwork.
    (D) The block chop event requires climbing skills.

This is the end of
the **TOSEL** Actual Test.
Thank you.

# Actual Test 4

# Section I

---

# Listening and Speaking

In SECTION I, you will be asked to demonstrate how well you understand spoken English. You will have approximately 25 minutes to complete this section. There are 30 questions separated into four parts, and directions are given for each part. You must mark your answers on the answer sheet provided.

**Part** ① **Listen and Recognize**

6 Questions

**Part** ② **Listen and Respond**

10 Questions

**Part** ③ **Short Conversations**

10 Questions

**Part** ④ **Talks**

4 Questions

**DIRECTIONS:** In this portion of the test, you will hear 6 short conversations. Select the picture from the three choices provided that best matches each conversation. Fill in the corresponding space on your answer sheet. The conversations are not printed in your test booklet and will be played twice.

1.

(A)

(B)

(C)

2.

(A)

(B)

(C)

3.

(A)

(B)

(C)

4.

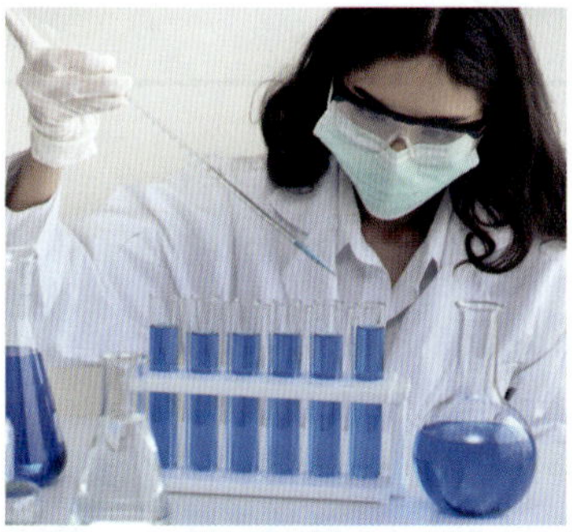

(A) 　　　　　　　　(B) 　　　　　　　　(C)

5.

(A) 　　　　　　　　(B) 　　　　　　　　(C)

6.

(A) 　　　　　　　　(B) 　　　　　　　　(C)

**DIRECTIONS:** In this portion of the test, you will hear 10 incomplete conversations. Listen carefully, and choose the best response to the last speaker from the choices provided. Fill in the corresponding space on your answer sheet. The conversations are not printed in your test booklet and will be played twice.

**7.**   What is the best response?

    (A) Does it hurt from texting?
    (B) Where is my thumb drive?
    (C) Is there another pair of glasses?
    (D) When does your leg cast come off?

**8.**   What is the best response?

    (A) This stool fits that old desk.
    (B) You can just have it for free.
    (C) I'll take the large one, please.
    (D) You'll see it in the bottom drawer.

**9.**   What is the best response?

    (A) Could I go next time?
    (B) Is the computer working?
    (C) Are you ready for school?
    (D) Can I have five more minutes?

**10.**   What is the best response?

    (A) They look pretty good.
    (B) Sure, that suit looks nice.
    (C) Yes, I have some sandals.
    (D) We had a great time there.

**11.**   What is the best response?

    (A) That kind of weather is perfect.
    (B) The venue hasn't been decided yet.
    (C) They are getting married in October.
    (D) This January is their third anniversary.

**12.**   What is the best response?

    (A) Sure do. Here you go.
    (B) Pardon me. That's my pen.
    (C) Never. You should pin it up.
    (D) Certainly. It's much appreciated.

**13.**   What is the best response?

    (A) They do not get along with cats.
    (B) She sensed he was quite hungry.
    (C) We often walk in the rain together.
    (D) He thinks you're going to feed him.

**14.**   What is the best response?

    (A) I'll take you to see my show.
    (B) I can, and you're invited, too.
    (C) I have, and I didn't like it either.
    (D) I've seen it and agree it's funny.

**15.**   What is the best response?

    (A) Can I get a refund on that item?
    (B) Were the employees there polite?
    (C) Should I complain to his manager?
    (D) Did you check at the information kiosk?

**16.**   What is the best response?

    (A) No one. I did it all myself.
    (B) Not anymore. It's all done.
    (C) Never again. I hate presentations.
    (D) No way. You should complain to her.

---

**DIRECTIONS:** In this portion of the test, you will hear a series of 10 short conversations. Choose the correct answer for each question from the choices provided and fill in the corresponding space on your answer sheet. The conversations are not printed in your test booklet and will be played twice.

---

17. What is the woman's purpose in the conversation?

    (A) to ask a group to be quieter
    (B) to make a complaint to the police
    (C) to get someone to help her move
    (D) to find directions to a neighborhood

18. Where does this conversation most likely take place?

    (A) in a kitchen
    (B) in a living room
    (C) at a movie theater
    (D) at a home goods store

19. What does the woman mean by "I'm the lead"?

    (A) She talks first in the play.
    (B) She plays the main character.
    (C) She is becoming class president.
    (D) She is on the cover of a newspaper.

20. When will the man go to a photo studio?

    (A) in the evening
    (B) on the weekend
    (C) during lunchtime
    (D) right after school

21. What most likely is the woman's job?

    (A) banker
    (B) cashier
    (C) librarian
    (D) accountant

22. What is the man's problem?

    (A) He lost his money.
    (B) He forgot his wallet.
    (C) He missed the subway.
    (D) He left money on the subway.

23. What will the woman most likely do next?

    (A) look at the man's drawings
    (B) write a new ending for a story
    (C) show some comics to the man
    (D) go to a market to look for comics

24. What is true about the woman?

    (A) She may not go to a dance.
    (B) She cannot dance anymore.
    (C) She does not want to see Ben.
    (D) She generally enjoys dance music.

25. What is the main topic of the conversation?

    (A) fine dust
    (B) first snow
    (C) slushy streets
    (D) snowman outside

26. What does the man ask the woman to do?

    (A) help him to build a raft
    (B) ask her uncle for a discount
    (C) teach him whitewater rafting
    (D) get tickets for whitewater rafting

**DIRECTIONS:** In this portion of the test, you will hear 2 talks. Listen carefully to each talk and answer the questions in your test booklet by choosing the best answer from the choices provided. Fill in the corresponding space on your answer sheet. The talks are not printed and will be played twice.

[27-28]

27.  What is the main topic of the announcement?

(A) cloudy skies
(B) high temperatures
(C) the aftermath of a flood
(D) a tropical storm warning

28.  According to the speaker, what should residents do?

(A) go to underground shelters
(B) swim only at marked beaches
(C) wear sunscreen before going out
(D) move valuable items in their homes

[29-30]

29.  Which is NOT a listed ingredient?

(A) boiled eggs
(B) heavy cream
(C) grated cheese
(D) raw vegetables

30.  Which is an instruction?

(A) Use a nonstick pan.
(B) Stuff the eggs with cheese.
(C) Add pepper and salt to taste.
(D) Wait for the vegetables to harden.

# Section II

---

# Reading and Writing

In SECTION II, you will be asked to demonstrate how well you understand written English. You will have approximately 35 minutes to complete this section. There are 35 questions separated into four parts, and directions are given for each part. You must mark your answers on the answer sheet provided.

| | | |
|---|---|---|
| **Part** | **5** | **Picture Description**<br>6 Questions |
| **Part** | **6** | **Sentence Completion**<br>10 Questions |
| **Part** | **7** | **Practical Reading Comprehension**<br>13 Questions |
| **Part** | **8** | **General Reading Comprehension**<br>6 Questions |

**DIRECTIONS:** In this portion of the test, you will be shown 6 pictures and corresponding incomplete sentences. From the choices provided, choose the word or words that match each picture and complete the sentence. Then, fill in the corresponding space on your answer sheet.

31.

This region of the country is ___________ for its apples. People come from all over to taste them.

(A) happy
(B) tender
(C) abrupt
(D) famous

32.

My amazing dad raised three kids on his own. I will always _________ him as a role model.

(A) look up to
(B) catch sight of
(C) come out with
(D) stay away from

33.

For my graduation exam, I have to _________ over 400 terms. It's too much to remember!

(A) run by heart
(B) run by clock
(C) learn by heart
(D) learn by clock

**34.**

She promised to be there at noon, and she arrived _________ on time—12 o'clock sharp.

(A) right
(B) stuck
(C) raced
(D) straight

**35.**

I need to run to the washroom. Can you _________ my seat? I'll be back in a minute.

(A) free
(B) give
(C) save
(D) make

**36.**

Kathy's feeling a bit under _________, so she's not going to school today.

(A) the cloud
(B) the thunder
(C) the weather
(D) the lightning

**DIRECTIONS:** In this portion of the test, you will be given 10 incomplete sentences. From the choices provided, choose the word or words that correctly complete the sentence. Then, fill in the corresponding space on your answer sheet.

---

**37.** What _______ the reason for the school to change its policy on soda?

(A) was
(B) were
(C) could
(D) might

**38.** That's the best movie _______ ever seen.

(A) that I
(B) I have
(C) have I
(D) when that

**39.** I met her when I _______ to Taiwan last year.

(A) went
(B) visited
(C) were been
(D) have been

**40.** Martin went home sick. He said he _______ feeling very well.

(A) been
(B) wasn't
(C) weren't
(D) not been

**41.** You'll be _______ with a thicker pillow. I'll get you one.

(A) nearly so comfortable
(B) much more comfortable
(C) more much comfortable
(D) nearly much comfortable

**42.** All the kids _______ town enjoy playing in that park.

(A) in
(B) to
(C) on
(D) for

**43.** He was _______ disappointed that he did not win the prize.

(A) bitter
(B) bitters
(C) bitterly
(D) bittering

**44.** I wonder whether _______ his driving test or not.

(A) passed Jim
(B) Jim passed
(C) did Jim pass
(D) Jim had pass

**45.** I am completely _______ by this artwork. I'd like to learn more about it.

(A) intrigue
(B) intrigues
(C) intrigued
(D) intriguing

**46.** If _______ it would be raining, we never would have started this hike.

(A) had we known
(B) we had known
(C) known we had
(D) had known we

Questions 47-48. Refer to the following sign.

**47.** What is the main purpose of the sign?

(A) to clarify visitors' rights
(B) to outline rules for visitors
(C) to explain how to register for a visit
(D) to notify visitors of new park features

**48.** According to the sign, which of the following is true?

(A) Snacks are sold at the park.
(B) Pet rabbits are permitted entry.
(C) Vaccinations are conducted at the site.
(D) Up to 15 dogs can enter simultaneously.

Questions 49-51. Refer to the following information.

## 5-day Summer Brain Camp

(Camp runs Monday - Friday, 7:30 AM to 6:30 PM.
Drop-off and pick-up at the UCN Kids' Camp main lobby.
Lunch included.)

### Camp 1: Robotics
### 4th grade and up
Work in teams to design and make a roller coaster model. Then go to
the Everafterland amusement park for a behind-the-scenes tour before trying out
real roller coasters.

### Camp 2: Aviation
### 5th grade and up
Construct and launch mini-rockets and learn all about different kinds of flight.
Visit airline academies (Uwe Air, Air Gecko) and get a tour of the Pinnington
International Airport.

### Camp 3: Conservation
### 6th grade and up
Go boating and fishing with staff of the Pinnington Conservation Commission.
Learn all about wildlife conservation.

---

**49.** How many hours do kids spend in each camp in total?

(A) 40
(B) 45
(C) 55
(D) 60

**50.** Which experience is NOT offered at the camps?

(A) sitting in a rocket
(B) taking a boat ride
(C) touring an airport
(D) riding a roller coaster

**51.** Who would most likely benefit from Camp 3?

(A) a fifth grade student
(B) a student who likes nature
(C) someone wanting to windsurf
(D) someone interested in art history

**Questions 52-55.** Refer to the following message chain.

**52.** Where is Kelly most likely writing from?

(A) a car
(B) a bus
(C) a cafe
(D) a bookstore

**53.** What does Kelly suggest Jon and Aki do?

(A) go home
(B) go by the sea
(C) take Highway A5
(D) walk to the bridge

**54.** When does Jon first suggest meeting?

(A) this afternoon
(B) tonight
(C) next week
(D) in two weeks

**55.** What does Aki mean by "I'm on board for lunch being on Jon and me"?

(A) He and Jon will make a new plan.
(B) He and Jon are enjoying their day.
(C) He and Jon will pay for Kelly's lunch.
(D) He and Jon are committed to meeting.

Questions 56-59. Refer to the following assessment.

**Name:** Afia Olowe
**Project:** Impressionism

**Teacher:** Mrs. Falade
**Date Submitted:** Dec 5, 2019

|   | Criterion | Student's Self Assessment | Teacher's Assessment |
|---|---|---|---|
| 1 | Produced high-quality, original work. | 8 | 9 |
| 2 | Demonstrated knowledge of core principles. | 8 | 8.5 |
| 3 | Showed technical skill and craftsmanship in the medium used for this project. | 9 | 8.5 |
| 4 | Made an effort. Used time well during class to do the project. | 9 | 9 |

Rating 1 (lowest) to 10 (highest)
Projects with total teacher's scores of 38 and above will be displayed at the festival.

**Overall impressions:** Nice effort in using <u>complementary</u> colors. In particular, the bridge has a nice color blend. Note that more work is needed on using various types of brushstrokes.

56. Who most likely, is Mrs. Falade?

(A) Afia's art teacher
(B) Afia's math teacher
(C) Afia's history teacher
(D) Afia's social studies teacher

57. What is true about Afia's total self-assessment score?

(A) It is the same as that given by the teacher.
(B) It is 1 point lower than that given by the teacher.
(C) It is 1 point higher than that given by the teacher.
(D) It means that Afia's project will be displayed at the festival.

58. Which of the following is NOT included in the criteria?

(A) originality
(B) use of time
(C) technical skill
(D) ability to collaborate

59. The underlined "complementary" is most similar to:

(A) whimsical
(B) affordable
(C) softhearted
(D) harmonizing

# General Reading Comprehension

**DIRECTIONS:** In this portion of the test, you will be provided with two longer reading passages. For the first passage, complete the blanks in the passage summary using the words provided. Fill in your choices in the corresponding spaces on your answer sheet. The second passage will be followed by four questions. For each question, choose the best answer according to the passage.

**Questions 60-61.** Read the passage and answer the questions.

> Look in the lunchbox of an innocent school child and you may find within it a sandwich. Yet sandwiches themselves may not have such innocent origins. Named after John Montagu, the 4th Earl of Sandwich, one story about the sandwich is that it got its start due to gambling. As legend has it, Lord Sandwich was constantly at the card table. An addicted gambler, he would play night and day without taking a break to eat. He was looking for a way to eat meat without getting his hands dirty while he was playing cards. The solution his servants came up with was two pieces of toasted bread with salted beef in the middle.

Summary:

The sandwich may have been invented due to the gambling problem of the Earl of Sandwich. Lord Sandwich played cards for long hours with no _____[A]_____ breaks. He wanted to be able to eat without _____[B]_____ the game. The solution was to put beef in between slices of bread.

60. Choose the most suitable word for blank [A], connecting the summary to the passage.

(A) dining
(B) music
(C) school
(D) looking

61. Choose the most suitable word for blank [B], connecting the summary to the passage.

(A) losing
(B) playing
(C) pausing
(D) legalizing

Questions 62-65. Read the passage and answer the questions.

[1] Jaguars are large cats found in the Americas, from the Southern United States, to Mexico, Central America, and South America. The third largest species of cat after lions and tigers, jaguars range in length from 90 to 190 centimeters and in weight from 28 to 90 kilograms. These large <u>felines</u> roam the dense tropical rainforests and grasslands that comprise their main habitat.

[2] Jaguars behave much like tigers, but most closely resemble African leopards due to their spots. Jaguars are larger, however, and their spots differ from those of a leopard. While leopards have spots shaped like rings, the spots on jaguars are filled with dots in the middle.

[3] Skilled hunters, jaguars possess a bite more powerful than a lion's. The bite of a jaguar is so strong, in fact, that it can crush the prey's skull. A jaguar's prey includes any kind of animal found in its habitat. Because jaguars are powerful swimmers, they can hunt anything in the rivers of their habitat, from fish to turtles, and even a type of small alligators called caimans. And on land, their prey includes everything from tiny mice to large domestic cows and deer.

62. Which is the best title for the passage?

(A) Spotted Cats of the Plains
(B) The Cat with the Strongest Bite
(C) Jaguars: Habitat, Appearance, Hunt
(D) Wild Cats: Jaguars versus Leopards

63. Which of the following is mentioned about jaguars?

(A) Most are found in Mexico.
(B) They are hunted by alligators.
(C) Their spots are filled with dots.
(D) Many have golden brown coats.

64. The underlined "felines" is closest in meaning to:

(A) cats
(B) animals
(C) hunters
(D) mammals

65. According to the passage, which of the following can be inferred about jaguars?

(A) They cannot get fully wet.
(B) They very rarely climb trees.
(C) They sometimes eat farm animals.
(D) They can thrive on the plains of Africa.

# This is the end of
# the TOSEL Actual Test.
# Thank you.

# Appendix

## A

| | |
|---|---|
| a ton of | 아주 많은 |
| aboveground | adj. 지상의 |
| abrupt | adj. 갑작스러운 |
| absolute | adj. 완전한 |
| accidentally | adv. 우연히, 뜻하지 않게, 잘못하여 |
| accomplished | adj. 기량이 뛰어난 |
| account | n. 계정 |
| accountant | n. 회계사 |
| accuracy | n. 정확도 |
| advise | v.조언하다,권고하다 |
| afford | v. (…을 할·살) 여유가 되다 |
| after school | 방과 후 |
| aftermath | n. 여파, 후유증 |
| air pollutants | 공기 오염물질 |
| alignment | n. 가지런함, (정치적)지지 |
| allergic | adj. 알레르기가 있는 |
| alter | v. 바꾸다 |
| altogether | adv. 완전히, 전적으로 |
| amount | n. (무엇의)양 |
| annoy | v. 짜증나게 하다 |
| applicant | n. 지원자 |
| application | n. 응용 프로그램, 지원[신청], 적용, 응용 |
| approve | v. 찬성하다, 승인하다, 인가하다 |
| appoximately | adv. 거의, 대략 |
| Arabic | n. 아랍어; adj. 아랍어[문학]의 |
| as soon as | … 하자마자 |
| assembly | n. 조회, 모임 |

| | |
|---|---|
| at fault | 잘못해서 |
| at the very latest | 아무리 늦어도 |
| ATM | n. 현금 자동 입출금기 |
| attorney | n. 변호사 |
| aunt | n. 고모, 이모, (외)숙모 |
| available | adj. 구할[이용할]수 있는, 시간[여유]이 있는 |
| awful | adj. 끔찍한 |

## B

| | |
|---|---|
| ballroom | n. 무도회장 |
| barely | adj. 간신히, 가까스로, 빠듯하게 |
| be aware | ~을 알다, 인지하다 |
| be in trouble | 난경에 처하다 |
| be out of control | 통제력을 벗어나다 |
| be supposed to | ~하기로 되어 있다[~해야 한다] |
| beach | n. 해변 |
| beat | v. 휘저어 섞다 |
| beneath | prep. 아래에, (수준 등이)…보다 못한 |
| bite | v. 묻다; n. 무는 행위 |
| bitterly | adv. 몹시 |
| blame | v. …을 탓하다[책임으로 보다] |
| block | v. 차단하다 |
| blogger | n. 블로그를 만드는 사람 |
| blow | v. (코를)풀다 |
| board | n. 판자; v. 승선하다 |
| boring | adj. 재미없는 |
| bowling | n. 볼링 |
| broadcast | v. 방송하다, 광고하다; n. 방송 |
| bruise | v. 멍[흠]이 생기다[생기게 하다] |

| brush off | v. (솔질로)털다 |
| --- | --- |
| bumper to bumper | adj. 차가 꽉 들어찬 |
| burn | n. 화상, 덴 상처; v. (불이)타오르다 |
| by accident | 실수로, 우연히 |
| bylaw | n. 조례, 내규 |

**C**

| canine | n. 개; adj. 개의 |
| --- | --- |
| capable of | ~할 수 있는 |
| carry | v. (이동 중에)들고[데리고] 있다 |
| cast iron | n. 무쇠 |
| catch sight of | 흘끗 보다 |
| cedar | n. 삼나무, 향나무 |
| Celsius | adj. 섭씨의 |
| century | n. 100년 |
| cereal | n. 곡물; 시리얼[가공 곡물] |
| charge | n. 혐의, 요금, v. 청구하다, 충전하다 |
| cheat | v. 부정행위를 하다 |
| check | v. 확인하다, 점검하다 |
| cheer | v. 응원하다 |
| chemical | n. 화학물질 |
| chemistry set | 화학실험 용품 |
| class president | 반장 |
| clock | n. 시계 |
| close | adj. (사이가)가까운, 친(밀)한 |
| coach | v. 코치하다, 지도하다 |
| coal mine | n. 석탄 광산 |
| come out with | ~을 사람들에게 선보이다 |
| comfortable | adj. 편한 |

| committed to | ~에 전념하는 |
| --- | --- |
| commonly | adv. 흔히, 보통 |
| competition | n. 대회 |
| complementary | adj. 상호보완적인 |
| comprehend | v. 이해하다 |
| concentrate | v. 집중하다 |
| concern | v. 걱정하다 |
| conditon | n. 상태 |
| conduct | v. (특정한 활동을)하다; 지휘하다; 안내하다 |
| confidence | n. 자신감 |
| confrontation | n. 대립, 대치 |
| consist of | ~로 구성되다 |
| contemporary | adj. 현대의, 동시대의 |
| content | n. 내용[물] |
| continent | n. 대륙 |
| contribution | n. 공헌, 기여, 기부금 |
| controversial | adj. 논란이 많은 |
| convert | v. 전환하다 |
| coolest | 최고로 멋진 |
| cousin | n. 사촌 |
| cower | v. (겁을 먹고)몸을 숙이다 [웅크리다] |
| crack | n. 금 |
| cruise ship | n. 유람선 |
| current | n. (물, 공기의)흐름, 해류, 기류; adj. 현재의 |
| cutting-edge | adj. 최첨단의 |

**D**

| dance | n. 춤 |
| --- | --- |

| dash cam | n. 차량용 블랙박스 |
| deadline | n. 기한, 마감 시간 |
| deer | n. 사슴 |
| delight | n. 기쁨[즐거움], v. 기쁨을 주다 |
| deny | v. 부인하다 |
| dessert | n. 디저트, 후식 |
| destination | n. 도착지 |
| detention | n. 방과 후 남게 하기 |
| diagonally | adv. 대각선으로, 비스듬하게 |
| diet | n. 식단 |
| dimension | n. (높이·너비·길이의) 치수 |
| dining room | n. 식당 |
| diploma | n. 졸업증, 학위증 |
| direction | n. 방향 |
| discount | n. 할인 |
| display case | n. 진열장 |
| diverse | adj. 다양한 |
| dock | n. 부두, 선창, 독 |
| don't bother | 신경 쓰지 마, 수고할 것 없다 |
| drawer | n. 서랍 |
| dress up | 옷을 갖춰 입다, 격식을 차려 입다 |
| drift | n. 이동, 표류 |
| drive | v. 태워다 주다 |
| driver's license | n. 운전면허증 |
| drone | n. 무인항공기 |
| dust | v. (고운 가루를) 뿌리다 |

## E

| earbud | n. 초소형 헤드폰 |

| economy | n. 경기, 경제 |
| elusive | adj. 찾기 힘든 |
| elderly | adj. 연세가 드신 |
| emotion | n. 감정, 정서 |
| endless | adj. 끝이 없는 |
| energy conservation | 에너지 절약 |
| enter | v. 출전시키다, 참가시키다 |
| entirely | adj. 전적으로 |
| entrant | n. 참가자 |
| equal | adj. 동일한 |
| essential item | 필수 품목 |
| exchange rate | 환율 |
| expiry date | n. 유통기한 |
| extraordinary | adj. 놀라운 |
| eye patch | n. 안대 |

## F

| fade | v. (색깔이)바래다[희미해지다] |
| fascinate | v. 마음을 사로잡다, 매혹하다 |
| famous | adj. 유명한 |
| fat | n. 지방 |
| fat chance | n. 가망 없음, 매우 희박한 가능성 |
| feed | v. 먹이다 |
| feline | n. 고양잇과 동물 |
| figure out | ~을 이해하다[알아내다], 해결하다 |
| film | n. 영화 |
| fine | adj. 아주 가는 |
| fine dust | n. 미세먼지 |
| first-aid kit | n. 구급상자 |

| | | | | |
|---|---|---|---|---|
| fix up | 수리하다 | | harmonizing | adj. 조화되는 |
| flake | n. 눈송이(=snowflakes) | | haunted | adj. 귀신이 나오는 |
| flashlight | n. 손전등 | | headache | n. 두통 |
| flood | n. 홍수; v. 물에 잠기다, 침수되다 | | heavy cream | 유지분이 많은 크림 |
| foggy | adj. 안개낀 | | helmet | n. 헬멧 |
| for a while | 잠시동안 | | help | v. 돕다 |
| free | v. 석방시키다, 풀어주다 | | hidden | adj. 숨겨진 |
| frittata | n. 채소,치즈 등을 달걀에 섞어 만든 오믈렛 | | hide | v. 감추다[숨기다] |
| furniture | n. 가구 | | hilarious | adj. 아주 우스운, 재미있는 |
| | | | hire | v. 고용하다 |
| **G** | | | historic | adj. 역사적인 |
| gazer | n. 응시[주시]하는 사람 | | How come? | 왜?, 어째서? |
| get sick | 탈이 나다 | | hunt | v. 사냥하다 |
| ghost | n. 유령 | | **I** | |
| good deal | 만족스러운 제안, 다수, 다량 | | idiot | n. 바보, 멍청이 |
| goods | n. 상품, 제품 | | in demand | 수요가 많은 |
| gorgeous | adj. 멋진 | | in spite of | ~에도 불구하고 |
| grass | n. 풀, 잔디 | | in step | 보조를 맞추어 |
| grasp | v. 꽉 잡다 | | incredibly | adv. 놀라울 정도로 |
| grated | adj. 갈은 | | immediately | adv. 즉시 |
| guest | n. 손님, 하객 | | indoor | adj. 실내의 |
| guy | n. 남자 | | information kiosk | n. 안내소, 안내 부스 |
| gym | n. 체육관 | | ingredient | n. (특히 요리 등의)재료[성분] |
| **H** | | | injure | v. (특히 사고로)부상을 입다[입히다] |
| hall | n. 홀[회관/-실](회의, 식사, 콘서트 등을 위한 큰 방이나 건물) | | inmate | n. 수감자 |
| handle | v. 다루다 | | inning | n. (야구에서 9회중의 한) 회 |
| hang out | 많은 시간을 보내다 | | ironically | adv. 반어적으로 |
| hardly | adv. 거의 ~ 않다 | | | |

| instrument | n. 악기 |
| --- | --- |
| intention | n. 의도 |
| intrigue | v. 흥미를 불러일으키다 |
| introduce oneself | 자기소개하다 |
| introduction | n. (사람) 소개, 도입, 전래 |

**J**

| join | v. 등록하다 |
| --- | --- |
| junk | n. 쓸모없는 물건, 폐물, 쓰레기 |

**K**

| keep in touch | 연락하고 지내자 |
| --- | --- |

**L**

| latest | adj. 최신의 |
| --- | --- |
| large | adj. 큰 |
| laundry | n. 세탁(물), 세탁소 |
| leakage | n. 누출 |
| leave | v. 떠나다 |
| legalizing | adj. 합법화하는 |
| level | n. 단계 |
| licensing | n. 허가 |
| link | v. 연결하다, 접속하다 |
| lock | v. 잠그다 |
| locker | n. 사물함 |
| log | n. 통나무 |
| log into | 접속하다 |
| loop | n. (올가미나 동그라미 모양의)고리 |
| loose | adj. 마음대로 돌아다니는; (조직, 통제가) 느슨한; 헐렁한 |
| lower | v. 낮추다 |

| lumberjack | n. 벌목꾼 |
| --- | --- |

**M**

| magnify | v. (렌즈, 현미경 등으로)(크기, 소리를) 확대하다; (중요성을) 과장하다 |
| --- | --- |
| make up one's mind | 결심하다 |
| marginalize | v. 하찮은 존재 같은 기분이 들게 하다[존재로 만들다] |
| marinated | adj. 절인 |
| mark | v.위치를 표시하다 |
| market | n. 시장 |
| marketing | n. 마케팅 |
| marry | v. (...와)결혼하다, 주례하다, (~에게)결혼시키다 |
| mate | n. 짝 |
| maximize | v. 극대화하다 |
| mean to | ...할 셈이다 |
| melt | v. 녹다[녹이다] |
| memorial | n. 기념비(적인 것); adj. (죽은 사람을)기념하기 위한, 추도[추모]의 |
| mention | v. 말하다, 언급하다 |
| merit | v. (칭찬, 관심 등을)받을 만하다; n. 장점 |
| merry | adj. 즐거운 |
| mess up | (~을) 엉망으로 만들다 |
| mile | n. 마일 |
| minimum order | 최소 주문량 |
| misbehave | v. 버릇없이 굴다 |
| miss | v. 그리워하다 |
| mistake | n. 실수, 잘못; v. 오해하다 |
| mobile app | n. 모바일 어플 |
| mock interview | 모의 면접 |

| motion sickness | n. 멀미 |
| --- | --- |

**N**

| nail | n. 손톱 |
| --- | --- |
| negotiation | n. 협상 |
| never mind | 신경 쓰지 마; 걱정하지 마 |
| new | adj. 새로운 |
| no less | (놀람,감탄을 나타냄) 역시 |
| nocturnal | adj. 야행성의 |
| nominate | v. 지명하다 |
| note | v. 알아차리다, 주목하다, 언급하다 |
| nowhere | adv. 아무데도[어디에도](...않다[없다]) |
| nuclear power | n. 원자력 발전 |

**O**

| occasion | n. (어떤 일이 일어나는 특정한)때[기회/경우], 행사 |
| --- | --- |
| on board | 동의하다 |
| on foot | 걸어서 |
| once | conj. ... 할 때 |
| operation | n. 운영 |
| orientation | n. 오리엔테이션, 예비 교육 |
| otherwise | adj. 그외에는 |
| out of shape | 건강이 안 좋은[몸매가 엉망인] |
| outdoor | adv. 야외의 |
| overall | adj. 대부분, 전체의 |
| overdo | v. 지나치게 하다, 과장하다, 지나치게 많이 쓰다[이용하다] |
| overseas | adj. 해외[외국/국외]의, 해외에[로] |

**P**

| pair | n. 짝 |
| --- | --- |

| panel | n. 판 |
| --- | --- |
| pass | v. 통과하다, 합격하다 |
| path | n. 길 |
| pavement | n. 보도, 인도, 포장 지역 |
| paw | n. (동물의 발톱이 달린)발 |
| percussionist | n. 타악기 연주자 |
| performance | n. 공연, 연주회, (개인의)연기[연주], 실적, 성과 |
| periodic | adj. 주기적인 |
| permanent | adj. 영구[영속]적인 |
| permit holder | n. 허가권자 |
| pet | n. 반려동물 |
| pharmacy | n. 약국 |
| phenomenon | n. 현상 |
| physics | n. 물리학 |
| pile | n. 포개(쌓아)놓은 것, 더미, 무더기 |
| pile up | 쌓이다 |
| plain | n. 평원, 평지 |
| playtime | n. 노는 시간 |
| planner | n. 일정 계획표 |
| pleasant | adj. 즐거운, 기분 좋은 |
| prank | n. (농담으로 하는)장난 |
| plumber | n. 배관공 |
| policy | n. 정책 |
| populous | adj. 인구가 많은 |
| precious | adj. 소중한 |
| preparation | n. 준비 |
| preschool | n. 유치원 |
| pressure | n. 압력 |

| previous | adj. 이전의 |
| --- | --- |
| price | n. 가격 |
| profession | n. 직업 |
| punishment | n. 벌 |
| purchase | v. 구매하다 |
| push-up | n. 팔굽혀펴기 |

## Q

| quit | v. (하던 일을) 그만두다 |
| --- | --- |
| quite | adv. 꽤, 상당히 |

## R

| racism | n. 인종차별 |
| --- | --- |
| racket | n. 시끄러운 소리, 소음, (테니스 등의)라켓 |
| raft | n. 뗏목 |
| rafting | n. 래프팅 |
| rage | n. 분노 |
| rally | n. 집회[대회], 경주 |
| range from A to B | (범위가) A에서 B 사이이다 |
| rate | n. 요금 |
| raw | adj. 날 것의 |
| recipe | n. 요리법, 레시피 |
| recommend | v. 추천하다, 권고하다 |
| reduce | v. 줄이다 |
| regarding | prep. ~에 관하여 |
| regulation | n. 규정 |
| relative | n. 친척 |
| release | v. 방출하다 |
| remind | v. 상기시키다 |
| reminder | n. 상기시키는[생각나게 하는] 것 |

| remote | n. 리모컨 |
| --- | --- |
| remote control | n. 리모콘 |
| remove | v. 제거하다 |
| report | n. 보고서; v. 알리다 |
| request | v. 요청하다 |
| reset | v. 다시 맞추다 |
| resident | n. 거주자 |
| residential neighborhood | n. 주택가 |
| responsibility | n. 책임, 맡은 일 |
| restore | v. 복원하다 |
| reveal | v. 드러내다 |
| right of way | n. 통행권 |
| ring | v. (종이[을])울리다; n. 종소리 |
| risky | adj. 위험한 |
| roof | n. 지붕 |
| rope | n. 밧줄 |
| rot | v. 썩다, 부패하다 |
| rotator | n. 회전하는 것 |
| router | n. 라우터 |
| ruin | v. 엉망으로 만들다, 망치다 |
| run | v. 출마[입후보]하다 |
| runners | n. 운동화 |

## S

| safety | n. 안전 |
| --- | --- |
| saw | n. 톱; v. 톱질하다 |
| say out loud | 크게 소리내어 말하다 |
| schedule | v. 일정[시간 계획]을 잡다, 예정하다 |
| scoop | n. 큰 숟갈, 스쿱 |

| | | | | |
|---|---|---|---|---|
| scraper | n. 긁개 | | sniff | v. 코를 훌쩍이다 |
| seat belt | n. 안전벨트 | | soft-hearted | adj. 마음씨 고운, 인정 많은 |
| secondhand | adj. 중고의 | | solitary | adj. 혼자 하는 |
| senior | n. 고령자, 노인 | | sound | n. 소리; adj. 다치지[손상되지] 않은, 이상 없는 |
| seniors' home | 양로원 | | spare | adj. 남는, 여분의, 예비용의 |
| separate compartment | 분리된 칸 | | species | n. 종 |
| separately | adj. 따로따로, 별도로 | | speed limit | n. 제한 속도 |
| severe | adj. 심각한 | | spicy | adj. 매운, 양념 맛이 강한 |
| shabby | adj. 허름한, 낡은 | | spit | v. 뱉다 |
| shade | n. 색조 | | splitting | adj. 깨질듯한 |
| shallow | adj. 얕은, 피상적인 | | squeeze | v. 짜다, 짜내다, (좁은 곳에)밀어[집어] 넣다 |
| ship | v. 수송하다, 출하하다, 선적하다 | | spot | n. (특정한) 곳 |
| shore | n. (바다호수 따위)기슭, 해안[해변] | | stare | v. 빤히 쳐다보다, 응시하다 |
| shovel | v. 삽질하다 | | stick | v. 붙이다 |
| significantly | adv. 상당히[크게] | | sticky-note | n. 포스트잇(쉽게 떼었다 붙였다 할 수 있는 메모지) |
| silly | adj. 어리석은, 바보 같은, 우스꽝스러운, 유치한 | | stitch | n. 바늘땀; v. 봉합하다 |
| sleeping bag | n. 침낭 | | stool | n. (등받이와 팔걸이가 없는)의자 |
| sleepy | adj. 졸린 | | stop A from B | A가 B하는 것을 멈추게 하다 |
| slice | n. 조각 | | strain | n. 무리 |
| slip | v. 미끄러지다 | | struggle | v. 애쓰다 |
| slippers | n. 슬리퍼 | | stub | v. (~에) 발가락이 차이다 |
| slope | n. 비탈길 | | stuck on | ~에 빠져[미쳐, 반해] |
| slow | adj. 느린 | | stuff | v. 채우다; n. 물건 |
| slushy | adj. 눈 녹은, 진흙탕의, 진창의 | | stuffed | adj. 잔뜩 먹은 |
| smart | v. 욱신[따끔]거리다, 쓰리다 | | stunning | adj. 아름다운 |
| smart cookie | 영리한 녀석 | | subject to | ~되기 쉽다 |
| smart features | 스마트 기능 | | substance | n. 물질 |

| | |
|---|---|
| sugar | n. 설탕, 당분 |
| sugary | adj. 단 |
| suit | n. 신사복[숙녀복] 정장; v. 어울리다 |
| sunrise | n. 동틀녘, 일출 |
| sunset | n. 노을 |
| supplier | n. 공급업체 |
| support | v. 지탱하다, 받치다 |
| supposedly | adj. 아마도 |
| susceptible | adj. ~에 민감한, 걸리기 쉬운 |
| sweetheart | n. 다정한 사람; 애인; 자기(호칭) |
| swell | v. 붓다, 부풀다 |
| swift | adj. 재빠른, 신속한 |
| swipe | v. (카드를)읽히다 |
| swivel chair | 회전의자 |

| T | |
|---|---|
| take a look at | ~을 한 번 보다 |
| take out | 가지고 나가다, 들어내다, 취득하다 |
| tattoo | n. 문신 |
| tease | v. 놀리다 |
| temperament | n. 기질, 성질 |
| temporary | adj. 일시적인, 임시의 |
| tender | adj. (고기 등이) 부드러운 |
| thrive | v. 번성하다, 성공하다, 무럭무럭 자라다 |
| thumb drive | n. 플래시 드라이브(컴퓨터의 휴대용 저장장치) |
| tidy up | 정리하다 |
| tip | v. 기울이다 |
| tonight | adv. 오늘 밤에 |
| towel | n. 수건 |

| | |
|---|---|
| transform | v. 변형시키다 |
| trash | n. 쓰레기 |
| trick | n. (사람들을 즐겁게 하는) 마술 |
| trickery | n. 속임수 |
| try-out | n. 선발, 오디션; v. 시험해보다, 오디션 보다 |
| turbulence | n. 난기류 |
| turnout | n. 참가자의 수, 투표율 |
| turtle | n. 바다 거북, (모든 종류의)거북 |
| typhoon | n. 태풍 |

| U | |
|---|---|
| undergo | v. 겪다, 받다 |
| underground shelter | 지하 대피소 |
| unexpected | adj. 뜻밖의, 예상 밖의 |
| unhealthy | adj. 건강에 해로운 |
| unmarinated | adj. 절이지 않은 |
| urge | v. 설득하다 |
| used goods | 중고물품 |
| user agreement (=contract) | 이용자 약관 |

| V | |
|---|---|
| value | v. 소중하게 생각하다; n. 가치 |
| vehicle | n. 차량, 탈 것 |
| vent | v. (감정, 분통을) 터뜨리다 |
| venue | n. 장소 |
| versatile | adj. 다재다능한 |
| vertical | adj. 수직의, 세로의 |
| victim | n. 피해자, 희생물 |
| viewer | n. 시청자 |

| voting | n. 투표 |
| --- | --- |
| **W** | |
| wallpaper | n. 벽지 |
| washroom | n. 화장실 |
| water content | 수분 함량 |
| waterfront | n. 해안가, 부둣가, 물가 |
| way | n. 길; adj. 훨씬 |
| wear | v. 입다 [쓰다, 끼다, 착용하다] |
| What are you up to?(=What are you doing?) | 무엇을 하고 있니? |
| whether | conj. ...인지(아닌지), ...이든(아니든 |
| while | conj. ...하는 동안[사이]; n. 잠깐, 잠시 |
| whimsical | adj. 변덕스러운, 별난, 기발한 |
| whitewater | n. 급류 |
| wireless | adj. 무선의 |
| wildcat | n. 들고양이 |
| wispy | adj. 성긴 |
| wooden | adj. 나무로 된 |
| worth | adj. ~의 가치가 있는 |
| wreck | v. 깨다, 파괴하다 |

# 국제영어능력인증시험 (TOSEL)

* 연습을 위한 OMR 카드 샘플입니다.

| HIGH JUNIOR | 한글이름 | 감독확인 |
| --- | --- | --- |

## 수 험 번 호

(1)

(2)

## SECTION I

| 문항 | A B C D | 문항 | A B C D |
| --- | --- | --- | --- |
| 1 | A B C | 16 | A B C D |
| 2 | A B C | 17 | A B C D |
| 3 | A B C | 18 | A B C D |
| 4 | A B C | 19 | A B C D |
| 5 | A B C | 20 | A B C D |
| 6 | A B C | 21 | A B C D |
| 7 | A B C D | 22 | A B C D |
| 8 | A B C D | 23 | A B C D |
| 9 | A B C | 24 | A B C D |
| 10 | A B C | 25 | A B C D |
| 11 | A B C D | 26 | A B C D |
| 12 | A B C D | 27 | A B C D |
| 13 | A B C D | 28 | A B C D |
| 14 | A B C D | 29 | A B C D |
| 15 | A B C D | 30 | A B C D |

## SECTION II

| 문항 | A B C D | 문항 | A B C D | 문항 | A B C D |
| --- | --- | --- | --- | --- | --- |
| 31 | A B C D | 46 | A B C D | 61 | A B C D |
| 32 | A B C D | 47 | A B C D | 62 | A B C D |
| 33 | A B C D | 48 | A B C D | 63 | A B C D |
| 34 | A B C D | 49 | A B C D | 64 | A B C D |
| 35 | A B C D | 50 | A B C D | 65 | A B C D |
| 36 | A B C D | 51 | A B C D | | |
| 37 | A B C D | 52 | A B C D | | |
| 38 | A B C D | 53 | A B C D | | |
| 39 | A B C D | 54 | A B C D | | |
| 40 | A B C D | 55 | A B C D | | |
| 41 | A B C D | 56 | A B C D | | |
| 42 | A B C D | 57 | A B C D | | |
| 43 | A B C D | 58 | A B C D | | |
| 44 | A B C D | 59 | A B C D | | |
| 45 | A B C D | 60 | A B C D | | |

### 주 의 사 항

1. 수험번호 및 답안은 검은색 사인펜을 사용해서 <보기>와 같이 표기합니다.
   <보기> 바른표기 : ●  틀린표기 : ⊘ ⊗ ⊙ ◑ ◉
2. 수험번호(1)에는 아라비아 숫자로 쓰고, (2)에는 해당란에 ● 표기합니다.
3. 답안 수정은 수정 테이프로 흔적을 깨끗이 지웁니다.
4. 수험번호 및 답안 작성란 이외의 여백에 낙서를 하지 마시기 바랍니다. 이로 인한 불이익은 수험자 본인 책임입니다.
5. 마킹오류로 채점 불가능한 답안은 0점 처리되오니, 이점 유의하시기 바랍니다.

* 정기시험 OMR로 사용이 불가합니다.

국제토셀위원회

# 국제영어능력인증시험 (TOSEL)



**HIGH JUNIOR**

한글이름

감독확인

## 수 험 번 호

(1)

(2)

## SECTION I

| 문항 | A B C D | 문항 | A B C D |
|---|---|---|---|
| 1 | A B C | 16 | A B C D |
| 2 | A B C | 17 | A B C D |
| 3 | A B C | 18 | A B C D |
| 4 | A B C | 19 | A B C D |
| 5 | A B C | 20 | A B C D |
| 6 | A B C | 21 | A B C D |
| 7 | A B C D | 22 | A B C D |
| 8 | A B C D | 23 | A B C D |
| 9 | A B C D | 24 | A B C D |
| 10 | A B C D | 25 | A B C D |
| 11 | A B C D | 26 | A B C D |
| 12 | A B C D | 27 | A B C D |
| 13 | A B C D | 28 | A B C D |
| 14 | A B C D | 29 | A B C D |
| 15 | A B C D | 30 | A B C D |

## SECTION II

| 문항 | A B C D | 문항 | A B C D | 문항 | A B C D |
|---|---|---|---|---|---|
| 31 | A B C D | 46 | A B C D | 61 | A B C D |
| 32 | A B C D | 47 | A B C D | 62 | A B C D |
| 33 | A B C D | 48 | A B C D | 63 | A B C D |
| 34 | A B C D | 49 | A B C D | 64 | A B C D |
| 35 | A B C D | 50 | A B C D | 65 | A B C D |
| 36 | A B C D | 51 | A B C D | | |
| 37 | A B C D | 52 | A B C D | | |
| 38 | A B C D | 53 | A B C D | | |
| 39 | A B C D | 54 | A B C D | | |
| 40 | A B C D | 55 | A B C D | | |
| 41 | A B C D | 56 | A B C D | | |
| 42 | A B C D | 57 | A B C D | | |
| 43 | A B C D | 58 | A B C D | | |
| 44 | A B C D | 59 | A B C D | | |
| 45 | A B C D | 60 | A B C D | | |

## 주 의 사 항

1. 수험번호 및 답안은 검은색 사인펜을 사용해서 <보기>와 같이 표기합니다.
   <보기> 바른표기 : ● 틀린표기 : ⊘ ⊗ ⊙ ◐ ◎

2. 수험번호(1)에는 아라비아 숫자로 쓰고, (2)에는 해당란에 ● 표기합니다.

3. 답안 수정은 수정 테이프로 흔적을 깨끗이 지웁니다.

4. 수험번호 및 답안 작성란 이외의 여백에 낙서를 하지 마시기 바랍니다. 이로 인한 불이익은 수험자 본인 책임입니다.

5. 마킹오류로 채점 불가능한 답안은 0점 처리되오니, 이점 유의하시기 바랍니다.



국제토셀위원회

# 국제영어능력인증시험 (TOSEL)



**HIGH JUNIOR**

한글이름

감독확인

## 수험번호

(1)

(2)

## SECTION I

| 문항 | A B C D | 문항 | A B C D |
|---|---|---|---|
| 1 | A B C | 16 | A B C D |
| 2 | A B C | 17 | A B C D |
| 3 | A B C | 18 | A B C D |
| 4 | A B C | 19 | A B C D |
| 5 | A B C | 20 | A B C D |
| 6 | A B C | 21 | A B C D |
| 7 | A B C D | 22 | A B C D |
| 8 | A B C D | 23 | A B C D |
| 9 | A B C D | 24 | A B C D |
| 10 | A B C D | 25 | A B C D |
| 11 | A B C D | 26 | A B C D |
| 12 | A B C D | 27 | A B C D |
| 13 | A B C D | 28 | A B C D |
| 14 | A B C D | 29 | A B C D |
| 15 | A B C D | 30 | A B C D |

## SECTION II

| 문항 | A B C D | 문항 | A B C D | 문항 | A B C D |
|---|---|---|---|---|---|
| 31 | A B C D | 46 | A B C D | 61 | A B C D |
| 32 | A B C D | 47 | A B C D | 62 | A B C D |
| 33 | A B C D | 48 | A B C D | 63 | A B C D |
| 34 | A B C D | 49 | A B C D | 64 | A B C D |
| 35 | A B C D | 50 | A B C D | 65 | A B C D |
| 36 | A B C D | 51 | A B C D | | |
| 37 | A B C D | 52 | A B C D | | |
| 38 | A B C D | 53 | A B C D | | |
| 39 | A B C D | 54 | A B C D | | |
| 40 | A B C D | 55 | A B C D | | |
| 41 | A B C D | 56 | A B C D | | |
| 42 | A B C D | 57 | A B C D | | |
| 43 | A B C D | 58 | A B C D | | |
| 44 | A B C D | 59 | A B C D | | |
| 45 | A B C D | 60 | A B C D | | |

### 주의사항

1. 수험번호 및 답안은 검은색 사인펜을 사용해서 <보기>와 같이 표기합니다.
   <보기> 바른표기 : ● 틀린표기 : ⊘ ⊗ ⊙ ◖ ◎

2. 수험번호(1)에는 아라비아 숫자로 쓰고, (2)에는 해당란에 ● 표기합니다.

3. 답안 수정은 수정 테이프로 흔적을 깨끗이 지웁니다.

4. 수험번호 및 답안 작성란 이외의 여백에 낙서를 하지 마시기 바랍니다. 이로 인한 불이익은 수험자 본인 책임입니다.

5. 마킹오류로 채점 불가능한 답안은 0점 처리되오니, 이점 유의하시기 바랍니다.



국제토셀위원회

# 국제영어능력인증시험 (TOSEL)



**HIGH JUNIOR**

한글이름

감독확인

## 수 험 번 호

(1)

(2)

| SECTION I | | | | | | | | |
|---|---|---|---|---|---|---|---|---|
| 문항 | A B C D | 문항 | A B C D | 문항 | A B C D | 문항 | A B C D | 문항 A B C D |
| 1 | A B C | 16 | A B C D | 31 | A B C D | 46 | A B C D | 61 A B C D |
| 2 | A B C | 17 | A B C D | 32 | A B C D | 47 | A B C D | 62 A B C D |
| 3 | A B C | 18 | A B C D | 33 | A B C D | 48 | A B C D | 63 A B C D |
| 4 | A B C | 19 | A B C D | 34 | A B C D | 49 | A B C D | 64 A B C D |
| 5 | A B C | 20 | A B C D | 35 | A B C D | 50 | A B C D | 65 A B C D |
| 6 | A B C | 21 | A B C D | 36 | A B C D | 51 | A B C D | |
| 7 | A B C D | 22 | A B C D | 37 | A B C D | 52 | A B C D | |
| 8 | A B C D | 23 | A B C D | 38 | A B C D | 53 | A B C D | |
| 9 | A B C D | 24 | A B C D | 39 | A B C D | 54 | A B C D | |
| 10 | A B C D | 25 | A B C D | 40 | A B C D | 55 | A B C D | |
| 11 | A B C D | 26 | A B C D | 41 | A B C D | 56 | A B C D | |
| 12 | A B C D | 27 | A B C D | 42 | A B C D | 57 | A B C D | |
| 13 | A B C D | 28 | A B C D | 43 | A B C D | 58 | A B C D | |
| 14 | A B C D | 29 | A B C D | 44 | A B C D | 59 | A B C D | |
| 15 | A B C D | 30 | A B C D | 45 | A B C D | 60 | A B C D | |

**SECTION I** (문항 1–30) / **SECTION II** (문항 31–65)

### 주의사항

1. 수험번호 및 답안은 검은색 사인펜을 사용해서 <보기>와 같이 표기합니다.
   <보기> 바른표기 : ● 틀린표기 : ✔ ✗ ⊙ ◑ ◓
2. 수험번호(1)에는 아라비아 숫자로 쓰고, (2)에는 해당란에 ● 표기합니다.
3. 답안 수정은 수정 테이프로 흔적을 깨끗이 지웁니다.
4. 수험번호 및 답안 작성란 이외의 여백에 낙서를 하지 마시기 바랍니다. 이로 인한 불이익은 수험자 본인 책임입니다.
5. 마킹오류로 채점 불가능한 답안은 0점 처리되오니, 이점 유의하시기 바랍니다.



국제토셀위원회

# TOSEL® Lab

## TOSEL Lab이란?

**공동기획**
- 고려대학교 문과대학 언어정보연구소
- 고려대학교 공과대학 기계학습 및 빅 데이터연구원
- 국제토셀위원회

**엄선된 100만 명의 응시자 성적 데이터를 활용한
AI기반 데이터 공유 및 가치 고도화 플랫폼**

국내외 15,000여 개 학교·학원 단체응시인원 중 엄선한 100만 명 이상의 실제 TOSEL 성적 데이터와, 정부(과학기술정보통신부)의 연구지원으로 개발된 **맞춤식 AI 빅데이터 기반 영어성장 플랫폼**입니다.

## TOSEL Lab Brand Identity

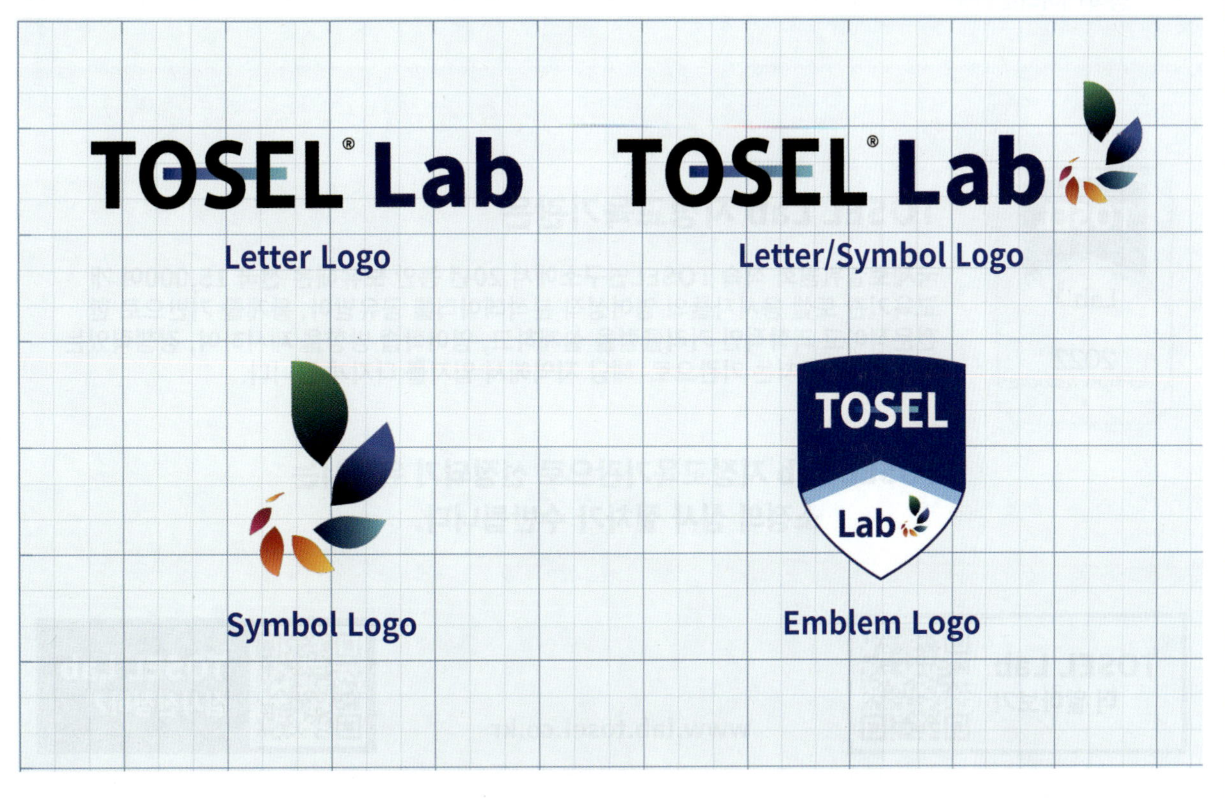

# 교재를 100% 활용하는 TOSEL Lab 지정교육기관의 노하우!

## Teaching Materials

TOSEL에서 제공하는 수업 자료로
교재 학습을 더욱 효과적으로 진행!

## Study Content

철저한 자기주도학습 콘텐츠로
교재 수업후 효과적인 복습!

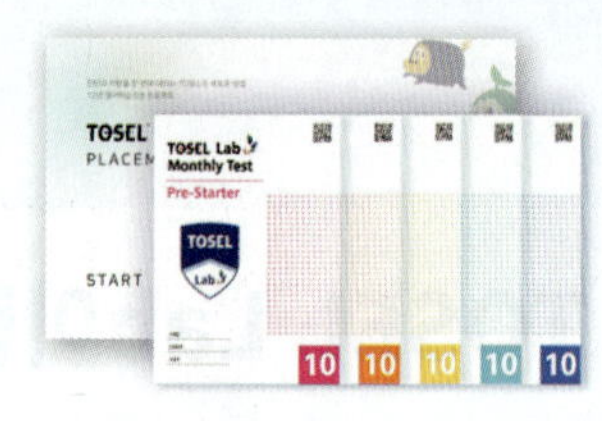


## Test Content

교재 학습과 더불어 학생 맞춤형
시험으로 실력 점검 및 향상

## Book Content

100만 명으로 엄선된 TOSEL
성적 데이터로 탄생!

국제토셀위원회는 TOSEL Lab 지정교육기관에서 교재로
수업하는 학원을 위해 교재를 잘 활용할 수 있는 다양한
콘텐츠를 제공 및 지원합니다.

**TOSEL Lab 지정교육기관을 위한 콘텐츠로
더욱 효과적인 수업을 경험하세요.**

## TOSEL Lab 지정교육기관은

국제토셀위원회 직속 TOSEL연구소에서 20년 동안 보유해온 전국 15,000여 개
교육기관 토셀 응시자들의 영어성적 분석데이터를 공유받아, 통계를 기반으로 한
전문적이고 과학적인 커리큘럼을 설계하고, 영어학습 방향을 제시하여, 경쟁력있는
기관, 잘 가르치는 기관으로 해당 지역에서 입지를 다지게 됩니다.

**TOSEL Lab 지정교육기관으로 선정되기 위해서는
소정의 심사 절차가 수반됩니다.**

**TOSEL Lab**
더 알아보기

www.lab.tosel.co.kr

# TOSEL

## 실전문제집 2

# HIGH JUNIOR

## 정답과 해설

# TOSEL®
## 실전문제집 ②

# High Junior
## 정답 및 해설

# TOSEL High Junior

## 실전 1회



---

## SECTION I  LISTENING AND SPEAKING

**Part 1. Listen and Recognize (p.14)**

**1.** W: Honey, wear your helmet. Safety comes first.
　M: Do I have to? I mean, it's just a 10-minute bike ride.
정답 (B)
해석 여: 얘, 너의 헬멧을 써. 안전이 먼저야.
　　남: 꼭 그래야만 해? 내 말은, 10분만 자전거 탈 거잖아.
풀이 여자가 헬멧을 써야 한다고 했으므로 (B)가 정답이다.
Words and Phrases  wear 쓰다 | helmet 헬멧 | safety 안전

**2.** M: Are those people wearing face masks for fashion?
　W: What? No, they are for blocking air pollutants and fine dust.
정답 (B)
해석 남: 저 사람들 패션으로 얼굴 마스크 쓰고 있는 거야?
　　여: 뭐라고? 아니, 저것들은 공기 오염물질들과 미세먼지 차단을 위한
　　　　거야.
풀이 사람들이 미세먼지 차단을 위한 마스크를 쓰고 있다고 했으므로 (B)가 정답
　　이다. (C)는 'mask'를 이용한 오답이다.
Words and Phrases  wear 입다 [쓰다, 끼다, 착용하다] | block 차단하다 |
　　　　　　　　air pollutants 공기 오염물질 | fine dust 미세먼지

**3.** W: Will you stop that? It's very unhealthy.
　M: I can't help it. Biting my nails helps me relax and
　　concentrate.
정답 (C)
해석 여: 그것 좀 그만할래? 그것은 건강에 매우 해로워.
　　남: 난 어쩔 수가 없어. 내 손톱들을 물어뜯는 것이 나를 편안하게 하고
　　　　내가 집중하도록 도와줘.
풀이 남자가 손톱을 물어뜯는다고 했으므로 (C)가 정답이다.
Words and Phrases  unhealthy 건강에 해로운 | bite 물다 | nail 손톱 |
　　　　　　　　help 돕다 | concentrate 집중하다

**4.** M: That was the coolest card trick I've ever seen! I'm
　　impressed!
　W: Ha ha, it's my hidden talent. Glad you liked my amateur
　　trickery.
정답 (A)
해석 남: 저것은 내가 본 것 중의 가장 멋진 카드 마술이었어! 정말 멋진데!
　　여: 하하, 그게 내 숨겨진 재주야. 내 아마추어 속임수를 좋아해줘서
　　　　다행이다.
풀이 카드를 이용한 마술에 관해 이야기하고 있으므로 (A)가 정답이다.
Words and Phrases  coolest 최고로 멋진 | hidden 숨겨진 |
　　　　　　　　trickery 속임수 | trick (사람들을 즐겁게 하는) 마술

**5.** W: I'm looking for a new mouse pad that can support my wrist.
　M: Try this one. It'll reduce the pressure and strain.
정답 (C)
해석 여: 저는 제 손목을 지탱할 수 있는 새 마우스 패드를 찾고 있어요.
　　남: 이것을 사용해보세요. 그것이 압력과 무리를 줄여줄 거예요.
풀이 손목을 지탱할 수 있는 마우스 패드에 관해 이야기하고 있으므로 (C)가 정
　　답이다. (B)는 'wrist'와 'strain'을 통해 연상하도록 유도한 오답이다.
Words and Phrases  new 새로운 | support 지탱하다, 받치다 |
　　　　　　　　reduce 줄이다 | pressure 압력 | strain 무리

**6.** W: There's a ton of snow piling up on the roof.
　M: I'll hire somebody to shovel it off.
정답 (A)
해석 여: 지붕 위에 아주 많은 눈이 쌓이고 있어.
　　남: 그것을 삽질할 누군가를 고용할게.
풀이 지붕에 쌓인 눈을 삽질하는 것에 관해 이야기하고 있으므로 (A)가 정답이
　　다. (B)와 (C)는 'snow'를 통해 연상하도록 유도한 오답이다.
Words and Phrases  a ton of 아주 많은 | pile up 쌓이다 | roof 지붕 |
　　　　　　　　hire 고용하다 | shovel 삽질하다

**Part 2. Listen and Respond (p.16)**

**7.** W: How much are these slippers?
　M: ________________
　　**(A) Seven thousand won for the pair.**
　　(B) My feet are cold in those sandals.
　　(C) Right around the corner is a store.
　　(D) The exchange rate from won to dollars.

해석　여: 이 슬리퍼들은 얼마인가요?

　　　남: ______________

　　　(A) 한 짝에 7천원입니다.

　　　(B) 그 샌들을 신으면 나의 발이 춥다.

　　　(C) 모퉁이를 돌면 바로 가게입니다.

　　　(D) 원에서 달러로의 환율입니다.

풀이　슬리퍼의 가격을 묻는 말에 한 짝에 7천원이라고 답하는 (A)가 정답이다.

Words and Phrases　slippers 슬리퍼 | pair 짝 | exchange rate 환율

**8.** M: I left my locker key at home.

　　　W: ______________

　　　(A) Let's paint over it.

　　　(B) Let's remind her again.

　　　**(C) Let's go back and get it.**

　　　(D) Let's lock all the windows.

해석　남: 나는 내 사물함 열쇠를 집에 놓고 왔어.

　　　여: ______________

　　　(A) 우리 그것 위에 페인트칠하자.

　　　(B) 우리 그녀에게 다시 한번 상기시키자.

　　　(C) 우리 돌아가서 그것을 가져오자.

　　　(D) 우리 창문들을 모두 잠그자.

풀이　열쇠를 집에 두고 왔다는 말에 돌아가서 가져오자고 제안하는 (C)가 정답이다.

Words and Phrases　locker 사물함 | remind 상기시키다 | lock 잠그다

**9.** W: What an extraordinary film! What did you think?

　　　M: ______________

　　　(A) I can take you there.

　　　**(B) I was also impressed.**

　　　(C) This is a delicious pie.

　　　(D) That's the biggest they had.

해석　여: 너무 놀라운 영화다! 넌 어떤 거 같아?

　　　남: ______________

　　　(A) 내가 너를 거기에 데려다 줄 수 있어.

　　　(B) 나에게도 인상 깊었어.

　　　(C) 이것은 맛있는 파이야.

　　　(D) 저것이 그들이 가진 것 중 가장 큰 것이야.

풀이　영화에 대해 어떻게 생각하냐는 질문에 자신도 인상 깊었다며 공감해주는 (B)가 정답이다.

Words and Phrases　extraordinary 놀라운 | film 영화

**10.** M: That clock is five minutes slow.

　　　W: ______________

　　　(A) Yes. You can run around.

　　　(B) Naturally. This is your day.

　　　(C) Of course. I'll let you know.

　　　**(D) You're right. I'll reset the time.**

해석　남: 저 시계는 5분 느려.

　　　여: ______________

　　　(A) 응, 넌 뛰어다닐 수 있어.

　　　(B) 물론이지. 오늘은 너의 날이야.

　　　(C) 당연하지. 내가 알려줄게.

　　　(D) 네가 맞아. 내가 시간을 다시 맞출게.

풀이　시계가 느리다는 말에 시간을 다시 맞추겠다고 대답하는 (D)가 정답이다.

Words and Phrases　clock 시계 | slow 느린 | reset 다시 맞추다

**11.** W: This computer game is boring.

　　　M: ______________

　　　(A) Ten people were there.

　　　(B) There are a few names.

　　　(C) This video is almost over.

　　　**(D) The next level is more exciting.**

해석　여: 이 컴퓨터 게임은 재미없어.

　　　남: ______________

　　　(A) 열 명이 거기에 있었어.

　　　(B) 거기에 몇 개의 이름들이 있어.

　　　(C) 이 영상은 거의 끝났어.

　　　(D) 그 다음 단계는 더 흥미로워.

풀이　컴퓨터 게임이 재미없다는 말에 다음 단계는 더 흥미롭다고 말하는 (D)가 정답이다.

Words and Phrases　boring 재미없는 | level 단계

**12.** M: It's too early to go to bed.

　　　W: ______________

　　　(A) They're the same price.

　　　**(B) But I'm sleepy right now.**

　　　(C) Your sleeping bag is here.

　　　(D) I can reach the light for you.

해석　남: 취침하기에는 너무 일러.

　　　여: ______________

　　　(A) 그것들은 같은 가격이야.

　　　(B) 하지만 난 지금 졸려.

　　　(C) 너의 침낭은 여기에 있어.

　　　(D) 내가 너 대신 불을 꺼줄게.

풀이　취침하기에는 너무 이르다는 말에 이미 졸리다고 말하는 (B)가 정답이다.

Words and Phrases　price 가격 | sleepy 졸린 | sleeping bag 침낭

**13.** W: This sunset is gorgeous, isn't it?

　　　M: ______________

　　　(A) I'm not sure of its name.

　　　**(B) It is absolutely stunning.**

　　　(C) That's as far as I can walk.

　　　(D) Let's wait until the sun rises.

해석　여: 이 노을이 멋지다, 안 그래?

　　　남: ______________

　　　(A) 나는 그것의 이름이 확실하지 않아.

　　　(B) 그것은 굉장히 아름다워.

　　　(C) 나는 저기까지만 걸을 수 있어.

　　　(D) 해가 뜰 때까지 기다리자.

풀이　노을이 멋지지 않냐고 묻는 말에 아름답다고 공감해주는 (B)가 정답이다.

Words and Phrases　sunset 노을 | gorgeous 멋진 | stunning 아름다운 |
　　　　　　　　　　　as far as ~까지

**14.** W: How did that cat get so large?

    M: _________________

      (A) About five years old.

      (B) We got him a week ago.

      (C) She's a great little puppy.

      **(D) He was always quite heavy.**

해석 여: 저 고양이는 어떻게 저렇게 컸니?

    남: _________________

      (A) 다섯 살 정도야.

      (B) 우리는 그를 일주일 전에 데리고 왔어.

      (C) 그녀는 정말 좋은 작은 강아지야.

      **(D) 그는 늘 꽤 무거웠어.**

풀이 고양이가 어떻게 저렇게 컸냐는 질문에 항상 꽤 무거웠다고 대답하는 (D)가 정답이다.

Words and Phrases  large 큰 | quite 꽤


**15.** W: I feel really out of shape.

    M: _________________

      **(A) Why not join a gym?**

      (B) How about a little pie?

      (C) Is math really that hard?

      (D) Would art class help me?

해석 여: 나는 정말 몸매가 엉망이야.

    남: _________________

      **(A) 체육관에 등록하는 건 어때?**

      (B) 파이 조금 어때?

      (C) 수학이 정말 그렇게 어려워?

      (D) 미술 수업이 나에게 도움이 될까?

풀이 몸매가 좋지 않은 것처럼 느껴진다는 말에 체육관에 등록할 것을 권유하는 (A)가 정답이다.

Words and Phrases  out of shape 건강이 안 좋은[몸매가 엉망인] | join 등록하다 | gym 체육관


**16.** M: They say that hotel ballroom is haunted.

    W: _________________

      (A) Weren't his legs tired?

      (B) Do they hunt for deer?

      **(C) So it supposedly has ghosts?**

      (D) Don't you dance better than her?

해석 남: 그들은 저 호텔 무도회장에서 귀신이 나온다고 말해.

    여: _________________

      (A) 그의 다리들은 안 피곤했대?

      (B) 그들은 사슴을 사냥해?

      **(C) 그래서 그곳에 아마 유령이 있다고?**

      (D) 네가 그녀보다 춤을 더 잘 추지 않아?

풀이 호텔 무도회장에 귀신이 나온다는 이야기에 되묻는 반응을 하는 (C)가 정답이다.

Words and Phrases  ballroom 무도회장 | haunted 귀신이 나오는 | hunt 사냥하다 | deer 사슴 | supposedly 아마도 | ghost 유령 | dance 춤


**Part 3.** Short Conversations (p.17)

**17.** W: How much is this pork?

    M: Ten dollars a kilogram. How much would you like?

    W: Just a little bit. A few slices, actually.

    M: The minimum order is 100 grams.

    W: I guess, I'll take just 100, then. Oh, and how much is your beef?

    M: Marinated beef or unmarinated?

    Q: Where does this conversation most likely take place?

      (A) bakery

      **(B) butcher's**

      (C) barber shop

      (D) beauty shop

해석 여: 이 돼지고기는 얼마인가요?

    남: 1킬로그램에 10달러요. 얼만큼 원하세요?

    여: 그냥 조금만요. 사실, 몇 조각들이요.

    남: 최소 주문량은 100그램입니다.

    여: 그럼, 저는 그냥 100그램 가져갈게요. 아, 그리고 소고기는 얼마인가요?

    남: 절인 고기요 아니면 절이지 않은 고기요?

    질문: 이 대화가 이루어질 장소로 가장 적절한 곳은 어디인가?

      (A) 빵집

      **(B) 정육점**

      (C) 이발소

      (D) 미용실

풀이 "How much is this pork?"를 통해 고기를 구매하기 위해 대화를 하고 있음을 알 수 있으므로 (B)가 정답이다.

Words and Phrases  slice 조각 | minimum order 최소 주문량 | marinated 절인 | unmarinated 절이지 않은


**18.** M: Can you lower the sound of the television? I have a splitting headache.

    W: If I turn it down any further, I won't hear it.

    M: Aren't you supposed to be studying?

    W: I finished everything I need to do.

    M: Well, no matter what, that TV volume needs to be lowered.

    W: Okay. Let me find the remote.

    Q: What does the man ask the woman to do?

      **(A) turn down a TV**

      (B) fix a broken TV set

      (C) take out a barking dog

      (D) finish her music homework

해석 남: 텔레비전의 소리를 낮춰 줄 수 있어? 난 깨질듯한 두통이 있어.

    여: 만약 내가 그것을 더 이상 낮추면, 내가 그것을 들을 수 없을 거야.

    남: 너 공부하고 있어야 하는 거 아니야?

    여: 내가 해야 할 모든 것들을 다 했어.

    남: 글쎄, 어쨌든, 저 티비 소리는 낮춰져야만 해.

    여: 알았어. 내가 리모콘을 찾아볼게.

    질문: 남자는 여자에게 무엇을 요청하는가?

(A) 티비 소리 낮추기
(B) 고장난 티비 고치기
(C) 짖는 개 데리고 나가기
(D) 그녀의 음악 숙제 끝내기

**풀이** 'that TV volume needs to be lowered'를 통해 텔레비전의 소리를 낮춰 줄 것을 요구하고 있음을 알 수 있으므로 (A)가 정답이다.

**Words and Phrases** lower 낮추다 | sound 소리 | splitting 깨질듯한 | headache 두통 | remote 리모컨

**19.** W: What brings you to my office, Silvio?
M: I'm concerned about my future.
W: Concerned in what way?
M: I want to be a doctor, but my parents want me to study engineering.
W: Ah, yes. Career plan differences.
M: How can I follow my own path without disappointing them?
Q: What profession does the boy want to have?
(A) artist
**(B) doctor**
(C) lawyer
(D) engineer

**해석** 여: Silvio, 무엇이 너를 나의 사무실에 오게 했니?
남: 저는 제 미래에 대해 걱정돼요.
여: 어떤 방식으로 걱정이 되니?
남: 저는 의사가 되고 싶은데, 저희 부모님은 제가 공학을 공부하기를 바라세요.
여: 아, 그래. 진로 계획 차이.
남: 어떻게 하면 그들을 실망시키지 않고 저의 길을 갈 수 있을까요?
질문: 소년은 어떤 직업을 갖고 싶어 하는가?
(A) 예술가
**(B) 의사**
(C) 변호사
(D) 엔지니어

**풀이** "I want to be a doctor."를 통해 소년이 의사가 되고자 함을 알 수 있으므로 (B)가 정답이다.

**Words and Phrases** concern 걱정하다 | path 길 | profession 직업

**20.** M: McNulty Lanes. How can I help you?
W: Hello, yes. Can I ask about rates?
M: It's 6 dollars per game for adults and 5.50 for students under 15 and seniors.
W: Does that include shoe rental?
M: No, bowling shoes are three dollars extra per bowler.
W: Okay, thanks for the information.
Q: Why does the woman call the man?
(A) to reserve a tennis court
**(B) to ask about bowling rates**
(C) to inquire about a driver's license
(D) to learn the dates of a shopping sale

**해석** 남: McNulty Lanes. 어떻게 도와드릴까요?
여: 안녕하세요, 네. 요금에 대해서 물어봐도 될까요?
남: 각 게임마다 어른들은 6달러씩이고, 15살 이하와 노인들은 5.50입니다.
여: 신발 대여까지 포함한 것인가요?
남: 아니요, 볼링화는 볼링 치는 사람당 3달러씩 추가입니다.
여: 알겠습니다, 정보 감사합니다.
질문: 왜 여자는 남자에게 전화를 하는가?
(A) 테니스장을 예약하기 위해서
**(B) 볼링 요금을 물어보기 위해서**
(C) 운전면허에 대해 물어보기 위해서
(D) 쇼핑 세일의 날짜를 알기 위해서

**풀이** "Can I ask about rates?"를 통해 볼링 요금을 묻고자 여자가 전화했음을 알 수 있으므로 (B)가 정답이다.

**Words and Phrases** rate 요금 | senior 고령자, 노인 | driver's license 운전면허증

**21.** W: Is that the outfit you're wearing to Nana's birthday party?
M: Yeah, why?
W: Isn't it looking a bit shabby?
M: It's a little old, but it still fits.
W: What about your nice blue sweater instead?
M: Fine. I'll go change.
Q: What is the main topic of the conversation?
(A) gift wrapping
**(B) a clothing choice**
(C) a dinner guest list
(D) transportation options

**해석** 여: 그 의상이 Nana의 생일파티에 입고 갈 옷이야?
남: 응, 왜?
여: 조금 허름해 보이지 않아?
남: 조금 오래 됐는데, 아직 맞아.
여: 그거 대신 너가 갖고 있는 예쁜 파란색 스웨터는 어때?
남: 알았어. 가서 갈아입을게.
질문: 대화의 주제는 무엇인가?
(A) 선물 포장
**(B) 옷 선택**
(C) 저녁 손님 목록
(D) 교통수단 선택지들

**풀이** "Is that the outfit you're wearing to Nana's birthday party?"를 통해 남자의 옷차림에 관해 이야기하고 있음을 알 수 있으므로 (B)가 정답이다.

**Words and Phrases** shabby 허름한, 낡은

**22.** M: Do you have wifi here?
W: Yes, we do.
M: I guess it's not connected. It doesn't seem to be working.
W: Oh, let me check that the router is plugged in. … Ah ha. It's not! I'll just plug it in and reset it.
M: Perfect.
W: Sorry about that. It should be working now.
Q: What is the man's problem?

(A) He woke up late for work.

(B) He does not know the password.

**(C) The internet connection is not working.**

(D) There is nowhere to plug in his computer.

해석 남: 여기 와이파이 있어요?

여: 네, 있어요.

남: 연결이 안 된 것 같아요. 작동 안 하고 있는 것 같아요.

여: 오, 라우터가 꽂혀 있는지 확인해 볼게요…. 아하. 안 꽂혀 있네요. 지금 꽂고 다시 초기화 할게요.

남: 완벽해요.

여: 죄송해요. 이제 작동할 거예요.

질문: 남자의 문제는 무엇인가?

(A) 그는 일하러 가야 하는데 늦게 일어났다.

(B) 그는 비밀번호를 모른다.

(C) 인터넷 연결이 작동하지 않는다.

(D) 그의 컴퓨터를 꽂을 수 있는 곳이 없다.

풀이 "It doesn't seem to be working."을 통해 인터넷 연결이 원활하지 않음을 알 수 있으므로 (C)가 정답이다.

Words and Phrases  router 라우터 ｜ reset 다시 맞추다

---

**23.** W: This one has great energy conservation.

M: That's a plus.

W: It's got a separate compartment just for ice cream, and of course for ice cubes.

M: And you say it's got smart features?

W: Exactly. It lets you know if you are low on frozen food.

M: It certainly seems very sleek and modern.

Q: What is the likely relationship between the speakers?

(A) car sales clerk - customer

**(B) freezer sales clerk - customer**

(C) barbecue sales clerk - colleague

(D) telephone sales clerk - colleague

해석 여: 이것은 에너지 절약이 좋아요.

남: 그건 좋은 점이네요.

여: 아이스크림, 그리고 당연히 얼음을 위한 분리된 칸이 있어요.

남: 그리고 그건 스마트 기능이 있다고요?

여: 맞아요. 냉동 식품이 부족하면 알려줘요.

남: 그건 확실히 매우 매끈하고 모던하네요.

질문: 화자들은 어떤 관계인가?

(A) 자동차 판매자 – 구매자

(B) 냉동고 판매자 – 구매자

(C) 바베큐 판매자 – 동료

(D) 전화기 판매자 – 동료

풀이 냉동고의 특징에 관해 이야기하고 있는 것으로 보아 두 사람이 냉동고 판매자와 구매자 관계임을 알 수 있으므로 (B)가 정답이다.

Words and Phrases  energy conservation 에너지 절약 ｜ separate compartment 분리된 칸 ｜ smart features 스마트 기능

---

**24.** M: The bank has a new mobile app. Have you tried it?

W: No, I'm not into doing my banking that way.

M: What? How come?

W: I think it's risky.

M: Riskier than an ATM?

W: Yes, it exposes you to hackers.

Q: What does the woman mean by "that way"?

**(A) via mobile app**

(B) in person at a bank

(C) through a cryptocurrency

(D) at an automatic teller machine

해석 남: 그 은행은 새로운 모바일 어플이 있어. 한번 사용해봤어?

여: 아니, 나는 그런 방식으로 뱅킹을 하지 않아.

남: 정말? 왜?

여: 위험하다고 생각해.

남: 현금 자동 입출금기보다 위험하다고?

여: 응, 해커들한테 노출될 수 있어.

질문: 여자가 말한 "that way"는 무슨 의미인가?

(A) 모바일 어플을 통해

(B) 직접 은행 가서

(C) 가상화폐를 통해

(D) 현금 자동 입출금기에서

풀이 "The bank has a new mobile app."이라는 앞 문장을 통해 'that way'가 의미하는 것이 'a new mobile app'임을 알 수 있으므로 (A)가 정답이다.

Words and Phrases  mobile app 모바일 어플 ｜ risky 위험한 ｜ ATM 현금 자동 입출금기

---

**25.** W: What's up with your thumb?

M: A little accident in the workshop.

W: Looks pretty bad. You sure it was just a little accident?

M: Well, I was moving some glass panels, and one slipped. I tried to catch it.

W: Yikes!

M: Yeah. I ended up with three stitches.

Q: How did the man hurt his thumb?

**(A) moving glass**

(B) falling at work

(C) opening a window

(D) picking up a broken cup

해석 여: 너 엄지손가락 왜 그래?

남: 워크샵에서 약간의 사고가 있었어.

여: 안 좋아 보여. 너 정말 작은 사고가 맞아?

남: 음, 유리 판들을 옮기다가 하나가 미끄러졌어. 그래서 잡으려고 했어.

여: 앗!

남: 응. 결국 세 바늘 꿰맸어.

질문: 어떻게 하다가 남자가 엄지손가락을 다치게 되었는가?

(A) 유리를 옮기다가

(B) 일에서 넘어져서

(C) 창문을 열다가

(D) 깨진 컵을 줍다가

풀이 "I was moving some glass panels, and one slipped."를 통해 유리를
옮기다 사고가 났음을 알 수 있으므로 (A)가 정답이다.

Words and Phrases  panel 판 | slip 미끄러지다 | stitch 바늘땀, 봉합하다

**26**. M: Why is it so foggy this morning?

W: That's the way it is in the mornings.

M: It wasn't like this yesterday in town.

W: We're in the mountains. This is normal winter weather.

M: Well, we are not going to have a good view from the top of the
mountain!

W: Okay. We'll wait another hour for the fog to clear before
heading up.

Q: What is the woman's plan?

(A) going into town

(B) organizing a winter trip

**(C) delaying a trip up a hill**

(D) waiting to hike down a slope

해석  남: 오늘 아침 왜 이렇게 안개가 많이 꼈어?

여: 그게 매일 아침의 모습이야.

남: 어제 마을은 이렇지 않았는데.

여: 우리는 산에 있잖아. 이것이 평범한 겨울 날씨야.

남: 그렇다면, 산 꼭대기에서 좋은 광경을 보지는 못하겠다.

여: 알았어. 안개가 걷힐 때까지 한 시간 더 기다렸다가 올라가자.

질문: 여자의 계획은 무엇인가?

(A) 마을에 가는 것

(B) 겨울 여행을 기획하는 것

(C) 꼭대기로 가는 여행을 미루는 것

(D) 산 비탈길 내려오는 거 기다리기

풀이  "We'll wait another hour for the fog to clear before heading up."
를 통해 안개가 걷힐 때까지 한 시간을 기다릴 것임을 알 수 있으므로
(C)가 정답이다.

Words and Phrases  foggy 안개 낀 | slope 비탈길


**Part 4.Talks (p.18)**

[27-28]

W: Need extra help with your homework? Are you struggling in math,
science, or Korean classes? Did you know that other students can help
you? Welcome to Brain 3000! At Brain 3000, senior high school students sit down with freshmen to help them with homework troubles.
And it's all for free! To get a tutor, just see Mrs. Travali at the school
office. She will help you sign up for this amazing program to increase
your confidence with your school work!

**27.** What is Brain 3000?

(A) a self-help online course

(B) a teaching and learning robot

(C) a professional tutoring organization

**(D) a student-to-student tutoring program**

**28.** How can students apply to use Brain 3000?

**(A) by visiting Mrs. Travali**

(B) by paying a senior student

(C) by completing an online form

(D) by purchasing a corporate product

해석  여: 숙제하는데 추가적인 도움이 필요한가요? 수학, 과학 또는 한국어 수업
들에서 애먹고 있나요? 다른 학생들이 도와줄 수 있다는 거 알고 있었나요?
Brain 3000에 온 것을 환영합니다. Brain 3000에서는 고등학교 3학년
선배들이 신입생과 같이 앉아서 그들의 숙제 어려움을 도와줍니다. 그리고
그것은 전부 무료입니다! 강습을 받고 싶다면, 학교 사무실에 Travali 씨를
찾아가세요. 그녀가 당신의 학교 과제에 대한 자신감을 높여줄 수 있는
엄청난 프로그램을 신청하는 것을 도와줄 것입니다.

27. Brain 3000이 무엇인가?

(A) 자기계발 온라인 강좌

(B) 교육용 로봇

(C) 전문적인 과외 기관

(D) 학생 대 학생 과외 프로그램

28. 학생들은 Brain 3000을 어떻게 신청해야 하는가?

(A) Travali씨를 찾아감으로써

(B) 선배에게 돈을 지불함으로써

(C) 온라인 신청서 양식을 완성함으로써

(D) 기업 상품을 구매함으로써

풀이  본문에서 뇌 3000에 대한 설명으로 선배와 신입생이 함께 앉아서 진행한
다고 했으므로 27번의 정답은 (D)이다.

본문에서 강습을 받고 싶은 학생들은 학교 사무실에 Travali씨를 만나라고
했으므로 28번의 정답은 (A)이다.

Words and Phrases  struggle 애쓰다 | confidence 자신감

[29-30]

M: Here is the schedule for our class field trip. In the morning, we catch
the 7:30 ferry to Harper Island, arriving at 8:00. There we will visit the
infamous Albray Prison. This was a maximum security prison that was
notorious for its harsh treatment of inmates in the early 1900s. We'll
first watch a movie about the history and then take a guided tour of the
prison. At noon we take the ferry back for lunch on the mainland.

**29.** How long is the ferry ride to Harper Island?

**(A) half an hour**

(B) one hour

(C) an hour and a half

(D) two hours

**30.** What will the class do on Harper Island?

(A) have lunch

**(B) tour an old prison**

(C) walk through fields

(D) talk to asylum inmates

29. Harper 섬까지 배 타고 얼마나 걸리는가?
   **(A) 30분**
   (B) 한 시간
   (C) 한 시간 반
   (D) 두 시간

30. 반은 Harper 섬에 가서 무엇을 할 예정인가?
   (A) 점심 먹기
   **(B) 오래된 감옥을 구경하기**
   (C) 들판을 걷기
   (D) 정신병원 환자들과 이야기하기

풀이 본문에서 7:30에 배를 타고 8:00에 Harper섬에 도착한다고 했으므로 29번의 정답은 (A)이다.

본문에서 영화를 보고 감옥을 구경한다고 했으므로 30번의 정답은 (B)이다.

Words and Phrases  infamous 악명 높은 | notorious 악명 높은 | inmate 수감자

## SECTION II  READING AND WRITING

**Part 5.** Picture Description (p.20)

31. This milk has already gone bad, and it's not even past its
   ____________!
   **(A) expiry date**
   (B) food period
   (C) rotten hours
   (D) eating deadline
해석 이 우유는 상했어, 그리고 그것은 유통기한도 지나지 않았어!
   **(A) 유통기한**
   (B) 음식 기간
   (C) 썩은 시간
   (D) 먹는 기한
풀이 우유가 유통기한이 지나지도 않았는데 상했다는 의미를 완성하기 위해서 '유통기한'라는 뜻을 가진 'expiry date'라는 표현을 사용할 수 있으므로 (A)가 정답이다.
Words and Phrases  expiry date 유통기한

32. Jimmy got on the wrong train __________ and ended up
   miles away from his destination.
   (A) for sale
   (B) by heart

(C) for good
**(D) by accident**
해석 Jimmy는 실수로 잘못된 기차를 탔고 목적지와 먼 곳에 도착했다.
   (A) 판매하는
   (B) 외워서
   (C) 영원히
   **(D) 실수로**
풀이 Jimmy는 실수로 잘못된 기차를 타서 목적지와 먼 곳에 도착했다는 의미를 완성하기 위해 '실수로'라는 뜻을 가진 'by accident'라는 표현을 사용할 수 있으므로 (D)가 정답이다.
Words and Phrases  mile 마일 | destination 목적지 | by accident 실수로, 우연히

33. The preschool teacher teaches kids to __________ the room themselves after playtime.
   (A) put on
   **(B) tidy up**
   (C) build in
   (D) throw out
해석 유치원 선생님은 아이들이 놀이 후 방을 스스로 치우도록 가르친다.
   (A) 입다
   **(B) 치우다**
   (C) 만들다
   (D) 버리다
풀이 유치원 선생님이 놀이 후 아이들이 치우도록 가르친다는 의미를 완성하기 위해 '치우다'라는 뜻을 가진 'tidy up'라는 표현을 사용할 수 있으므로 (B)가 정답이다.
Words and Phrases  preschool 유치원 | playtime 노는 시간

34. Ironically, the summer water sports competition will take ______________ in late autumn this year.
   (A) spot
   **(B) place**
   (C) venue
   (D) location
해석 모순적으로, 여름 수상 스포츠 대회는 이번 년도 늦가을에 개최될 예정이다.
   (A) 차지하다
   **(B) 개최되다**
   (C) 장소
   (D) 위치
풀이 이번 년도에는 여름 수상 스포츠 대회가 늦가을에 열릴 거라는 의미를 완성하기 위해 '개최되다'라는 뜻을 가진 'take place'라는 표현을 사용할 수 있으므로 (B)가 정답이다.
Words and Phrases  ironically 반어적으로 | competition 대회 | venue 장소

35. I held a bucket until the plumber came to fix water ______________ from the ceiling.
   (A) reveal
   (B) handle
   **(C) leakage**
   (D) discovery
해석 나는 배관공이 누수를 고치기 위해 올 때까지 통을 들고 있었다.

(A) 드러내다
(B) 다루다
(C) 누출
(D) 발견

**풀이** 배관공이 누수를 고칠 때까지 기다린 의미를 완성하기 위해 '누수'라는
뜻을 가진 'water leakage'라는 표현을 사용할 수 있으므로 (C)가
정답이다.

**Words and Phrases**  plumber 배관공 | reveal 드러내다 | handle 다루다 |
leakage 누출

**36.** Our plane made it through the turbulence, and we're all safe
and ________________ on the ground now.
(A) solid
**(B) sound**
(C) strong
(D)sincere

**해석** 우리 비행기는 난기류를 통과해서 지금 안전히 지상에 도착했다.
(A) 단단한
(B) 다치지[손상되지] 않은, 이상 없는
(C) 강한
(D) 진실된

**풀이** 비행기가 난기류를 만났지만 지금은 안전히 도착했다는 의미를 완성하기
위해 '무사히, 탈 없이'이라는 뜻을 가진 'safe and sound'라는 표현을 사
용할 수 있으므로 (B)가 정답이다.

**Words and Phrases**  turbulence 난기류 |
sound 다치지[손상되지] 않은, 이상 없는

**Part 6.** Sentence Completion (p.22)

**37.** One of Jen's best friends ________________ nominated for a
prize.
(A) be
**(B) was**
(C) may
(D) were

**해석** Jen의 친구 중 한 명이 상 후보에 올랐다.
(A) be동사원형
(B) be동사 3인칭 과거 단수
(C) ~일지도 모른다
(D) be동사 3인칭 과거 복수

**풀이** 빈칸에는 동사가 와야 하며, Jen의 친구 중 한 명을 언급하기 때문에 be
의 단수 과거형이 필요하므로 (B)가 정답이다. (D)의 경우 복수 과거형이
므로 오답이다.

**Words and Phrases**  nominate 지명하다

**38.** You will be ____________ sorry if you don't stop teasing your
sister right now!
**(A) very**
(B) such
(C) extreme
(D) absolute

**해석** 너는 지금 당장 여동생을 놀리는 것을 멈추지 않으면 매우 후회할 것이야!
(A) 매우
(B) 그런
(C) 지나친
(D) 완전한

**풀이** 빈칸에는 매우 후회할 것이라는 의미를 완성하기 위해 'very'라는 단어를
사용할 수 있으므로 (A)가 정답이다.

**Words and Phrases**  tease 놀리다 | absolute 완전한

**39.** If you look ________________ your right, you'll see the
famous Tokyo Tower.
(A) in
**(B) to**
(C) for
(D) from

**해석** 너의 오른쪽으로 보면, 유명한 도쿄타워가 보일 거야.
(A) ~안에
(B) ~쪽으로
(C) ~위해
(D) ~에서

**풀이** 빈칸에는 오른쪽으로 본다는 의미를 완성하기 위해 'to'라는 단어를 사용
할 수 있다. 'Look to your right'은 '오른쪽을 봐'라는 뜻을 가지고 있으므
로 (B)가 정답이다.

**Words and Phrases**  famous 유명한

**40.** This elderly gentleman may ______________ some help with
his bags.
**(A) need**
(B) needing
(C) be need
(D) be have need

**해석** 이 연세가 드신 남성분은 그의 가방들 때문에 도움이 필요할 수도 있다.
(A) 필요하다
(B) 필요하고 있다
(C) 필요가 있다
(D) 필요가 있었다

**풀이** 빈칸에는 연세가 드신 남성분이 가방이 많아서 도움이 필요하다는 의미
를 완성하기 위해 'need'라는 단어를 사용할 수 있으므로 (A)가 정답이다.
'May'와 같은 조동사 뒤에는 동사원형이 와야 된다.

**Words and Phrases**  elderly 연세가 드신

**41.** If you cheat on your assignments, your punishment will be
______________.
**(A) swift**
(B) swifts
(C) swiftly
(D) swifting

**해석** 너는 과제를 하면서 부정행위를 하면, 너의 벌은 재빠를 것이다.
(A) 재빠른
(B) 틀린 표현
(C) 재빠르게
(D) 틀린 표현

**풀이** 빈칸에 과제를 하면서 부정행위를 하면 재빠른 벌을 내릴 것이라는 의미를 완성하기 위해 (A)가 정답이다. 'swift'라는 형용사를 사용해야 된다.

**Words and Phrases** cheat 부정행위를 하다 | punishment 벌 | swift 재빠른, 신속한

**42.** I discovered I ______________ old smelly cheese in my locker. I threw the cheese out, and my locker smells better.

    **(A) had left**

    (B) have left

    (C) had to leave

    (D) have to leave

**해석** 나는 사물함에 오래되고 냄새나는 치즈를 남겨두었었다는 걸 알게 됐다. 나는 치즈를 버려서 사물함 냄새가 좋아졌다.

    (A) 남겨두었었다

    (B) 남겨두었다

    (C) 남겨둬야만 했다

    (D) 남겨둬야만 한다

**풀이** 나는 사물함에 치즈를 예전에 남겨뒀다는 의미를 완성하기 위해 'had left' 라는 표현을 사용할 수 있으므로 (A)가 정답이다.

**Words and Phrases** locker 사물함

**43.** The wooden chest, ______________ to Maria by her grandmother, sat in the dining room.

    (A) give

    (B) gave

    **(C) given**

    (D) giving

**해석** Maria의 할머니가 Maria에게 준 나무 상자는 거실에 있었다.

    (A) 주다

    (B) 줬다

    (C) 주어진

    (D) 기부

**풀이** 나무 상자가 Maria의 할머니로부터 Maria에게 주어진 것이므로 (C)가 정답이다.

**Words and Phrases** wooden 나무로 된 | dining room 식당

**44.** There's the guy ______________ was telling you about.

    **(A) I**

    (B) that

    (C) who

    (D) what

**해석** 저기 내가 너에게 말해주었던 남자가 있어.

    (A) 내가

    (B) 관계대명사(주격/목적격)

    (C) 관계대명사(주격)

    (D) 복합관계대명사

**풀이** 'the guy' 다음에 목적격 관계대명사 'that'이나 'whom'이 생략되었으며, 내가 봤던 남자를 언급하고 있으므로 '나'라는 뜻을 가진 (A)가 정답이다.

**Words and Phrases** guy 남자

**45.** Don't forget ______________ your seat belt. The roads are icy, and wearing a seat belt is the law.

    (A) buckled

    (B) buckling

    **(C) to buckle**

    (D) that buckled

**해석** 안전벨트 매는 걸 잊지 마. 도로는 얼음으로 뒤덮였고 안전벨트를 매는 것이 법이야.

    (A) 맨

    (B) 동명사

    **(C) 부정사**

    (D) 저것이 매는

**풀이** 'forget' 다음에 부정사가 오면 '~할 것을 잊다'라는 의미이며, 안전벨트를 매는 것을 잊지 말라는 의미로 (C)가 정답이다.

**Words and Phrases** seat belt 안전벨트

**46.** ______________ simply asked someone for directions, we would not be lost now.

    (A) We had

    **(B) Had we**

    (C) If had we

    (D) If we would

**해석** 우리가 단순히 누구에게 길을 물어봤더라면, 우리는 지금 길을 잃지 않았을 것이다.

    (A) 우리는 ~있다

    **(B) 우리가 ~했었으면**

    (C) 만약 우리가 ~했었으면

    (D) 우리가 ~한다면

**풀이** 가정법 과거완료 문형으로 'If'가 생략되면 주어와 동사가 도치되며, 빈칸에는 '누구에게 길을 물어봤더라면' 이라는 뜻을 완성해야 하므로 (B)가 정답이다. (C)는 주어와 동사 순서가 올바르지 않으므로 오답이다.

**Words and Phrases** direction 방향



[47-48]

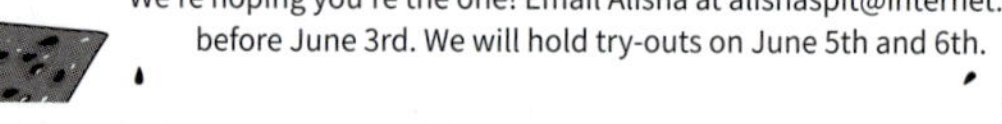



**47.** What is the purpose of the notice?

    (A) to announce a fair

    **(B) to find a teammate**

    (C) to get competition judges

    (D) to advertise a job opening

**48.** Which of the following is NOT mentioned?

    (A) types of events

    (B) how to join the team

    **(C) how often a fair is held**

    (D) how many people are still needed

### 해석

수박씨 뱉는 사람 모집!

31번째 Casitas 박람회에 포함된 수박씨 뱉기 이벤트에 참여하기 위해 팀을 만들고 있다. 우리는 두 가지 이벤트에 참여할 것이다: 거리 이벤트와 정확성 이벤트.

아래의 것을 할 수 있으면 참여하라:

1) 수박씨를 엄청 멀리 뱉을 수 있다

2) 수박씨를 정확히 타겟에 맞출 수 있다

우리 팀은 이미 두 명의 뛰어난 참가자가 있고 세 번째가 필요하다. 우리는 당신이 그 한 사람이길 바란다! 6월 3일 전까지 alishaspit@internet.net으로 Alisha에게 이메일을 보내라. 6월 5일과 6일에 테스트를 진행할 예정이다.

47. 이 안내문의 목적은 무엇인가?

    (A) 박람회를 소개하기 위해

    (B) 팀원을 모집하기 위해

    (C) 대회 심사위원을 구하기 위해

    (D) 일자리를 광고하기 위해

48. 다음 중 언급되지 않은 것은?

    (A) 이벤트의 종류

    (B) 팀에 합류하는 방법

    (C) 박람회가 얼마나 자주 열리는지

    (D) 아직 몇 명의 팀원이 필요한지

풀이   안내문 제목은 'Watermelon Seed Spitters Needed'이기 때문에 수박씨를 뱉을 수 있는 사람을 모집하는 숭인걸 일 수 있다. 본문에서는 수박씨 뱉기 대회에 함께 나갈 팀원을 모집하고 있다는 내용이므로 47번의 정답은 (B)이다.

본문에는 31번째 박람회라고만 언급을 하고 박람회가 얼마나 자주 열리는 지 언급되지 않음으로 48번의 정답은 (C)이다.

Words and Phrases   spit 뱉다 | accuracy 정확도 | accomplished 기량이 뛰어난



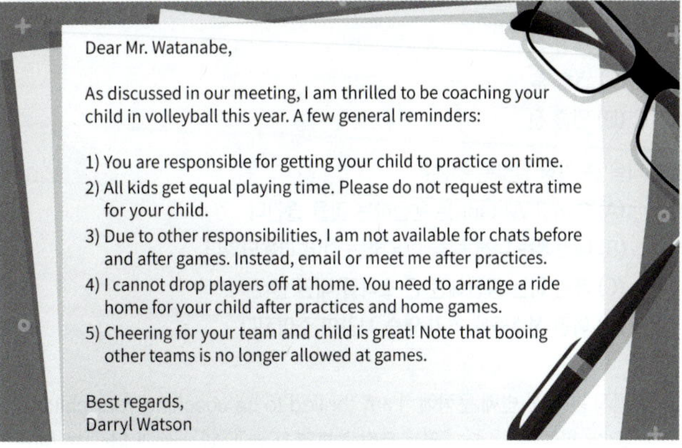


**49.** What is the most likely relationship between Darryl Watson and Mr. Watanabe?

    (A) driver - player

    **(B) coach - parent**

    (C) principal - vice-principal

    (D) debate organizer - debater

**50.** When can Mr. Watanabe meet Darryl Watson?

    (A) after games

    (B) before games

    **(C) after practices**

    (D) before practices

**51.** Which of the following is most likely true?

    (A) Darryl Watson enjoys driving.

    **(B) Booing teams used to be permitted.**

    (C) Loud noise is not allowed during games.

    (D) Some players are allowed extra playing time.

### 해석

Mr. Watanabe에게,

우리 회의에서 논의했듯이, 이번 년도에 당신의 아이의 배구 코치가 되어 기쁩니다. 몇 가지 안내사항을 드리겠습니다:

1. 당신은 연습 시간에 아이를 시간에 맞춰서 데려다주는 책임이 있습니다.

2. 모든 아이들은 동일한 연습 시간을 갖습니다. 당신의 아이를 위해 추가 연습 시간을 요청하지 마세요.

3. 다른 맡은 일들 때문에, 게임 전과 후에 이야기할 시간이 없습니다. 대신, 이메일을 보내거나 연습 후에 만나러 올 수 있습니다.

4. 저는 선수들을 집에 데려다 줄 수 없습니다. 연습과 게임 후에 집까지 데려다 줘야 합니다.

5. 당신의 팀과 아이를 응원하는 것은 좋습니다! 하지만 다른 팀을 야유 하는 것은 더 이상 허용되지 않습니다.

Darryl Watson

49. Darryl Watson과 Mr. Watanabe의 관계로 가장 적절한 것은 무엇인가?

    (A) 운전자 – 선수

    (B) 코치 – 학부모

    (C) 교장 선생님 – 부교장 선생님

    (D) 토론 주최자 – 토론자

**50.** Mr. Watanabe는 언제 Darryl Watson을 만날 수 있는가?

(A) 게임 후

(B) 게임 전

(C) 연습 후

(D) 연습 전

**51.** 다음 중 가장 알맞는 것은?

(A) Darryl Watson은 운전하는 것을 즐긴다.

(B) 예전에는 다른 팀을 아유하는 것이 허용되었다.

(C) 게임 하는 동안에는 큰 소리를 내면 안 된다.

(D) 어떤 선수들은 추가 연습 시간이 주어진다.

**풀이** 편지 본문 첫 번째 문장에 "I am thrilled to be coaching your child in volleyball this year."라는 문장을 통해 Darryl Watson과 Mr. Watanabe는 코치와 학부모 관계라는 것을 알 수 있으므로 49번의 정답은 (B)이다.

본문 3번에 의하면 학부모들은 코치를 연습 후에 만날 수 있으므로 50번의 정답은 (C)이다.

본문 5번에 있는 "Note that booing other teams is no longer allowed at games."라는 문장에서 'no longer'는 '더 이상 ~않다'라는 의미로 예전에는 가능했으나 현재는 안 된다는 의미이므로 51번의 정답은 (B)이다.

**Words and Phrases** coach 코치하다, 지도하다 | reminder 상기시키는 것 | equal 동일한 | request 요청하다 | responsibility 책임, 맡은 일 | arrange a ride 차편을 마련하다

[52-55]

**Hours: Spring and Summer 2019**

| May 20 to May 26 | Sat, Sun, Mon: 11:00 AM to 6:00 PM / Tues, Wed, Thurs, Friday: 12:30 AM to 6:00 PM |
| --- | --- |
| May 27 to June 25 | Daily: 11:00 AM to 6:00 PM |
| June 26 to September 4 | Daily: 10:00 AM to 8:00 PM |
| September 5 to September 10 | Daily: 11:00 AM to 6:00 PM |

**52.** What is the schedule for?

(A) a roller coaster

(B) a flower garden

(C) an ocean museum

(D) **an urban water park**

**53.** Which of the following is mentioned?

(A) A child has been hurt.

(B) A ride is being repaired.

(C) **A park has been flooded.**

(D) A mall had storm damage.

**54.** According to the schedule, what is true about July 5, 2019?

(A) The park closes at 6:00 PM.

(B) **The park closes at 8:00 PM.**

(C) The park is guaranteed to be open.

(D) The park is closed before 11:00 AM.

**55.** The underlined word "updates" is closest in meaning to:

(A) **news**

(B) slides

(C) renovations

(D) improvements

**해석**

날씨에 따라 Inner City Splash Park의 운영 날짜와 시간은 변경 될 수 있다.

현재 상황:

오늘 날짜: 2019년 3월 10일

참고: Inner City Splash Park는 홍수 피해로 인해 현재 운영하지 않고 수리 중이다. 최근 소식을 위해 다시 오라.

시간: 2019년 봄과 여름

5월 20일부터 5월 26일:

토-월: 오전 11시부터 오후 6시

화-금: 오후 12시 반부터 오후 6시

5월 27일부터 6월 25일: 매일 오전 11시부터 오후 6시

6월 26일부터 9월 4일: 매일 오전 10시부터 오후 8시

9월 5일부터 9월 10일: 매일 오전 11시부터 오후 6시

**52.** 이건 무엇을 위한 시간표인가?

(A) 롤러코스터

(B) 꽃밭

(C) 해양 박물관

(D) 도심 워터파크

**53.** 다음 중 언급된 것은?

(A) 아이가 한 명 다쳤다.

(B) 놀이기구 중 하나를 고치고 있다.

(C) 워터파크에 홍수가 났다.

(D) 쇼핑몰이 폭풍 피해를 입었다.

**54.** 스케줄에 의하면, 2019년 7월 5일에 대해 사실인 것은?

(A) 워터파크는 6시에 문을 닫는다.

(B) 워터파크는 8시에 문을 닫는다.

(C) 워터파크는 반드시 열려 있을 것이다.

(D) 워터파크는 오전 11시 전에 문을 닫는다.

**55.** 밑줄 친 단어 "updates"와 가장 유사한 뜻을 가진 단어는:

(A) 소식

(B) 미끄럼틀

(C) 수리

(D) 개선

풀이 **풀이** Inner City Splash Park는 워터파크의 이름이므로 52번의 정답은 (D)이다.

안내문 본문에 워터파크에 홍수가 나서 현재 운영하지 않고 수리 중이라고 나와 있으므로 53번의 정답은 (C)이다.

스케줄에 6월 26일부터 9월 4일까지 워터파크의 운영시간이 오전 10시부터 오후 8시까지라고 나와 있다. 7월 5일은 그 사이에 있으니 오후 8시에 문을 닫으므로 54번의 정답은 (B)이다.

"Check back for the latest updates."는 최근 소식을 확인하기 위해 다시 방문하라는 의미로 'updates'는 '소식'이라는 뜻을 가진 'news'와 가장 유사하므로 55번의 정답은 (A)이다.

**Words and Phrases** operation 운영 | subject to ~되기 쉽다 | condition 상태 | undergo 겪다, 받다 | latest 최신의

## [56–59]

**Product: Shilana Curling Iron**

**Product details**
- Product dimensions: 1 X 11 X 10 inches; 0.5 kg
- Shipping weight: 1 kg
- Item model number: X345
- Average customer review: 4.5 out of 5 stars; 13 customer reviews

**Reviews**

Marta: This thing is fantastic! It's got a timer, so you won't fry your hair by letting the iron get too hot on your hair. Previous curling irons I've had couldn't make the same claim….

Wendy: Even on my very fine, wispy hair, this held the curls in. Amazing.

Miki: This was not for me. The automatic rotator grasps your hair too tight and the iron just stays there. I couldn't get it out of my hair easily.

**56.** What is the shipping weight of the product?
(A) half a kilogram
**(B) one kilogram**
(C) one and a half kilograms
(D) two kilograms

**57.** What can be inferred about Marta?
(A) She has bought two Shilana iron.
**(B) She has previously burned her hair.**
(C) She normally wears her hair straight.
(D) She ruined her hair on her Shilana iron.

**58.** What does Wendy say about her hair?
**(A) It is thin.**
(B) It is long.
(C) It is thick.
(D) It has tight curls.

**59.** What does Miki mean by "it"?
(A) a curl
(B) a plug
**(C) the iron**
(D) the cord

**해석**

> 제품: Shilana 고데기
> 제품 세부사항:
> 제품 치수: 1 X 11 X 10 인치, 0.5kg
> 운송 무게: 1kg
> 제품 모델 번호: X345
> 평균 고객 리뷰: 5점 만점에 4.5점, 13개의 고객 리뷰
> 리뷰:
> Marta: 이것은 기가 막혀요! 타이머 기능을 가지고 있기 때문에, 고데기가 뜨거워서 머리가 탈 걱정은 안해도 돼요. 이전에 사용했던 고데기에 대해서는 똑같이 이야기할 수 없어요…
> Wendy: 나의 매우 얇고 숱이 적은 머리에도 컬이 생겼어요. 놀라워요.
> Miki: 이 제품은 저에게 안 맞았어요. 자동 회전자는 머리카락을 너무 세게 잡고 고데기가 그냥 그 자리에 머물러요. 그것을 머리카락에서 쉽게 빼낼 수 없어요.

56. 제품의 운송 무게는 무엇인가?
(A) 0.5 킬로그램
(B) 1 킬로그램
(C) 1.5 킬로그램
(D) 2 킬로그램

57. Marta에 대해 추론할 수 있는 것은 무엇인가?
(A) 그녀는 Shilana 고데기를 두 개 구매했다.
(B) 그녀는 이전에 머리를 태운 적이 있다.
(C) 그녀는 주로 머리를 곧게 핀다.
(D) 그녀는 Shilana 고데기 때문에 머리를 망쳤다.

58. Wendy가 자신의 머리카락에 대해 언급한 것은?
(A) 머리카락이 얇다.
(B) 머리카락이 길다.
(C) 머리카락이 두껍다.
(D) 두꺼운 컬을 가지고 있다.

59. Miki가 말한 'it'이 무엇인가?
(A) 컬
(B) 플러그
(C) 고데기
(D) 코드

**풀이** 본문 내용 중 제품 세부사항 아래 운송 무게는 1kg이라고 나와있으므로 56번의 정답은 (B)이다.

Marta는 Shilana 고데기를 칭찬하면서 고데기가 너무 뜨거워지지 않는 것이 좋다고 했다. 하지만 이전에 사용했던 고데기는 이런 기능이 없었다고 했으므로 57번의 정답은 (B)이다.

Wendy가 쓴 리뷰에서 본인은 얇고 머리 숱이 없다고 했으므로 58번의 정답은 (A)이다.

Miki가 후기에서 '그것'을 머리카락에서 쉽게 뺄 수 없었다고 했기에 그것은 고데기일 것이므로 59번의 정답은 (C)이다.

**Words and Phrases** dimension (높이·너비·길이의) 치수 | previous 이전의 | fine 아주 가는 | wispy 성긴 | rotator 회전하는 것 | grasp 꽉 잡다

[60–61]

Bobcats are meat-eating wildcats that are quite common in North America. However, despite their large population numbers, they are rarely seen by humans, perhaps because they are nocturnal. These elusive animals are approximately twice the size of domestic house cats. Their furry coats are usually brown or a brownish red color. Bobcats are extremely powerful hunters, and are capable of capturing prey much larger than themselves. They sneak up on prey and jump on their victims at the last minute, with leaps of up to 3 meters. Bobcats are solitary animals. Unlike dogs or wolves, who travel in packs, bobcats travel and hunt alone.

Summary:

Bobcats are __[A]__ , undomesticated cats that are populous in North America. They do not often get spotted by people. Most bobcats have brown or brownish fur. They are good at hunting and can catch prey that are bigger than their body size. They __[B]__ approach their prey. They also travel alone.

**60.** Choose the most suitable word for blank [A], connecting the summary to the passage.
(A) hairless
(B) miniature
**(C) carnivorous**
(D) endangered

**61.** Choose the most suitable word for blank [B], connecting the summary to the passage.
(A) rarely
(B) noisily
(C) foolishly
**(D) stealthily**

해석　보브캣은 북미에서 꽤 흔한, 고기를 먹는 야생 고양이이다. 그러나, 그들의 많은 개체수에도 불구하고, 아마도 그들은 야행성이기 때문에, 인간에게 거의 보이지 않는다. 이러한 찾기 힘든 동물들은 집고양이의 약 두 배 크기이다. 그들의 가득한 털들은 보통 갈색이거나 갈색 빛이 도는 붉은색이다. 보브캣은 굉장히 강한 사냥꾼이고, 그들보다 훨씬 큰 먹이를 잡을 수 있다. 그들은 먹이를 향해 몰래 다가가 마지막 순간에 그 희생양을 향해 3미터까지 뛰어오른다. 보브캣은 혼자 사는 동물이다. 무리를 지어 이동하는 개나 늑대와는 달리, 보브캣은 혼자 이동하고 사냥한다.

요약:

보브캣은 북미에 그 수가 많은 육식성의, 길들여지지 않은 고양이다. 그들은 사람들에게 자주 눈에 띄지 않는다. 대부분의 보브캣은 갈색이나 갈색빛의 털을 가진다. 그들은 사냥에 능하고 그들의 몸 크기보다 큰 먹이를 잡을 수 있다. 그들은 은밀하게 먹이에게 다가간다. 그들은 또한 혼자 이동한다.

**60.** 본문과 요약본을 연결할 수 있는, 빈칸 [A]에 들어갈 가장 적절한 단어를 고르시오.
(A) 털이 없는
(B) 아주 작은
(C) 육식의
(D) 멸종 위기에 처한

**61.** 본문과 요약본을 연결할 수 있는, 빈칸 [B]에 들어갈 가장 적절한 단어를 고르시오.
(A) 드물게
(B) 시끄럽게
(C) 어리석게
(D) 몰래

풀이　본문에 보브캣은 'meat-eating'이라고 했으므로 61번의 정답은 (C)이다.

본문에 보브캣은 먹이를 향해 살금살금 다가간다고 언급했고 몰래 다가간다는 것과 같은 의미이므로 62번의 정답은 (D)이다.

Words and Phrases　wildcat 들고양이 | nocturnal 야행성의 | elusive 찾기 힘든 | approximately 거의, 대략 | capable of ~할 수 있는 | victim 희생물 | solitary 혼자 하는 | populous 인구가 많은

[62–65]

[1] The famous Sistine Chapel, in the Vatican, Italy, was built in 1481. It was immediately filled with beautiful artwork by master artists. By 1512, the Michelangelo had painted the famous ceiling. In 1541, the last artwork by the artist Rafael was finished. These precious artworks lasted centuries. However, by the 1980s, a problem was clear. The artworks had probably lost a lot of their original colors. The decision was made to clean and restore the art.

[2] This was extremely controversial. Supporters of the restoration noted that there were centuries of water damage to the ceiling. The water damage had created cracks. The cracks had let salt through, which had whitened the paintings. However, art historians noted that the restoration may have altered the paintings significantly from their original state. It is not always clear what techniques a master painter like Michelangelo was using. Modern restorers must make guesses about the intention of the original artists. Critics of the decision to restore the paintings worried that some of those guesses were wrong.

[3] In short, art restoration in general is often controversial. However, when it comes to paintings as important as those in the Sistine Chapel, the controversies have been endless.

**62.** Which of the following would be the best title for the passage?
(A) The Art and Style of Michelangelo
(B) The Man Who Painted the Sistine Chapel
**(C) The Sistine Chapel Restoration Controversy**
(D) The People Who Restored the Sistine Chapel

**63.** According to the passage, what did salt do?

   (A) create the paintings

   **(B) lighten the artworks**

   (C) darken the artworks

   (D) preserve the paintings

**64.** What does the underlined "This" mean?

   **(A) the decision to restore the art**

   (B) the mistakes made by Michelangelo

   (C) the company hired to work on the art

   (D) the cost to fix the art in the Sistine Chapel

**65.** According to the passage, what is most likely true about restoring the Sistine Chapel?

   (A) It is overly expensive.

   (B) It has all been finished.

   **(C) It will always be controversial.**

   (D) It is what the original artist wants.

65. 본문에 의하면, 시스티나 성당을 복원시키는 것에 대해 가장 알맞은 것은?

   (A) 그것은 몹시 비싸다.

   (B) 그것은 다 끝났다.

   (C) 그것은 항상 논란이 있을 것이다.

   (D) 그것은 원래 화가가 원하는 것이다.

**풀이** 본문은 시스티나 성당의 복원 문제를 다루고 있으므로 62번의 정답은 (C)이다.

본문에 소금은 그림을 하얗게 만들었다고 했다. 하얗게 변하는 것은 밝게 해줬다는 의미와 동일하므로 63번의 정답은 (B)이다.

'This'라는 단어가 나오기 전 단락에 "The decision was made to clean and restore the art"라는 문장이 나온다. 미술 작품들을 복원하기로 결정 했다는 뜻이므로 64번의 정답은 (A)이다.

본문 마지막 문장에 의하면 시스티나 성당의 복원 작업에 대한 논란은 끝이 없을 거라고 나와 있으므로 65번의 정답은 (C)이다.

**Words and Phrases** immediately 즉시 | century 100년 | restore 복원하다 | controversial 논란이 많은 | crack 금 | alter 바꾸다 | significantly 상당히[크게] | intention 의도 | endless 끝이 없는

**해석** [1] 이탈리아에 있는 바티칸 시국에 위치한 유명한 시스티나 성당은 1481년도에 지어졌다. 그것은 즉시 명화가의 아름다운 예술 작품으로 채워졌다. 1512년이 되었을 때 미켈란젤로가 유명한 천정을 그렸다. 1541년도에 화가 Rafael의 마지막 작품이 완성 되었다. 이러한 귀중한 예술 작품은 수백 년 동안 지속 되었다. 하지만, 1980년대에 한 가지 문제가 분명했다. 미술 작품들은 아마도 본래 색을 잃었을 것이다. 미술 작품을 깨끗히 하고 복원하기로 결정했다.

[2] 이것은 매우 논란이 많았다. 복원을 지지하는 사람들은 천장에 수백 년 간 수피해가 있었다는 사실에 주목했다. 수피해는 금을 만들었다. 그 금은 소금이 통과할 수 있도록 했고, 이는 그림을 하얗게 만들었다. 하지만, 미술사가는 복원이 그림의 본래 상태를 많이 변형시켰을 수도 있다는 사실에 주목했다. 미켈란젤로와 같은 명화가가 어떤 기법을 사용했는지 항상 명확하지 않다. 현대 복원 전문가는 원래 화가들의 의도에 대해 추측을 해야 된다. 그림을 복원하기로 한 결정에 대한 비평가들은 이러한 추측이 잘못 되었다고 우려한나.

[3] 요컨대, 미술 복원은 대체로 논란이 많다. 하지만, 시스티나 성당에 있는 그림들과 같이 중요한 그림들에 관해서라면, 논란은 끝이 없다.

62. 본문의 가장 적절한 제목은 무엇인가?

   (A) 미켈란젤로의 그림과 스타일

   (B) 시스티나 성당을 그림 남자

   (C) 시스티나 성당의 복원 논란

   (D) 시스티나 성당을 복원한 사람들

63. 본문에 의하면, 소금은 무엇을 했는가?

   (A) 그림을 만들었다

   (B) 미술 작품을 밝게 했다

   (C) 미술 작품을 어둡게 했다

   (D) 그림을 보호했다

64. 밑줄 친 "This"는 무슨 의미인가?

   (A) 미술 작품을 복원시키기로 한 결정

   (B) 미켈란젤로가 저지른 잘못

   (C) 그림 작업을 위해 고용된 회사

   (D) 시스티나 성당의 미술 작품을 고치기 위한 비용

# 실전 2회

## Section I  Listening and Speaking

|     |     |     |     |     |
|-----|-----|-----|-----|-----|
| 1 (C) | 2 (C) | 3 (A) | 4 (C) | 5 (B) |
| 6 (A) | 7 (B) | 8 (A) | 9 (B) | 10 (C) |
| 11 (A) | 12 (A) | 13 (D) | 14 (C) | 15 (B) |
| 16 (B) | 17 (D) | 18 (A) | 19 (A) | 20 (C) |
| 21 (D) | 22 (C) | 23 (B) | 24 (D) | 25 (B) |
| 26 (C) | 27 (A) | 28 (C) | 29 (D) | 30 (B) |

## Section II  Reading and Writing

|     |     |     |     |     |
|-----|-----|-----|-----|-----|
| 31 (C) | 32 (B) | 33 (D) | 34 (C) | 35 (D) |
| 36 (D) | 37 (B) | 38 (C) | 39 (B) | 40 (D) |
| 41 (A) | 42 (D) | 43 (C) | 44 (B) | 45 (B) |
| 46 (C) | 47 (B) | 48 (B) | 49 (A) | 50 (A) |
| 51 (C) | 52 (C) | 53 (A) | 54 (D) | 55 (A) |
| 56 (D) | 57 (C) | 58 (C) | 59 (C) | 60 (D) |
| 61 (B) | 62 (B) | 63 (C) | 64 (C) | 65 (A) |

---

## SECTION I  LISTENING AND SPEAKING

**Part 1.** Listen and Recognize (p.32)

**1.** W: Why did Jamie have to leave the party so early?
   M: His cat is home alone. You know he cares about his pet.

정답 (C)

해석 여: 왜 Jamie가 그 파티를 그렇게 일찍 떠나야 했니?
   남: 그의 고양이가 집에 혼자 있어. 너는 그가 얼마나 그의 반려동물을 신경 쓰는지 알잖아.

풀이 Jamie가 고양이를 기르고 있고, 그가 그의 반려동물을 신경 쓴다고 했으므로 고양이를 안고 있는 (C)가 정답이다. (A), (B)는 'pet'을 통해 연상하도록 유도한 오답이다.

Words and Phrases  leave 떠나다

**2.** M: Yesterday's blackout was so unexpected.
   W: What a pain. I had to use a flashlight to read my book.

정답 (C)

해석 남: 어제의 정전은 너무 뜻밖이었어.
   여: 정말 괴로웠어. 나는 내 책을 읽으려고 손전등을 써야만 했어.

풀이 여자가 어제 정전으로 인해 책을 읽으려고 손전등을 써야만 했으므로 어둠 속에서 손전등을 들고 있는 (C)가 정답이다. (B)는 'light'를 통해 연상하도록 유도한 오답이다.

Words and Phrases  unexpected 뜻밖의, 예상 밖의 | flashlight 손전등

**3.** W: The sandwiches here are way too spicy to enjoy.
   M: I can see that. Your face is as red as a strawberry.

정답 (A)

해석 여: 여기 샌드위치들은 너무 많이 매워서 즐길 수 없어.
   남: 그런 것 같아. 너의 얼굴이 딸기만큼 빨개.

풀이 여자가 샌드위치가 너무 맵다고 했으므로 샌드위치를 들고 혓바닥을 내밀고 있는 (A)가 정답이다. (B)는 'red'를 통해, (C)는 'strawberry'를 통해 연상하도록 유도한 오답이다.

Words and Phrases  spicy 매운, 양념 맛이 강한

**4.** M: Can I take a look at your science project?
   W: Sure. My onion in a cup started to grow a week ago!

정답 (C)

해석 남: 내가 너의 과학 프로젝트를 한번 봐도 되니?
   여: 물론이지. 컵 안에 있는 내 양파가 일주일 전에 자라기 시작했어!

풀이 여자의 과학 프로젝트가 컵에서 양파를 기르는 것이므로 양파가 컵에서 자라는 (C)가 정답이다. (A)는 'cup'을 통해, (B)는 'onion'을 통해 연상하도록 유도한 오답이다.

Words and Phrases  take a look at ~을 한 번 보다

**5.** W: These wireless earbuds are now in high demand. What're they for?
   M: You don't have to worry about them getting all twisted in your pocket.

정답 (B)

해석 여: 이 무선 이어폰들이 지금 수요가 많네. 그것들은 무엇을 위한 거니?
   남: 너는 그것들이 너의 주머니 안에서 모두 꼬이는 것을 걱정하지 않아도 돼.

풀이 여자와 남자가 무선 이어폰에 대해서 이야기하고 있으므로 무선 이어폰이 등장한 (B)가 정답이다. (A)는 'ear'를 통해, (C)는 'earbud'를 통해 연상하도록 유도한 오답이다.

Words and Phrases  wireless 무선의 | earbud 초소형 헤드폰 | in demand 수요가 많은

**6.** M: That idiot on the cellphone is crossing right in the middle of the road!
   W: He's lucky that driver saw him and stopped.

정답 (A)

해석 남: 핸드폰을 보고 있는 저 바보가 그 도로 한가운데를 건너는 중이야!
   여: 운 좋게도 저 운전자가 그를 보고 멈췄어.

풀이 남자가 핸드폰을 보고 있는 사람이 도로 한가운데를 건너고 있다고 말했으므로 핸드폰을 든 사람이 도로를 건너고 있는 (A)가 정답이다. (B)는 'crossing right in the middle of the road'에서 'cross'와 'the road'를 통해, (C)는 'driver'를 통해 연상하도록 유도한 오답이다.

Words and Phrases  idiot 바보, 멍청이

**7.** W: Does Jenna enjoy being class president?

   M: ________________

     (A) Voting is in the gym.

     **(B) Absolutely. She loves it.**

     (C) I'm not running this year.

     (D) No, I can't. I was last year.

해석 여: Jenna가 반장이 된 것을 좋아하니?

   남: ________________

     (A) 투표는 체육관에서 해.

     **(B) 당연하지. 그녀는 그것을 좋아해.**

     (C) 나는 올해 출마하지 않아.

     (D) 아니, 나는 할 수 없어. 나는 작년에 했어.

풀이 여자는 Jenna가 반장이 된 것을 좋아하는지 묻고 있다. 이에 대해 "Absolutely. She loves it."이라고 대답하는 (B)가 정답이다. (C), (D)는 남자가 반장이 되는 것에 대한 내용이므로 오답이다.

Words and Phrases class president 반장 | voting 투표 | run 출마[입후보]하다

**8.** M: I can't find my wallet anywhere.

   W: ________________

     **(A) It's on the living room table.**

     (B) The waterfront is foggy today.

     (C) There's some soup in the fridge.

     (D) They're the second door on the left.

해석 남: 나는 어디에서도 내 지갑을 찾을 수 없어.

   여: ________________

     **(A) 그것은 거실 탁자 위에 있어.**

     (B) 오늘 해안가에 안개가 꼈어.

     (C) 냉장고에 수프가 있어.

     (D) 그들은 왼쪽에 두 번째 문이야.

풀이 지갑을 찾을 수 없다는 남자의 말에 그것이 거실 테이블 위에 있다는 (A)가 정답이다.

Words and Phrases waterfront 해안가, 부둣가, 물가

**9.** W: My back is totally killing me.

   M: ________________

     (A) Give it to me.

     **(B) Lie down for a while.**

     (C) Show me your locker.

     (D) Turn off the light then.

해석 여: 나의 등이 너무 아파 죽겠어.

   남: ________________

     (A) 나에게 줘.

     **(B) 잠깐 누워 있어.**

     (C) 너의 사물함을 보여줘.

     (D) 그럼 불을 꺼.

풀이 등이 너무 아프다는 여자의 말에 잠시 누우라는 (B)가 정답이다.

Words and Phrases for a while 잠시 동안 | locker 사물함

**10.** M: How early do we need to get up tomorrow?

   W: ________________

     (A) One way to go about it.

     (B) I'm ready when you're ready.

     **(C) By six-thirty at the very latest.**

     (D) I changed the battery in the clock.

해석 남: 우리가 내일 얼마나 일찍 일어나야 하지?

   여: ________________

     (A) 한 가지 방법이 있어.

     (B) 나는 너가 준비됐을 때 준비 돼.

     **(C) 아무리 늦어도 6시 반까지야.**

     (D) 내가 시계에 있는 배터리 교체했어.

풀이 내일 얼마나 일찍 일어나야 하냐고 묻는 남자의 말에 적어도 6시 30분에는 일어나야 한다는 (C)가 정답이다.

Words and Phrases at the very latest 아무리 늦어도

**11.** W: I miss my grandparents. I want to go see them over the holidays.

   M: ________________

     **(A) I miss mine, too.**

     (B) Yes, I'm on holiday.

     (C) No, she cannot come.

     (D) My grandpa told you, too.

해석 여: 나는 내 조부모님이 그리워. 나는 그분들을 연휴 동안에 뵈러 가고 싶어.

   남: ________________

     **(A) 나도 나의 조부모님이 그리워.**

     (B) 응, 나는 휴가 중이야.

     (C) 아니, 그녀는 올 수 없어.

     (D) 나의 할아버지가 너에게도 말해줬어.

풀이 조부모님이 보고 싶다는 여자의 말에 자신도 자신의 조부모님이 보고 싶다는 (A)가 정답이다.

Words and Phrases miss 그리워하다

**12.** M: How did you make this delicious pie?

   W: ________________

     **(A) It's an old family recipe.**

     (B) That's not where we sit.

     (C) These bananas are rotten.

     (D) He cooked the soup too long.

해석 남: 너는 어떻게 이 맛있는 파이를 만들었니?

   여: ________________

     **(A) 그것은 오래된 집안 요리법이야.**

     (B) 저기는 우리가 앉는 곳이 아니야.

     (C) 이 바나나들은 상했어.

     (D) 그는 그 수프를 너무 오래 요리했어.

풀이 맛있는 파이를 어떻게 만들었냐는 남자의 말에 집안의 요리법이라는 (A)가 정답이다.

Words and Phrases recipe 요리법, 레시피 | rot 썩다, 부패하다

**13.** W: What are you doing that's making so much noise?

    M: _______________

    (A) She called her friend.

    (B) We'll deny all charges.

    (C) You can always get a refill.

    **(D) I'm just hammering some boards.**

해석 여: 뭘 하느라 이렇게 시끄러워?

    남: _______________

    (A) 그녀는 그녀의 친구를 불렀어.

    (B) 우리는 모든 혐의를 부인할 것이다.

    (C) 너는 언제나 리필을 받을 수 있어.

    **(D) 나는 단지 판자 몇 개를 망치질하는 중이야.**

풀이 무엇을 하느라 시끄럽냐는 여자의 말에 망치질을 하고 있다는 (D)가 정답이다.

Words and Phrases   deny 부인하다 | charge 혐의 | board 판자

**14.** M: This comedian is hilarious.

    W: _______________

    (A) Never! It's not right to.

    (B) Hardly! I laughed so much.

    **(C) I know! I loved the last joke.**

    (D) Exactly! I was upset about it.

해석 남: 이 코미디언은 아주 재미있어.

    여: _______________

    (A) 절대로! 그것은 옳지 않아.

    (B) 거의 그렇지 않아! 나는 너무 웃었어.

    **(C) 내 말이! 나는 마지막 농담이 좋았어.**

    (D) 바로 그거야! 나는 그것에 대해 화가 났어.

풀이 코미디언이 정말 웃기다는 남자의 말에 동의하는 (C)가 정답이다.

Words and Phrases   hilarious 아주 재밌는 | hardly 거의 ~않다

**15.** W: This orange juice spilled all over my shopping bag!

    M: _______________

    (A) What would you like to drink?

    **(B) Did it ruin the stuff you bought?**

    (C) Are they from a supplier in Spain?

    (D) Should we put these tables together?

해석 여: 이 오렌지 주스가 내 쇼핑백에 온통 쏟아졌어!

    남: _______________

    (A) 너는 무엇을 마시고 싶니?

    **(B) 그게 네가 산 것들을 엉망으로 만들었니?**

    (C) 그것들이 스페인에 있는 공급업체에서 온 것이니?

    (D) 우리가 이 탁자들을 같이 붙여야 할까?

풀이 오렌지 주스를 쇼핑백에 쏟았다는 여자의 말에 주스가 산 물건들에 쏟아지지 않았는지 물어보는 (B)가 정답이다. (A)는 'orange juice'와 'drink'의 연관성을 이용한 오답이다.

Words and Phrases   ruin 엉망으로 만들다, 망치다 | supplier 공급업체

**16.** M: Are there nuts in that ice cream? I'm allergic.

    W: _______________

    (A) Two scoops are three dollars.

    **(B) That one does contain walnuts.**

    (C) We're sorry he couldn't enjoy it.

    (D) Vanilla is also my favorite flavor.

해석 남: 저 아이스크림에 견과류가 있을까요? 저는 알레르기가 있어요.

    여: _______________

    (A) 두 스쿱에 삼 달러입니다.

    **(B) 저것은 호두를 포함하고 있기는 해요.**

    (C) 그가 즐기지 못했다니 유감이에요.

    (D) 바닐라 또한 제가 가장 좋아하는 맛이에요.

풀이 아이스크림에 견과류가 있냐는 남자의 물음에 저것은 호두가 들었다는 (B)가 정답이다. (A), (D)는 'ice cream'과의 연관성을 이용한 오답이다.

Words and Phrases   allergic 알레르기가 있는 | scoop 큰 숟갈, 스쿱

---

**Part 3.** Short Conversations (p.35)

**17.** W: What instrument do you play in the school band?

    M: I'm a percussionist.

    W: So you play the drums?

    M: Well, I'd like to. Right now there's another drummer. I play the tambourine.

    W: That's it? Isn't that like playing the triangle?

    M: Hey, it's an important instrument. It's harder than it looks.

    Q: What does the man play in the band?

    (A) drums

    (B) recorder

    (C) accordion

    **(D) tambourine**

해석 여: 너는 학교 밴드에서 어떤 악기를 연주해?

    남: 나는 타악기 연주자야.

    여: 그럼 너는 드럼을 연주하는 거야?

    남: 글쎄, 나도 그러고 싶어. 지금은 다른 드럼 연주자가 있어. 나는 탬버린을 연주해.

    여: 그게 다야? 트라이앵글을 연주하는 거랑 같은 거 아냐?

    남: 야, 그것은 중요한 악기야. 보이는 것보다 더 어려워.

    질문: 남자는 그 밴드에서 무엇을 연주하는가?

    (A) 드럼

    (B) 리코더

    (C) 아코디언

    **(D) 탬버린**

풀이 여자가 드럼을 연주하냐고 물었을 때 남자가 탬버린을 연주한다고 말했으므로 (D)가 정답이다. (A)는 남자가 "Well, I'd like to. Right now there's another drummer."라고 말한 것을 이용해 혼동을 유도한 오답이다.

Words and Phrases   percussionist 타악기 연주자 | instrument 악기

**18.** M: Are you going by the pharmacy later?

    W: I wasn't, but I can stop by there.

    M: Do you think you can pick up a first-aid kit?

    W: Yeah, sure. How come?

    M: We don't have one in the car. We should.

    W: Okay, I'll get one for us.

    Q: What does the man ask the woman to do?

(A) **buy a medical kit**
(B) pick up cold medicine
(C) get a shoulder bandage
(D) ask the doctor a question

해석 남: 너는 이따가 그 약국에 들를 거야?
여: 아니었지만, 나는 거기에 들를 수 있어.
남: 네가 구급상자를 사올 수 있을 것 같아?
여: 그래, 물론이지. 왜?
남: 차에 없어. 우리 있어야 해.
여: 알겠어, 내가 우리를 위해서 하나 가져올게.
질문: 남자가 여자에게 요청한 것은?
(A) **의료용품 사기**
(B) 감기약 가져오기
(C) 어깨 붕대 가져오기
(D) 의사에게 질문하기

풀이 남자가 "Do you think you can pick up a first-aid kit?"라고 말하며
구급 상자를 사올 수 있냐고 묻고 있으므로 (A)가 정답이다. (B)는
'pharmacy'와 'medicine'의 연관성을 이용한 오답이다.

Words and Phrases  pharmacy 약국 | first-aid kit 구급상자 |
How come? 왜?, 어째서?


19. W: Two sweet potato lattes, please.
M: Hot or iced?
W: Uh, hot, please.
M: Is that for here or to go?
W: For here, please.
M: Do you have your own mugs? There's a discount if you
do.
Q: Where most likely are the speakers?
(A) **a cafe**
(B) a garden
(C) a supermarket
(D) a wedding hall

해석 여: 고구마 라떼 두 잔 주세요.
남: 뜨거운 것으로 드릴까요, 아니면 차가운 것으로 드릴까요?
여: 어, 뜨거운 거 주세요.
남: 여기서 드시고 가시나요, 아니면 **가지고** 가시나요?
여: 여기서 먹고 갈게요.
남: 개인 컵 있으세요? 있으시다면 할인이 됩니다.
질문: 화자들이 있는 장소로 가장 적절한 곳은 어디인가?
(A) **카페**
(B) 정원
(C) 슈퍼마켓
(D) 예식장

풀이 여자가 고구마 라떼를 주문하고 있고 남자가 그 주문을 받고 있다. 카페일
가능성이 높으므로 (A)가 정답이다.

Words and Phrases  discount 할인


20. M: Where did you get that jacket?
W: I'm not sure. At a secondhand shop, probably.
M: Oh, really? Do you usually shop secondhand?
W: For clothes, furniture, books, yes.
M: I guess I should start doing that. I just order everything
online.
W: I can recommend some great secondhand shops.
Q: What is the main topic of the conversation?
(A) deals on spring jackets
(B) where to buy textbooks
(C) **shopping at used goods stores**
(D) problems with shopping online

해석 남: 그 재킷은 어디서 났니?
여: 잘 모르겠어. 아마 중고 가게에서인 것 같아.
남: 오, 정말? 너는 주로 중고로 물건을 사니?
여: 옷, 가구, 책은.
남: 나도 그렇게 해야 할 것 같아. 나는 그냥 모든 것을 인터넷에서 사거든.
여: 내가 몇몇 훌륭한 중고 가게를 추천해줄 수 있어.
질문: 무엇에 관한 대화인가?
(A) 봄 재킷 행사
(B) 교과서를 어디에서 살지
(C) **중고물품 가게에서 쇼핑하기**
(D) 인터넷으로 쇼핑하는 것에 대한 문제

풀이 여자가 재킷을 중고 가게에서 구입했고 남자가 자신도 중고 가게에서 사기
시작해야겠다는 대화이므로 (C)가 정답이다.

Words and Phrases  secondhand 중고의 | furniture 가구 |
used goods 중고물품


21. W: Do you have anything to get glue off of glass?
M: What kind of glass are you talking about?
W: A window. My son stuck stickers all over.
M: Uh-oh. We do have scrapers.
W: Could that wreck the glass?
M: Not usually. Otherwise, there is a spray.
Q: What does the woman want?
(A) a new spray bottle
(B) a glass display case
(C) a set of stickers for her son
(D) **a way to remove sticker glue**

해석 여: 유리에서 접착제를 뗄 수 있는 것이 있나요?
남: 어떤 종류의 유리를 말씀하시는 거죠?
여: 창문이요. 저의 아들이 온통 스티커를 붙였어요.
남: 이런. 저희는 긁개를 가지고 있긴 합니다.
여: 저것이 유리를 깰 수 있나요?
남: 그렇진 않습니다. 그 외에는 스프레이가 있습니다.
질문: 여자가 원하는 것이 무엇인가?
(A) 새로운 스프레이 병
(B) 유리 진열장
(C) 그녀의 아들을 위한 스티커 세트
(D) **스티커 접착제를 제거하기 위한 방법**

풀이 여자가 유리에서 접착제를 뗄 수 있는 것을 찾고 있었고 그녀의 아들이 스
티커를 창문에 붙였다고 했으므로 (D)가 정답이다.

**22.** M: This graduation ceremony is so boring.

W: Shhhh, dear! Someone will hear you.

M: (Whispering) Well, why is it so long?

W: It's a large high school class. What do you expect?

M: I don't even see Meejung. Where is my precious little girl?

W: She's over to the right, dear. She'll have her diploma soon
enough.

Q: Who are the man and woman, most likely?

(A) readers in a library

(B) teachers at a school

**(C) parents of a student**

(D) students at a ceremony

해석  남: 이 졸업식은 정말 지루하네요.

여: 쉿, 여보! 누가 듣겠어요.

남: (속삭이며) 글쎄, 그것은 왜 이렇게 긴 거예요?

여: 학생이 많은 고등학교 반이잖아요. 무엇을 기대한 거예요?

남: 나는 심지어 미정이도 보이지 않아요. 내 소중한 딸은 어디에 있나요?

여: 그녀는 저기 오른쪽에 있잖아요, 여보. 그녀는 곧 졸업장을 받을
거예요.

질문: 남자와 여자는 누구일 가능성이 가장 높은가?

(A) 도서관에 있는 독자들

(B) 학교에 있는 선생님들

**(C) 한 학생의 부모님**

(D) 졸업식에 있는 학생들

풀이  여자가 남자를 'dear'로 부르고 남자가 "Where is my precious little
girl?" 라고 말해 자신의 딸이 참석하는 고등학교 졸업식에 왔음을 알 수
있고 남자와 여자는 부부이므로 (C)가 정답이다.

Words and Phrases  precious 소중한 ｜diploma 졸업증, 학위증

**23.** W: Are you all ready for your job interview tomorrow?

M: I think so.

W: How did you prepare?

M: I wrote out answers to questions and practiced saying them
out loud.

W: You should probably do a mock interview. I can help you with
that today.

M: Okay, that would be great. Let's meet after dinner.

Q: What does the man say he will do?

(A) offer interviewing tips

**(B) practice interview skills**

(C) make dinner for the woman

(D) drive the woman to an interview

해석  여: 너는 내일 면접 준비는 전부 다 했니?

남: 나는 그런 것 같아.

여: 너는 어떻게 준비했어?

남: 질문에 대한 답을 적고 그것들을 크게 소리내서 말하는 것을 연습했어.

여: 아마 너는 모의 면접을 하는 게 좋을 것 같아. 내가 오늘 그걸 도와줄게.

남: 좋아, 그러면 좋지. 저녁 후에 만나자.

질문: 남자가 할 것이라고 말한 것은 무엇인가?

(A) 면접 팁을 제공하기

**(B) 면접 기술을 연습하기**

(C) 여자를 위한 저녁 만들기

(D) 여자를 면접장으로 태워다주기

풀이  모의 면접을 하자는 여자의 제안에 남자가 알겠다고 대답을 했으므로 (B)가
정답이다. (A)는 남자가 면접팁을 제공하는 것이 아니므로 오답이다.

Words and Phrases  say out loud 크게 소리내어 말하다 ｜
mock interview 모의 면접 ｜drive 태워다 주다

**24.** M: What result did you get in the physics experiment?

W: I haven't done it yet.

M: What? How come?

W: I missed physics class yesterday because I was sick.

M: So are you off the hook for the experiment altogether?

W: No, I have to do it after school today.

Q: What does the man mean by "off the hook"?

(A) receiving a top grade

(B) failing an important class

(C) top of the class in physics

**(D) allowed not to do something**

해석  남: 너는 물리학 실험에서 어떤 결과를 얻었니?

여: 나는 그걸 아직 안했어.

남: 뭐라고? 어째서?

여: 어제 아파서 물리학 수업을 빠졌거든.

남: 그럼 너는 완전히 그 실험을 면제받았니?

여: 아니, 나는 그것을 오늘 방과 후에 해야 해.

질문: 남자가 "off the hook"라고 한 의미는 무엇인가?

(A) 최고 점수를 받은 것

(B) 중요한 수업을 낙제한 것

(C) 물리 수업에서 1등한 것

**(D) 무언가를 하지 않아도 되는 것**

풀이  여자가 아직 실험을 안했고 아파서 물리 수업에 빠졌다는 말에 대해 남자가
실험을 'off the hook'한 것이냐고 묻고 여자가 남자의 말에 대한 답으로
그렇지 않고 실험을 해야 한다고 답했으므로 (D)가 정답이다. (B)는 여자가
아파서 수업에 빠졌다는 말에 대한 연관성을 이용한 오답이다.

Words and Phrases  physics 물리학 ｜altogether 완전히, 전적으로 ｜
after school 방과 후

**25.** W: I'm interested in trying out for baseball this year.

M: Great! Try-outs are next Wednesday.

W: What do I need to bring to try-outs?

M: Shoes and clothes you can run in.

W: Do I need my own bat and glove?

M: Your own glove, eventually. But we have bats for you.

Q: What does the woman need for try-outs?

(A) her own bat and glove

**(B) gym clothes and runners**

(C) filled-out application forms

(D) permission from her parents

 여: 나는 올해 야구 팀 선발에 관심이 있어.

남: 좋아! 선발은 다음주 수요일이야.

여: 내가 선발에 무엇을 가져가야 해?

남: 네가 달릴 수 있는 신발과 옷.

여: 나의 야구방망이와 글러브가 필요하니?

남: 언젠가는 너의 글러브가 필요해. 하지만 우리가 너를 위한
야구방망이는 가지고 있어.

질문: 여자가 선발에 필요한 것은 무엇인가?

 (A) 그녀의 야구방망이와 글러브

 (B) 체육복과 운동화

 (C) 작성된 가입 신청서

 (D) 그녀의 부모님의 허락

풀이　무엇이 필요하냐는 여자의 물음에 남자의 대답은 여자가 뛸 수 있는 옷과
신발이라고 답했으므로 (B)가 정답이다. 야구 방망이는 준비가 되어있고
글러브는 나중에 필요하다고 했으므로 (A)는 오답이다.

Words and Phrases　try-out 선발, 오디션 | runners 운동화


**26**. M: What are you up to?

W: I'm trying to comprehend this user agreement.

M: What's it for?

W: It's to use this video streaming site. The user agreement is
impossible to comprehend.

M: I think they use confusing language on purpose.

W: Yeah, I feel like you need to be a lawyer to get it.

Q: What is the woman having trouble with?

 (A) updating her profile

 (B) cropping photographs

 **(C) understanding a user contract**

 (D) logging into her email account

해석　남: 지금 뭐하고 있니?

여: 이 이용자 약관을 이해하려고 노력하는 중이야.

남: 무엇을 위한 건데?

여: 그것은 이 비디오 스트리밍 사이트를 사용하기 위한 것이야  그 이용자
약관을 이해하는 것은 불가능해.

남: 내가 생각하기엔 그들이 일부러 헷갈리는 언어를 쓴 것 같아.

여: 맞아, 나는 네가 그걸 이해하기 위해선 변호사가 되어야 할 것 같다고
느껴.

질문: 여자가 무엇 때문에 어려움을 겪고 있는가?

 (A) 그녀의 프로필을 업데이트하는 것

 (B) 사진들을 잘라내는 것

 **(C) 이용자 약관을 이해하는 것**

 (D) 그녀의 이메일 계정에 접속하는 것

풀이　무엇을 하고 있냐는 남자의 말에 여자가 이용자 약관을 이해하려고 노력한
다고 대답하였고 이후에 여자가 그 이용자 약관이 이해하기 불가능하다고
말했으므로 (C)가 정답이다.

Words and Phrases　What are you up to?(=What are you doing?) 무엇을
하고 있니? | user agreement(=contract) 이용자 약관 |
comprehend 이해하다 | crop 잘라내다 |
account 계정 | log into 접속하다



**[27-28]**

W: We hope you enjoy the tour of this historic coal mine. As your pri-
mary guide, I will give you a short introduction aboveground. Then,
Hans here will take you down into the mine. He'll tell you about the
explosions that took place here in the early 1900s. I will join you again
at the end of the tour to guide you through our museum. You might
then wish to visit our gift shop to purchase some coal-related products.


**27.** What does the tour show?

 **(A) an old coal mine**

 (B) a weapons factory

 (C) an ancient art museum

 (D) a nuclear power exhibit

**28.** What can listeners do right after the tour?

 (A) talk to an engineer

 (B) see a fencing display

 **(C) buy things at a gift shop**

 (D) try mud-pack facial creams


해석　여: 저희는 여러분이 그 역사적인 석탄 광산 투어를 즐기셨으면 합니다. 여
러분의 주 가이드로서 제가 지상에서 짧은 소개를 해드리겠습니다. 그 다
음에, 여기에 있는 Hans가 여러분을 광산 아래로 데리고 갈 것입니다. 그
는 1900년대 초에 이곳에서 일어났던 그 폭발에 대해 설명해 줄 것입니다.
저는 투어의 마지막에 여러분들과 다시 만나 우리 박물관을 여러분께 안내
할 것입니다. 그리고 나서 여러분은 석탄과 관련된 상품들을 구매하기 위해
저희 기념품점을 방문하고 싶으실지도 모릅니다.


27. 그 투어가 보여주는 것은 무엇인가?

 (A) 오래된 석탄광산

 (B) 무기 공장

 (C) 고대 미술관

 (D) 원자력 발전 전시

28. 청자들이 투어 직후에 할 수 있는 것은 무엇인가?

 (A) 기술자와 대화하기

 (B) 펜싱 전시를 보기

 (C) 기념품점에서 물건을 사기

 (D) 진흙팩 크림을 발라보기


풀이　여자가 처음에 청자들에게 "We hope you enjoy the tour of this
historic coal mine."이라고 말하는 것을 보아 이 투어가 오래된 석탄 광산
에 대한 것임을 알 수 있으므로 27번의 정답은 (A)이다. (C)는 '~ to guide
you through our museum.'을 이용해 혼동을 유도한 오답이다.

여자가 "You might then wish to visit our gift shop to purchase
some coal-related products."라고 말하며 투어가 끝난 후 기념품점을
방문하고 싶어질지도 모른다고 말했으므로 28번의 정답은 (C)이다.


Words and Phrases　historic 역사적인 | coal mine 석탄 광산 |
aboveground 지상의 | purchase 구매하다 | nuclear
power 원자력 발전

[29-30]

M: Students, I am extremely disappointed about your behavior during the assembly. We invited in Chief Mornay from the fire department to help you learn important life-saving information. Did you listen quietly and politely? No. Many students were in conversations all throughout Chief Mornay's presentation. And students who were not talking were texting on their phones. You all know that phones are not allowed during school assemblies. I have cancelled this Friday's pizza party as punishment for this class's poor behavior.

**29.** Why is the man disappointed in the students?
    (A) They stole another student's lunch.
    (B) They pulled the fire alarm at school.
    (C) They used their phones during a test.
    **(D) They misbehaved during a presentation.**

**30.** What punishment will the students receive?
    (A) a lower grade
    **(B) no class party**
    (C) clean-up work
    (D) detention after school

해석 남: 학생들, 나는 조회시간 동안 너희들의 행동에 매우 실망했단다. 우리는 너희가 중요한 생명을 살릴 수 있는 정보를 배우는 데 도움을 주실 소방서의 Mornay 서장님을 초대했어. 너희들은 조용히 그리고 예의 있게 들었니? 아니. 많은 학생들이 Mornay 서장님의 발표 내내 떠들었어. 그리고 떠들고 있는 중이지 않았던 학생들은 휴대폰으로 문자를 보냈지. 너희는 모두 학교 조회 시간 동안에 휴대폰을 하면 안 된다는 것을 알고 있잖아. 나는 이 학급의 나쁜 태도 때문에 벌로 이번 주 금요일의 피자 파티를 취소했어.

29. 남자는 왜 학생들에게 실망했는가?
    (A) 그들이 다른 학생의 점심을 훔쳤다.
    (B) 그들이 학교의 화재경보기를 울렸다.
    (C) 그들이 시험 도중 휴대폰을 썼다.
    (D) 그들이 발표 도중에 버릇없이 굴었다.

30. 학생들이 받을 벌은 무엇인가?
    (A) 점수 감점
    (B) 학급 파티 취소
    (C) 청소
    (D) 방과 후에 남기

풀이 남자가 'disappointed about your behavior during the assembly'라고 말하고 'Many students were in conversations ~', 'students who were not talking were texting on their phones'라고 말한 것으로 보아 남자가 발표 동안의 학생들의 버릇 없는 행동에 실망했으므로 29번의 정답은 (D)이다. (B)는 'fire department'를 이용해 혼동을 유도한 오답이다.

남자가 "I have cancelled this Friday's pizza party as punishment for this class's poor behavior."라고 말해 학생들이 받을 벌은 학급 파티 취소이므로 30번의 정답은 (B)이다.



---

Words and Phrases assembly 조회, 모임 | punishment 벌 | misbehave 버릇없이 굴다 | detention 방과 후 남게 하기

## SECTION II READING AND WRITING

### Part 5. Picture Description (p.38)

**31.** The traveler couldn't afford a vehicle. She had to explore the desert ___________.
    (A) in step
    (B) in shoe
    **(C) on foot**
    (D) on walk

해석 그 여행자는 차를 살 형편이 안 됐다. 그녀는 사막을 걸어서 탐험해야 했다.
    (A) 보조를 맞추어
    (B) 틀린 표현
    (C) 걸어서
    (D) 틀린 표현

풀이 차를 구할 수 없었기 때문에 걸어서 가야 했으므로 '걸어서'라는 뜻을 가진 (C)가 정답이다.

Words and Phrases vehicle 차량, 탈 것 | afford (...을 살·할) 여유가 되다 | in step 보조를 맞추어 | on foot 걸어서

**32.** I'll miss you while you're gone. Please _________ in touch.
    (A) do
    **(B) keep**
    (C) bring
    (D) make

해석 네가 떠나는 동안 나는 네가 보고 싶을 거야. 계속 연락하고 지내자.
    (A) 하다
    (B) 유지하다
    (C) 가져오다
    (D) 만들다

풀이 두 사람이 헤어지고 나서 연락을 계속 하자는 의미를 완성하기 위해서 '(계속) 연락하고 지내자'라는 뜻을 가진 'keep in touch'라는 표현을 사용할 수 있으므로 (B)가 정답이다.

Words and Phrases keep in touch 연락하고 지내다

**33.** Jackson got bad grades on a test. He _________ his mind to study harder.
    (A) fixed up
    (B) took out
    (C) tried out
    **(D) made up**

해석 Jackson은 시험에서 나쁜 점수를 받았다. 그는 더 열심히 공부하기로 결심했다.
    (A) 수리하다
    (B) 가지고 나가다
    (C) 시험해 보다
    (D) 만들다, 정하다

풀이 Jackson이 시험 점수가 좋지 않아 공부를 더 열심히 하겠다는 결심을 했다는 의미를 완성하기 위해서 '결심하다'라는 뜻을 가진 (D)가 정답이다.

**34.** Please _______________ your card in the reader here and
enter your 4-digit password.
(A) tip
(B) link
**(C) swipe**
(D) check

해석  당신의 카드를 여기 리더기에 읽혀주시고 4자리 비밀번호를 입력해주세요.
(A) 기울이다
(B) 연결하다
(C) 읽히다
(D) 확인하다

풀이  카드 결제를 할 때 카드를 리더기에 읽히라는 의미를 완성하기 위해서
'(카드를) 읽히다'라는 뜻을 가진 (C)가 정답이다.



**35.** For some, boarding a cruise ship may not be pleasant due to
severe motion _______________.
(A) shake
(B) illusion
(C) disease
**(D) sickness**

해석  누군가에게 유람선을 타는 것이 심각한 멀미 때문에 즐겁지 않을 수 있다.
(A) 흔들림
(B) 환각
(C) 질환
(D) 아픔

풀이  유람선에 타는 것이 즐겁지 않은 이유가 멀미를 하기 때문이라는 의미를
완성하기 위해서 '멀미'라는 뜻을 가진 표현 (D)가 정답이다.



**36.** Liam built his own unique drone within just a few hours. He's
such a _______________!
(A) fine dust
(B) good deal
(C) fat chance
**(D) smart cookie**

해석  Liam이 그 자신만의 독특한 무인 항공기를 몇 시간 만에 만들었어. 그는
정말 영리한 녀석이야!
(A) 미세먼지
(B) 만족스러운 제안
(C) 가망 없음
(D) 영리한 녀석

풀이  Liam이 자신만의 독특한 무인항공기를 단지 몇 시간만에 만들었으므로 그
가 똑똑하다는 의미를 완성하기 위해 '영리한 녀석'이라는 뜻을 가진
(D)가 정답이다.



**Part 6.** Sentence Completion (p.40)

**37.** Do you know that girl in Grade 7 _______________ gave a
speech about racism?
(A) she
**(B) who**
(C) when
(D) where

해석  너는 인종차별에 대해 연설한 7학년 저 여자아이를 아니?
(A) 주격 대명사 she
(B) 주격 관계대명사 who
(C) 관계부사 when
(D) 관계부사 where

풀이  빈칸 뒤에 위치한 절은 주어가 없는 불완전한 절이다. 빈칸에는 선행사
'that girl in Grade 7'을 받아 주절과 종속절을 이어주는 주격 관계대명사
가 와야 하므로 (B)가 정답이다.



**38.** The typhoon victims were each provided _______________ a
box of essential items.
(A) at
(B) to
**(C) with**
(D) from

해석  태풍 피해자들은 각각 필수품 상자를 제공받았다.
(A) ~에게
(B) ~에서
(C) ~와
(D) ~로부디

풀이  'A에게 B를 제공하다'라는 표현인 'provide A with B'에서 A를 주어로
해서 수동태로 쓴 문장이므로 (C)가 정답이다.



**39.** We asked Robin if he _______________ any help with
preparations, but he told us not to worry.
(A) need
**(B) needed**
(C) will have a need
(D) would have need

해석  우리는 Robin에게 그가 준비에 어떤 도움이 필요한지 물었지만, 그는 우리
에게 걱정하지 말라고 말했다.
(A) 필요하다
(B) 필요했다
(C) 틀린 표현
(D) 틀린 표현

**풀이** 주절의 동사의 시제가 과거시제이다. 종속접속사 if가 이끄는 종속절에서도
동사의 시제가 과거시제가 되어야 하므로 과거동사 (B)가 정답이다.

**Words and Phrases**  preparation 준비

**40.** Stop doing those push-ups. You ______________ exercise so
soon after eating. You'll get sick.
(A) will
(B) might
(C) wouldn't
**(D) shouldn't**

**해석** 그 팔굽혀펴기를 그만 해라. 너는 식사 후에 너무 빨리 운동해서는 안 된다.
너는 탈이 날 것이다.
(A) ~할 것이다
(B) ~일지도 모른다
(C) ~하지 않을 것이다
**(D) ~해서는 안 된다**

**풀이** 팔굽혀펴기를 하지 말라고 말하고 탈이 날 것이라고 경고하고 있다. 운동을
해서는 안 된다는 충고의 의미인 조동사 'shouldn't'가 쓰여야 하므로
(D)가 정답이다.

**Words and Phrases**  push-up 팔굽혀펴기 | get sick 탈이 나다

**41.** Every student at our school ______________ aware of the
rules regarding skateboards on school grounds.
**(A) is**
(B) do
(C) are
(D) does

**해석** 학교의 모든 학생은 학교 운동장에서 스케이트보드에 대한 규칙을 알고
있다.
**(A) be동사 3인칭 단수형**
(B) 조동사 do
(C) be동사 복수형
(D) 조동사 do 3인칭 단수형

**풀이** 학교의 학생들이 학교 운동장에서 스케이트보드를 타는 것에 대한 규칙을 '
알고 있다'는 의미로 'be aware of'가 와야 하고 주어가 'Every student'
로 3인칭 단수 be동사가 와야 하므로 (A)가 정답이다.

**Words and Phrases**  be aware of ~을 알다 | regarding ~에 관하여

**42.** Don't you find it ______________ when people keep sniffing
instead of just blowing their nose?
(A) annoy
(B) is annoy
(C) annoyed
**(D) annoying**

**해석** 너는 사람들이 코를 푸는 것 대신 계속해서 코를 훌쩍이는 것이
짜증난다고 생각하지 않니?
(A) 짜증나게 하다
(B) 틀린 표현
(C) 짜증이 난
(D) 짜증스러운

**풀이** 5형식 동사 'find'의 목적격 보어이고 코를 풀지 않고 코를 계속 훌쩍이는
것이 짜증을 '나게' 하는 것이므로 현재분사인 (D)가 정답이다.

**Words and Phrases**  annoy 짜증나게 하다 | sniff 코를 훌쩍이다 |
blow (코를) 풀다

**43.** Kelly and I introduced ______________ to our new neighbors
yesterday.
(A) us
(B) ourself
**(C) ourselves**
(D) themselves

**해석** Kelly와 나는 어제 우리의 새로운 이웃에게 우리 스스로를 소개했다.
(A) 우리를
(B) 틀린 표현
(C) 우리 스스로를
(D) 그들 스스로를

**풀이** Kelly와 내가 새 이웃에게 스스로를 소개한 것이므로 나와 Kelly를 모두 이
를 수 있는 재귀대명사 'ourselves'가 와야 하므로 (C)가 정답이다. (D)는
'I'를 포함하지 않으므로 오답이다.

**Words and Phrases**  introduce oneself 자기소개하다

**44.** ______________ the heat, we played basketball outside.
(A) In spite
**(B) In spite of**
(C) Despite of
(D) Despite there was

**해석** 더위에도 불구하고 우리는 밖에서 농구를 했다.
(A) 틀린 표현
**(B) ~에도 불구하고**
(C) 틀린 표현
(D) 틀린 표현

**풀이** 더위에도 불구하고 밖에서 농구를 했다는 의미가 돼야 하므로 '비록 ~임에
도 불구하고'라는 의미인 (B)가 정답이다.

**Words and Phrases**  in spite of ~에도 불구하고

**45.** Abdul's teachers urged him ______________ his artwork in
the contest.
(A) enter
**(B) to enter**
(C) entering
(D) he should enter

**해석** Abdul의 선생님들이 그에게 그의 작품을 대회에 내보라고 설득했다.
(A) 내다
**(B) 내는 것을**
(C) 내는
(D) 어색한 표현

**풀이** Abdul의 선생님들이 Abdul에게 대회에 그의 작품을 내라는 것을 충고하
고 있고 'urge'의 목적격 보어인 to부정사가 와야 하므로 (B)가 정답이다.
(D)는 접속사가 없으므로 오답이다.

**Words and Phrases**  urge 설득하다 | enter 출전시키다, 참가시키다

**46.** It's entirely your choice whether _______________ go on the trip
with us.
    (A) if you
    (B) you or if
    **(C) or not you**
    (D) you or not

해석   네가 우리와 함께 여행을 갈지 말지는 전적으로 너의 선택이다.
    (A) 틀린 표현
    (B) 틀린 표현
    (C) 네가 ~말지는
    (D) 틀린 표현

풀이   '갈지 안 갈지'라는 의미를 나타내기 위해 접속사 'whether'가 올 수 있고
그 뒤에 'or not'을 붙여 선택권을 강조할 수 있다. 또한 'whether' 뒤에 완
전한 절이 와야 하는 접속사로 주어 'you'가 필요하므로 (C)가 정답이다.
(A)는 접속사 'whether' 뒤에 접속사 'if'가 나올 수 없으므로 오답이다.

Words and Phrases   entirely 전적으로

## Part 7. Practical Reading Comprehension (p.41)

**[47-48]**

**47.** What is the purpose of the poster?
    (A) to announce a clothing sale
    **(B) to advertise a performance festival**
    (C) to find applicants for an arts school
    (D) to notify the public of arts scholarships

**48.** What is true?
    (A) Acts come from ten countries.
    **(B) Outdoor performances are free.**
    (C) Indoor acts cost less for students.
    (D) Costume discounts are available for entrants.

해석

> Akita 공연단
> 2019년 7월 5일–10일
>
> 참가국: 알바니아, 중국, 도미니카, 핀란드, 일본, 라오스, 마다가스카르,
> 뉴질랜드 그리고 한국
>
> 페스티벌 장 무료 입장: 길거리 야외 공연을 무료로 보세요
> 실내 공연을 위한 티켓값: 1,500¥
> 티켓 10장을 세트로 10,000¥에 구매하세요.

47. 포스터의 목적은 무엇인가?
    (A) 의류 세일을 발표하기 위해
    (B) 공연 축제를 홍보하기 위해
    (C) 예술 학교를 위한 지원자들을 찾기 위해
    (D) 대중에게 예술 장학금을 공지하기 위해

48. 무엇이 사실인가?
    (A) 공연은 10개국에서 참여한다.
    (B) 야외 공연은 무료이다.
    (C) 실내 공연은 학생들에게 저렴하다.
    (D) 참가자들에게 복장 할인이 가능하다.

풀이   포스터의 제목이 'Akita Troupe'이고 'July 5-10, 2019', 'See outdoor
street performances at no charge', 'Tickets to indoor performances: 1,500¥'과 같은 공연의 날짜와 그 가격에 대한 정보가 있으므
로 47번의 정답은 (B)이다.

포스터에서 'See outdoor street performances at no charge'라고 했
으므로 48번의 정답은 (B)이다.

Words and Phrases   outdoor 야외의 | charge 요금; 청구하다; 충전하다 |
indoor 실내의 | applicant 지원자 | entrant 참가자

**[49-51]**

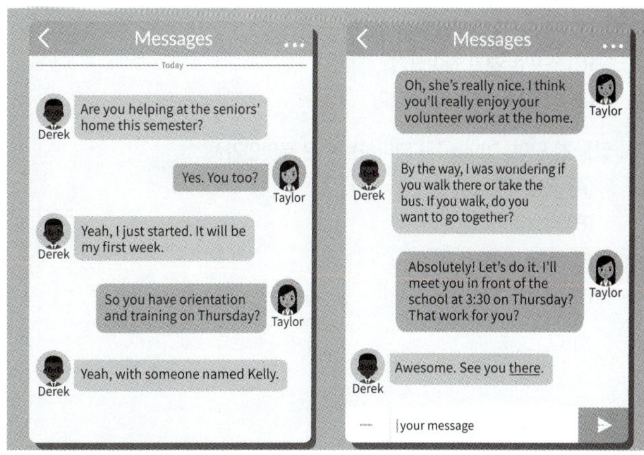


**49.** What is the most likely relationship between Derek and
Taylor?
    **(A) co-volunteers**
    (B) band musicians
    (C) student - teacher
    (D) basketball teammates

**50.** What will Derek do on Thursday?

(A) **receive training**

(B) teach a volunteer

(C) attend a sports match

(D) sing for senior citizens

**51.** What does the underlined "there" refer to?

(A) at home

(B) on a bus

(C) **outside a school**

(D) at a seniors' home

### 해석

> Derek: 이번 학기에 양로원 일을 도와주니?
>
> Taylor: 응. 너도?
>
> Derek: 응, 난 이제 막 시작했어. 이번 주가 내 첫 번째 주야.
>
> Taylor: 그럼 너는 목요일에 예비 교육이랑 훈련을 받겠네?
>
> Derek: 응, Kelly라는 사람하고.
>
> Taylor: 오, 그녀는 정말 친절해. 나는 네가 그 양로원에서 너의 봉사활동을 정말 즐길 거라고 생각해.
>
> Derek: 그나저나 나는 네가 걸어가는지 버스를 타는지 궁금했어. 만약에 너도 걸어가면 같이 걸어갈래?
>
> Taylor: 물론이지! 그러자. 내가 너를 목요일 3시 30분에 학교 앞에서 만날게. 괜찮지?
>
> Derek: 좋아. 거기에서 보자.

49. Derek과 Taylor의 관계로 가장 적절한 것은 무엇인가?

(A) 자원봉사 동료

(B) 밴드 음악가들

(C) 학생 – 선생님

(D) 농구 팀 동료

50. Derek이 목요일에 할 것은 무엇인가?

(A) 교육 받기

(B) 자원 봉사자 가르치기

(C) 스포츠 경기 참여하기

(D) 양로원에서 노래 부르기

51. 밑줄 친 단어, "there"가 의미하는 것은 무엇인가?

(A) 집에서

(B) 버스에서

(C) 학교 밖에서

(D) 양로원에서



**풀이**  Derek의 "Are you helping at the seniors' home this semester?"라는 물음에 Taylor가 "Yes. You too?"라고 대답하고 그 뒤 Derek이 그렇다고 대답한 것으로 보아 둘의 관계는 같은 곳에서 자원봉사를 하는 사람들이므로 49번의 정답은 (A)이다.

Taylor의 "So you have orientation and training on Thursday?"라는 물음에 Derek이 그렇다고 했고 Derek은 목요일에 교육을 받을 것이므로 50번의 정답은 (A)이다.

Taylor이 'I'll meet you in front of the school ~'라고 말한 것에 Derek이 "See you there."라고 대답했으므로 "there"가 가리키는 곳은 학교 밖이므로 51번의 정답은 (C)이다.

Words and Phrases  seniors' home 양로원 | orientation 오리엔테이션, 예비 교육

[52–55]

**52.** What does the video show?

(A) travel advice

(B) bicycle races

(C) **angry motorists**

(D) people opening toys

**53.** Which of the following is true?

(A) **The video was posted in 2017.**

(B) Viewers must be over 12 years old.

(C) There are 80 comments below the video.

(D) Watching the video requires a subscription.

**54.** What does Jaygirl claim?

(A) Someone moves too slowly.

(B) A taxi driver is mad for no reason.

(C) The video does not load properly.

(D) **Someone in a blue car makes a mistake.**

**55.** The underlined word "confrontations" is closest in meaning to:

(A) **fights**

(B) officers

(C) cameras

(D) permissions

---

영상

---

블랙박스 속 운전자의 분노!
화난 운전자들의 반응을 보세요--모두 블랙박스에 나와있습니다!

---

게시자 Kelida: 2017년 6월 3일
더 좋은 영상을 보려면 www.kelidashcam.wetube.com을 구독하세요!

댓글 76개

Willis: 인간들은 정말 끔찍할 수 있어. 어떤 사람이 할머니에게 천천히 운전하는 중이라고 소리를 질러?

Alexira: 아마 노인에게 소리 지르는 것은 좋지 못한 행동이긴 하지만, 저 할머니는 제한 속도보다 "훨씬" 더 느리게 갔다고.

Jaygirl: 5:34를 봐. 그 파란색 차에 있는 그 남자가 잘못인 것을 볼 수 있어. 그 노란색 택시가 먼저 지나갈 수 있었어. 그 택시 운전자가 화 난 게 놀랍지도 않아.

Heronutter: 왜 사람들은 그들이 운전 중일 때 인내하지 않을까? 운전자들은 대립을 피해야만 해.

---

52. 영상은 무엇을 보여주는가?

   (A) 여행 조언

   (B) 자전거 경주

   (C) 화가 난 운전자들

   (D) 장난감을 여는 사람들

53. 다음 중 사실인 것은 무엇인가?

   (A) 그 영상은 2017년에 게시되었다.

   (B) 시청자들은 12세 이상이어야 한다.

   (C) 영상 밑에 80개의 댓글이 달려 있다.

   (D) 영상을 보려면 구독해야 한다.

54. Jaygirl이 주장하는 것은 무엇인가?

   (A) 누군가가 너무 느리게 움직였다.

   (B) 택시 운전자가 아무 이유 없이 화를 냈다.

   (C) 그 비디오가 제대로 로딩되지 않는다.

   (D) 파란색 차에 있는 누군가가 실수를 했다.

55. 밑줄 친 "confrontations"와 가장 유사한 뜻을 가진 단어는:

   (A) 싸움

   (B) 경찰관들

   (C) 카메라들

   (D) 허락

풀이  영상 제목에 'ROAD RAGE!'라고 적혀있고 영상 설명에 'SEE ANGRY DRIVERS REACT'라고 쓰여있는 것을 보아 운전자들이 길에서 분노하는 내용을 담고 있다는 것을 알 수 있으므로 52번의 정답은 (C)이다.

영상 하단에 'Posted by Kelida: June 3, 2017'라고 쓰여있는 것으로 보아 영상은 2017년에 게시되었으므로 53번의 정답은 (A)이다. 하단에 'Subscribe to: www.kelidashcam.wetube.com for more great videos!'라고 구독을 유도하는 링크가 나와있었지만 반드시 해야 하는 것은 아니므로 (D)는 오답이다.

Jaygirl의 댓글에 "You can totally see that the guy in the blue car is at fault." 라고 하는 것으로 보아 Jaygirl은 파란색 차의 남자가 잘못했다고 주장하고 있음을 알 수 있으므로 54번의 정답은 (D)이다.

'confrontation'은 '대립, 대치'라는 뜻을 가진 단어로 55번의 정답은 (A)이다.

Words and Phrases  dash cam 차량용 블랙박스 | rage 분노 | awful 끔찍한 | way 길; 훨씬 | speed limit 제한 속도 | at fault 잘못해서, (...에 대해) 책임이 있어 | right of way 통행권 | confrontation 대립, 대치

**[56-59]**

Page 5    **Masonville Herald**    Masonville February 3, 2019

Local woman Gina Lee (42) has won her long-running negotiations with authorities to keep Drago, her 8-foot, 507-pound alligator. Said Lee of Drago, "He's such a sweetheart, and there have been no complaints from any neighbors."

Lee's attorney, Parma Denzig, said "We are fairly satisfied with the outcome of the case." City Hall employee Ken Harley said, "This case differed from many pet licensing cases in that Ms. Lee's original permit for Drago was granted when Drago was a little alligator. Once he passed the 5.5-foot mark, though, he no longer fit in the size restrictions for pets according to Masonville bylaws. We feel that the case's conclusion balances public safety and pet owners' rights."

56. Who most likely went to law school?

   (A) Drago

   (B) Gina Lee

   (C) Ken Harley

   **(D) Parma Denzig**

57. How long was Drago at the time the story was published?

   (A) 5 feet

   (B) 5.5 feet

   **(C) 8 feet**

   (D) 8.5 feet

58. What does Lee say about Drago?

   (A) He needs a mate.

   (B) He is getting too fat.

   **(C) He has a nice temperament.**

   (D) He eats more than she expected.

59. The underlined word "bylaws" is closest in meaning to:

   (A) federal rules

   (B) permit holders

   **(C) local regulations**

   (D) married relatives

> **Masonville 신문**
>
> 5면 　　　　　　　　　　　　　　Masonville, 2019년 2월 3일
>
> 우리 지역 여성 Gina Lee (42)가 그녀의 8피트, 507 파운드짜리 악어 Drago를 지키기 위한 당국과의 오랜 협상에서 승리했다. Drago의 주인 Lee 씨가 말했다, "그는 정말 다정하고, 어떤 이웃으로부터 불만이 없었어요." Lee 씨의 변호인인 Parma Denzig는 "우리는 그 사건의 결과에 상당히 만족합니다."라고 말했다. 시청 직원 Ken Harley는 "이 사건은 Lee 씨의 Drago 에 대한 원래의 허가가 Drago가 작은 악어였을 때 허가됐다는 점에서 많은 반려동물 허가 사례와 다릅니다. 하지만 그가 5.5피트 기록을 통과한 이상, 그는 Masonville의 조례에 따른 반려동물의 크기 제한에 더 이상 맞지 않습니다. 우리는 그 사건의 결론이 시민의 안전과 반려동물 주인의 권리의 균형을 맞췄다고 생각합니다."라고 말했다.

56. 로스쿨에 다녔을 사람으로 가장 적절한 것은 누구인가?
    (A) Drago
    (B) Gina Lee
    (C) Ken Harley
    (D) Parma Denzig

57. 기사가 발행되었을 때 Drago의 길이는 얼마였는가?
    (A) 5피트
    (B) 5.5피트
    (C) 8피트
    (D) 8.5피트

58. Lee가 Drago에 대해 무엇이라고 말하는가?
    (A) 그는 짝이 필요하다.
    (B) 그는 너무 살찌고 있는 중이다.
    (C) 그는 좋은 성격을 가졌다.
    (D) 그는 그녀가 예상한 것보다 더 먹는다.

59. 밑줄 친 단어 "bylaws"와 가장 유사한 뜻을 가진 단어는:
    (A) 연방법
    (B) 허가권자
    (C) 지역 규정
    (D) 결혼한 친척들

**풀이** Parma Denzig가 'Lee's attorney'이므로 가장 로스쿨에 다녔을 것으로 예상되므로 56번의 정답은 (D)이다.

'~ her 8-foot, 507-pound alligator ~'라고 나와있는 것으로 보아 기사 나왔을 당시의 Drago의 길이는 8피트이므로 57번의 정답은 (C)이다. (B) 는 Masonville의 반려동물 크기 규격이므로 오답이다.

Lee가 Drago에 대해 "He's such a sweetheart, and there have been no complaints from any neighbors."라고 말한 것으로 보아 Lee는 Drago가 좋은 성격을 가진 악어라고 말하고 있으므로 58번의 정답은 (C)이다.

'bylaw'는 '내규, 규칙; 조례, 지방법'이라는 뜻을 가진 단어로 59번의 정답은 (C)이다. (A)는 지방 조례보다 상위법인 연방법이라는 뜻이므로 오답이다.

**Words and Phrases**　negotiation 협상 | sweetheart 다정한 사람; 애인; 자기(호칭) | attorney 변호사 | licensing 허가 | once ... 할 때 | bylaw 조례, 내규 | mate 짝 | temperament 기질, 성질 | permit holder 허가권자 | regulation 규정 | relative 친척

## Part 8. General Reading Comprehension (p.45)

[60–61]

The world today is divided into six to seven continents: Africa, Antarctica, Australia, North America, South America, Asia, and Europe. (Some people put the last two together as "Eurasia".) One German researcher, Alfred Wegener, looked at their shapes, and thought that some of the continents maybe used to be connected. Particularly, South America and Africa looked like two puzzle pieces that fit together. In 1912, he proposed the theory of continental drift, meaning that the continents used to be joined together, had then separated, and were slowly moving around the globe. At the time, the theory was not accepted by many scientists. However, by the 1950s, scientists generally agreed that continental drift was a real phenomenon.

Summary:
Currently, the world's continents are divided. However, as Alfred Wegener noted in 1912, different continents have shapes like puzzle pieces. He hypothesized that the continents had once been connected and that they were now in a state of ___[A]___. His theory of "continental drift" was ___[B]___ controversial, but is now widely accepted.

60. Choose the most suitable word for blank [A], connecting the summary to the passage.
    (A) shock
    (B) union
    (C) danger
    (D) motion

61. Choose the most suitable word for blank [B], connecting the summary to the passage.
    (A) hardly
    (B) initially
    (C) particularly
    (D) surprisingly

해석 오늘날 세계는 아프리카, 남극, 호주, 북아메리카, 남미, 아시아, 유럽 등 6~7개 대륙으로 나뉜다. (어떤 사람들은 마지막 두 개를 "유라시아"라고 부른다). 독일의 한 연구원 Alfred Wegener는 그들의 모양을 보고, 몇몇 대륙이 아마도 예전에 연결되어 있었다고 생각했다. 특히, 남아메리카와 아프리카는 서로 맞는 두 개의 퍼즐 조각처럼 보였다. 1912년, 그는 대륙 이동설을 제안했는데, 이것은 그 대륙들이 서로 결합되어 있었고, 그 뒤 분리되고, 지구 주위를 천천히 움직이는 중이었다는 것을 의미한다. 그 당시에, 그 이론은 많은 과학자들에 의해 받아들여지지 않았다. 그러나, 1950년대에 이르러 과학자들은 일반적으로 대륙의 이동이 실제 현상이라는 데 동의했다.

요약:
현재, 세계의 대륙은 나뉘어져 있다. 그러나, 1912년에 Alfred Wegener가 알아차렸듯이, 다양한 대륙들은 퍼즐 조각과 같은 모양을 가지고 있다. 그는 대륙들이 한때 연결되었던 적이 있고, 이제는 <u>운동</u> 상태에 있다는 이론을 세웠다. 그의 "대륙 이동" 이론은 <u>처음에는</u> 논란이 많았으나, 지금은 널리 받아들여지고 있다.

60. 본문과 요약본을 연결할 수 있는, 빈칸 [A]에 들어갈 가장 적절한 단어를 고르시오.
    (A) 충격
    (B) 단합
    (C) 위험
    (D) 운동

61. 본문과 요약본을 연결할 수 있는, 빈칸 [B]에 들어갈 가장 적절한 단어를 고르시오.
    (A) 거의 ~않다
    (B) 처음에
    (C) 특히
    (D) 놀랍게도

풀이 Wegener의 가설에 대해 지문에서 'meaning that the continents used to be joined together, had then separated, and were slowly moving around the globe'라고 말하고 있으므로 60번의 정답은 (D)이다.

"At the time, the theory was not accepted by many scientists."라는 것으로 보아 대륙 이동설이 발표된 당시에 받아들여지지 않았으므로 61번의 정답은 (B)이다.

Words and Phrases continent 대륙 | drift 이동, 표류 | phenomenon 현상 | note 알아차리다; 주목하다; 언급하다

[62–65]

[1] First grown in Afghanistan in around 900 AD and now found in most countries, carrots are an incredibly versatile vegetable. There are many kinds of carrots. While many people may think of the color orange when they think of carrots, in fact there are at least twenty species of carrots, and these come in all kinds of shades from white, to yellow, to red, to purple.

[2] Carrots contain many substances that make them versatile for cooking. Fans of carrot cake and carrot muffins know that carrots are a very sugary vegetable. What they may not also know is how much water is in a carrot. Each carrot consists of approximately 88 percent water. Moreover, carrots are very high in beta-carotene, a chemical that is <u>converted</u> into vitamin A in the human body. However, healthy eaters should note that it is important to cook these vegetables to maximize the amount of beta-carotene each carrot releases.

[3] In conclusion, carrots are diverse and are found all over. Anyone with an interest in cooking and in health should consider carrots as a key part of their diet.

62. What is the main idea of the passage?
    (A) Carrots are disappearing.
    **(B) Carrots are very versatile.**
    (C) Carrots are extremely sugary.
    (D) Carrots are originally from Afghanistan.

63. Which of the following is mentioned about carrots?
    (A) their price
    (B) their diseases
    **(C) their water content**
    (D) their least popular color

64. The underlined word "converted" is closest in meaning to:
    (A) hired
    (B) stuffed
    **(C) transformed**
    (D) marginalized

65. According to the passage, what can be inferred about carrots?
    **(A) They are used in desserts.**
    (B) Most people eat them raw.
    (C) They are bad for our health.
    (D) Purple is their most popular color.

 [1] 서기 약 900년경 아프가니스탄에서 처음 재배되었고 현재 대부분의 나라에서 볼 수 있는 당근은 놀라울 정도로 다재다능한 채소이다. 당근에는 많은 종류가 있다. 많은 사람들이 당근을 생각할 때 주황색을 생각할지 모르지만, 사실은 적어도 20종의 당근이 있고, 이것들은 흰색, 노란색, 빨간색, 보라색까지 모든 종류의 색조로 나온다.

[2] 당근은 요리에 유용하게 쓰이는 많은 물질을 함유하고 있다. 당근 케이크와 당근 머핀을 좋아하는 사람들은 당근이 매우 단 야채라는 것을 알고 있다. 그들이 또 알지 못할지도 모르는 것은 당근에 얼마나 많은 물이 들어 있는지이다. 각각의 당근은 약 88 퍼센트의 물로 이루어져 있다. 게다가, 당근은 인체에서 비타민 A로 <u>전환되는</u> 화학 물질인 베타 카로틴이 매우 높다. 하지만, 건강한 식습관을 가진 사람들은 각 당근이 방출하는 베타 카로틴의 양을 최대화하기 위해 이러한 야채를 조리하는 것이 중요하다는 것을 알아야 한다.

[3] 결론적으로, 당근은 다양하고 곳곳에서 발견된다. 요리와 건강에 관심이 있는 사람은 누구나 당근을 식단의 주요 부분으로 생각해야 한다.

62. 이 지문의 요지는 무엇인가?
    (A) 당근이 사라지고 있다.
    (B) 당근은 유용하다.
    (C) 당근은 매우 달다.
    (D) 당근은 원래 아프가니스탄에서 왔다.

63. 다음 중 지문에서 당근에 대해 언급된 것은 무엇인가?
    (A) 그들의 가격
    (B) 그들의 질병
    (C) 그들의 수분 함량
    (D) 그들의 가장 유명하지 않은 색깔

64. 밑줄 친 단어 "converted"와 가장 유사한 뜻을 가진 단어는:
    (A) 고용된
    (B) 채워진
    (C) 변환되는
    (D) 소외된

65. 지문에 따르면 당근에 대해 추론할 수 있는 것은 무엇인가?
    (A) 그들은 디저트에 쓰일 수 있다.
    (B) 대부분의 사람들이 그것을 날 것으로 먹는다.
    (C) 그들은 건강에 좋지 않다.
    (D) 보라색이 그들의 가장 인기 있는 색깔이다.

풀이 [1] 문단에서 당근이 다재다능한 채소이며 종류가 많다고 언급하고 [2]에서는 당근이 지닌 영양 성분에 대해서 설명하고 그 다음 [3] 문단에서 당근을 식단의 주요 부분으로 여겨야 한다고 마무리하고 있다. 따라서 지문의 중심 소재는 당근의 유용함이므로 62번의 정답은 (B)이다.

[2]문단에서 "Each carrot consists of approximately 88 percent water." 라고 말한 것으로 당근에는 88%의 수분이 들어있다는 것을 알 수 있으므로 63번의 정답은 (C)이다.

'converted'는 '전환된'이라는 뜻을 나타내므로 64번의 정답은 (C)이다.

[2]문단에 "Fans of carrot cake and carrot muffins know that carrots are a very sugary vegetable."라고 언급된 것으로 보아 당근이 케이크나 머핀으로도 만들어 질 수 있다는 것을 알 수 있으므로 65번의 정답은 (A)이다.

Words and Phrases   incredibly 놀라울 정도로 | versatile 다재다능한 | species 종 | shade 색조 | substance 물질 | sugary 단 | consist of ~로 구성되다 | chemical 화학물질 | convert 전환하다 | maximize 극대화하다 | release 방출하다 | diverse 다양한 | diet 식단 | stuff 채우다; 물건 | transform 변형시키다 | marginalize 하찮은 존재 같은 기분이 들게 하다[존재로 만들다] | water content 수분 함량 | dessert 디저트, 후식 | raw 날 것의

# TOSEL High Junior

## 실전3회

**Section I** Listening and Speaking

1 (A)  2 (C)  3 (A)  4 (B)  5 (C)
6 (A)  7 (A)  8 (B)  9 (B) 10 (B)
11 (B) 12 (C) 13 (D) 14 (C) 15 (D)
16 (A) 17 (D) 18 (A) 19 (A) 20 (C)
21 (B) 22 (B) 23 (D) 24 (C) 25 (D)
26 (D) 27 (B) 28 (B) 29 (C) 30 (C)

**Section II** Reading and Writing

31 (C) 32 (A) 33 (D) 34 (C) 35 (A)
36 (A) 37 (C) 38 (A) 39 (C) 40 (D)
41 (B) 42 (C) 43 (B) 44 (C) 45 (B)
46 (D) 47 (D) 48 (D) 49 (C) 50 (B)
51 (B) 52 (A) 53 (B) 54 (D) 55 (B)
56 (B) 57 (C) 58 (B) 59 (D) 60 (D)
61 (A) 62 (D) 63 (A) 64 (B) 65 (A)

---

### SECTION I  LISTENING AND SPEAKING

**Part 1.** Listen and Recognize (p.50)

**1.** W: Look at the amount of trash left on this beach.
  M: It's like people don't even think!
정답 (A)
해석 여: 이 해변가에 버려진 쓰레기의 양 좀 봐.
  남: 사람들이 생각조차 하지 않는 것 같아!
풀이 여자가 해변가에 버려진 쓰레기의 양('the amount of trash left on this beach')를 언급하고 있으므로 (A)가 정답이다. (B)는 'beach'를 통해, (C)는 'trash'를 통해 연상하도록 유도한 오답이다.
Words and Phrases  amount (무엇의) 양 | trash 쓰레기 | beach 해변

**2.** M: Wait up! I can't go that fast.
  W: I'm riding at a normal pace and I'm even carrying your stuff in my basket!
정답 (C)
해석 남: 기다려! 난 그렇게 빨리 갈 수 없어.
  여: 난 보통 속도로 달리고 있는 중이고 심지어 너의 물건도 내 바구니에 있잖아!
풀이 여자가 남자보다 빠르게 자전거를 타면서, 바구니에 물건을 담고 ('carrying your stuff in my basket') 있는 사진 (C)가 정답이다. (A)는 'fast'를 통해 연상하도록 유도한 오답이다.
Words and Phrases  carry (이동 중에) 들고[데리고] 있다 | stuff 물건

**3.** W: The sofa's been moved to a new spot! The room looks good.
  M: Yeah, it really makes the room look brighter in front of that window.
정답 (A)
해석 여: 그 소파가 새로운 장소로 옮겨졌어! 그 방이 좋아 보여.
  남: 맞아, 그것은 저 창문 앞에 있어. 그 방이 더 밝아 보이게 만들어.
풀이 남자가 창문 앞에 ('in front of that window') 소파를 옮긴 것을 언급하고 있으므로 (A)가 정답이다. (C)는 'brighter'를 통해 연상하도록 유도한 오답이다.
Words and Phrases  spot (특정한) 곳

**4.** M: Are you free on the 28th? There's this indoor market at the mall.
  W: Let's see. What have I got marked in this sticky-note covered planner?
정답 (B)
해석 남: 너 28일에 시간 되니? 이번에 쇼핑몰에서 실내 시장이 열린다고 하거든.
  여: 한 번 볼게. 내가 포스트잇으로 가득 찬 이 수첩에 무엇을 써놨지?
풀이 여자가 포스트잇으로 뒤덮힌 수첩 ('sticky-note covered planner')을 언급하고 있으므로 (B)가 정답이다. (A)의 경우, 'planner'를 통해 연상하도록 유도한 오답이다.
Words and Phrases  sticky-note 포스트잇 (쉽게 떼었다 붙였다 할 수 있는 메모지) | planner 일정 계획표

**5.** W: Ms. Miller's class is out of control.
  M: She's been cowering, head covered, in front of her own students.
정답 (C)
해석 여: Miller 선생님의 수업은 통제 불능의 상태야.
  남: 그녀는 학생들 앞에서 웅크리고, 머리를 감싸고 있는 중이야.
풀이 선생님이 머리를 감싸고 웅크리고 ('cowering, head covered') 있다고 했으므로 (C)가 정답이다. (A)와 (B) 둘 다 'in front of her own students'를 통해 연상하도록 유도한 오답이다.
Words and Phrases  be out of control 통제력을 벗어나다 | cower (겁을 먹고) 몸을 숙이다 [웅그리다]

**6.** M: Look at him make that huge loop with the rope. That's impressive.
  W: Yeah, all while dancing! Not easy to do.
정답 (A)
해석 남: 그 밧줄을 가지고 저 큰 고리를 만들고 있는 남자를 봐. 아주 인상적이야.
  여: 맞아, 그것도 춤을 추면서! 쉽지 않은 일인데.
풀이 남자가 밧줄을 이용하여 고리를 만드는 ('make that huge loop with the rope') 사람을 가리키고 있으므로 (A)가 정답이다. (B)는 'loop'를 통해 연상하도록 유도한 오답이다.
Words and Phrases  loop (올가미나 동그라미 모양의) 고리 | rope 밧줄

**7.** W: It's nice out here, isn't it?

M: ________________

   **(A) Yes, the weather is great.**

   (B) No, they will meet us later.

   (C) No, the wallpaper is still good.

   (D) Yes, I can help you with the dishes.

해석 여: 여기 참 좋다, 그렇지 않니?

   남: ________________

   **(A) 맞아, 날씨가 참 좋네.**

   (B) 아니, 그들은 우리와 나중에 만날 거야.

   (C) 아니, 벽지는 여전히 괜찮아.

   (D) 그래, 내가 설거지 하는 것을 도울 수 있어.

풀이 여자가 이곳이 참 좋다고 ('nice out here') 말하자 날씨가 좋다고 동의하는 (A)가 정답이다.

Words and Phrases  wallpaper 벽지


**8.** M: What is the right kind of water for a pet turtle?

W: ________________

   (A) When are you getting me a dog?

   **(B) What size of turtle do you mean?**

   (C) Why is my cat eating so little food?

   (D) Where are you keeping your snake?

해석 남 : 반려 거북이한테 어떤 종류의 물이 좋을까?

   여: ________________

   (A) 나한테 언제 강아지를 줄래?

   **(B) 어떤 크기의 거북이를 말하는 거야?**

   (C) 왜 내 고양이는 음식을 적게 먹는 중이지?

   (D) 너의 뱀은 어디에 보관하고 있는 중이니?

풀이 남자가 자신의 거북이에게 알맞은 물을 알아보러 왔기 때문에 거북이의 크기, 상세한 정보에 대해서 되물어보는 (B)가 정답이다.

Words and Phrases  pet 반려동물 | turtle 바다 거북, (모든 종류의) 거북


**9.** W: Oh no! My favorite blogger has quit.

M: ________________

   (A) Is your screen the issue?

   **(B) What kind of blog was it?**

   (C) Who helps you with that blog?

   (D) Do you need to fix your mouse?

해석 여: 오 이런! 내가 가장 좋아하는 블로거가 그만뒀어.

   남: ________________

   (A) 화면에 문제가 있는 거야?

   **(B) 어떤 블로그였는데?**

   (C) 누가 저 블로그를 도와주니?

   (D) 너는 너의 마우스를 고칠 필요가 있니?

풀이 여자가 자신이 가장 좋아하는 블로거 ('my favorite blogger')에 대해 말하고 있으므로 블로그에 대한 질문하는 (B)가 정답이다.

Words and Phrases  blogger 블로그를 만드는 사람 | quit (하던 일을) 그만두다


**10.** M: How early do we need to wake up for the hike?

W: ________________

   (A)  This alarm clock has a nice ring.

   **(B)  We need to be up before sunrise.**

   (C) I have an extra pair of boots for you.

   (D) They have to be in bed by ten tonight.

해석 남: 그 등산을 위해서 우리는 얼마나 빨리 일어나야 될까?

   여: ________________

   (A) 이 알람시계는 좋은 소리를 가지고 있어.

   **(B) 우리는 해 뜨기 전에 일어나야 해.**

   (C) 난 널 위해 여분의 부츠를 가지고 있어.

   (D) 그들은 오늘 밤 10시까지 잠자리에 들어야 해.

풀이 남자가 등산을 위해 일어나야 하는 시간에 대해 묻고 있으므로 해 뜨기 전에 일어나야 한다는 (B)가 정답이다.

Words and Phrases  ring (종이[을]) 울리다, 종소리 | sunrise 동틀녘, 일출


**11.** W: Who else is coming to this thing?

M: ________________

   (A) The hall was so beautiful.

   **(B) I'm not sure of the guest list.**

   (C) I'll be there as soon as I can.

   (D) They are serving hamburgers.

해석 여: 여기에 또 누가 오는 거야?

   남: ________________

   (A) 그 홀이 너무 아름다웠어.

   **(B) 나도 손님 명단에 대해 잘 모르겠어.**

   (C) 나는 가능한 한 일찍 도착할게.

   (D) 그들은 햄버거를 제공하고 있어.

풀이 누가 오는 것인지 묻는 여자의 말에 확실하지 않다고 말하는 (B)가 정답이다. (C)의 경우, 'coming'과 'I'll be there'의 연관성을 이용한 오답이다.

Words and Phrases  hall 홀[회관/~실](회의, 식사, 콘서트 등을 위한 큰 방이나 건물) | guest 손님, 하객 | as soon as ...하자마자


**12.** M: What is in these big boxes?

W: ________________

   (A) Just leave yours on the corner.

   (B) Just wash the fruit you'll eat today.

   **(C) Just some old clothes I don't need.**

   (D) Just a bit of room is left in each one.

해석 남: 이 큰 상자들에 뭐가 들어있는 거야?

   여: ________________

   (A) 그냥 너의 것을 그 구석에 둬.

   (B) 그냥 너가 오늘 먹을 그 과일을 씻겨줘.

   **(C) 그냥 내가 필요로 하지 않는 낡은 옷가지들이야.**

   (D) 그냥 각각에 약간의 공간이 남아 있어.

풀이 남자가 상자에 무엇이 들어있는지 묻는 말에 옷가지가 들어 있다고 대답하는 (C)가 정답이다.

Words and Phrases  fruit 과일 | clothes 옷 | room 공간

**13.** W: How was the baseball game?

    M: _______________

       (A) That's the team I cheer for.

       (B) It will be in Wisley Stadium.

       (C) He was injured halfway through.

       **(D) The last inning was really exciting.**

**해석** 여: 그 야구 경기 어땠어?

    남: _______________

       (A) 그 팀이 바로 내가 응원하는 팀이야.

       (B) 그것은 Wisley 경기장에서 진행할 예정이야.

       (C) 그는 중반에 부상당했어.

       **(D) 마지막 회가 정말 재미있었어.**

**풀이** 야구 경기가 어땠냐는 질문에 정말 재미있었다는 (D)가 정답이다. (A)의 경우, 'baseball'과 'team'의 연관성을 이용한 오답이다. (B)의 경우, 시합 장소를 물어보는 질문이 아니라, 경기의 감상평을 물어보는 질문이므로 오답이다.

**Words and Phrases**  cheer 응원하다 | injure (특히 사고로) 부상을 입다 [입히다] | inning (야구에서 9회중의 한) 회

**14.** M: How come you don't see your aunt more?

    W: _______________

       (A) He is still living overseas.

       (B) You were going to be out all day.

       **(C) She and I have never been close.**

       (D) They are visiting us next summer.

**해석** 남: 어째서 너의 고모를 더 이상 안 보는 거니?

    여: _______________

       (A) 그는 여전히 해외에 계셔.

       (B) 너는 하루 종일 외출하려고 했었잖아.

       **(C) 나는 그녀와 친했던 적이 없어.**

       (D) 그들은 다음 여름에 우리를 방문할 예정이야.

**풀이** 고모를 더 이상 보지 않는 이유에 대해 친했던 적이 없었다고 답하는 (C)가 정답이다. (D)의 경우 'see'외 'visiting'의 연관성을 이용한 오답이다.

**Words and Phrases**  How come ~? 어째서 ~하니? | aunt 고모, 이모, (외)숙모 | overseas 해외[외국/국외]의, 해외에[로] | close (사이가) 가까운, 친(밀)한

**15.** W: What do you think of this report?

    M: _______________

       (A) Barely, but at least it is all done.

       (B) The more that come, the merrier.

       (C) Sure, I can add a few words to it.

       **(D) Great content, weak writing style.**

**해석** 여: 너는 이 보고서에 대해 어떻게 생각해?

    남: _______________

       (A) 간신히지만, 적어도 다 끝냈어.

       (B) 많이 올수록, 더 즐거워.

       (C) 그래, 내가 그것에 몇 가지를 첨언할 수 있을 것 같아.

       **(D) 내용은 훌륭하지만 문체는 빈약해.**

**풀이** 보고서에 대한 평가를 묻는 말에 평가를 내려주는 (D)가 정답이다. (A)의 경우, 'all done' 그리고 (C)의 경우, 'add a few words'를 통해 'report'를 연상하도록 유도한 오답이다.

**Words and Phrases**  report 보고서; 알리다 | barely 간신히, 가까스로, 빠듯하게 | merry 즐거운 | content 내용[물]

**16.** M: I feel stuffed. I think I overdid it at dinner.

    W: _______________

       **(A) Me, too. Let's walk it off.**

       (B) Me, neither. I'm so tired.

       (C) I can, too. I'll get dessert.

       (D) I can't, either. Let's sit down.

**해석** 남: 나는 배불러. 내 생각에 내가 저녁에 과식한 것 같아.

    여: _______________

       **(A) 나도. 산책 좀 하자.**

       (B) 나도 아니야. 나는 너무 피곤해.

       (C) 나 또한 가능해. 내가 후식을 가져올게.

       (D) 나 역시 안 될 것 같아. 앉아 있자.

**풀이** 배부르다는 남자의 말에 산책을 하자는 (A)가 정답이다. 나머지 선택지의 경우, 'tired', 'dessert', 'sit down' 모두 배부르다는 말에 대한 대답에 어색하므로 오답이다.

**Words and Phrases**  stuffed 잔뜩 먹은 | overdo 지나치게 하다, 과장하다; 지나치게 많이 쓰다[이용하다] | dessert 후식

## Part 3. Short Conversations (p.53)

**17.** W: I think there's something on your arm.

    M: Do you like it? Samrita did the design.

    W: Uh…Is it a permanent tattoo?

    M: No, it's just temporary. It'll fade over time.

    W: Aha… does it mean something?

    M: Yes. It means "Peace" in Arabic.

    Q: What is the main topic of the conversation?

       (A) dirty hands

       (B) interior design

       (C) a beaded bracelet

       **(D) a temporary tattoo**

**해석** 여: 팔에 그건 뭐야?

    남: 어때? Samrita가 그려줬는데.

    여: 어… 그거 영구 문신이야?

    남: 아니, 그것은 그냥 일시적인 거야. 시간이 지나면 사라질 거야.

    여: 아… 어떤 의미를 가지고 있는 거야?

    남: 그럼. "평화"라는 의미의 아랍어야.

    질문: 대화의 주제는 무엇인가?

       (A) 더러운 손

       (B) 실내 디자인

       (C) 구슬로 장식된 팔찌

       **(D) 일시적인 문신**

**풀이** 여자가 남자의 팔에 그려진 문신에 대해 물어보고 있다. 이에 대해 남자는 'it's just temporary'라고 말하며 일시적인 문신에 대해 얘기하고 있으므로 (D)가 정답이다. (B)의 경우, 'design'을 이용해 혼동을 유도한 오답이다.

**Words and Phrases**  permanent 영구[영속]적인 | tattoo 문신 | temporary 일시적인, 임시의 | fade (색깔이) 바래다[희미해지다] | Arabic 아랍어, 아랍어[문학]의

**18.** M: It's nowhere to be found!

W: What are you looking for?

M: The key to the outside gate at my cousin's house.

W: Why would you even have that?

M: I'm supposed to water his garden while he's away.

W: You should just call your cousin. He probably has a spare.

Q: What is the man's problem?

  **(A) He lost a key.**

  (B) He left a gate open.

  (C) He killed some plants.

  (D) He slipped in a garden.

해석 남: 어디에도 찾을 수가 없어!

여: 너는 무엇을 찾고 있는데?

남: 사촌 집 현관문 열쇠를 찾고 있어.

여: 왜 네가 그걸 가지고 있는 거야?

남: 그가 외출하는 동안 내가 그의 정원에 물을 주기로 했었거든.

여: 너는 먼저 사촌한테 연락해야 돼. 그는 아마 여분의 열쇠를 가지고 있을 거야.

질문: 남자는 무엇이 문제인가?

  (A) 그는 열쇠를 잃어버렸다.

  (B) 그는 문을 열어뒀다.

  (C) 그가 몇몇 식물들을 시들게 했다.

  (D) 그는 정원에서 미끄러져 넘어졌다.

풀이 두 번째 발화에서 여자가 "What are you looking for?"라고 남자에게 무엇을 찾고 있는지 묻고, 이에 대해 남자가 열쇠를 찾고 있다고 말하고 있으므로 (A)가 정답이다. (B)의 경우 'gate'를 (D)의 경우 'garden'을 다시 한 번 언급하며 혼동을 유도한 오답이다.

Words and Phrases  nowhere 아무데도[어디에도](...않다[없다]) | cousin 사촌 | be supposed to ~ 하기로 되어 있다 [~해야 한다] | spare 남는; 여분의, 예비용의

**19.** W: Ouch! That smarts!

M: What happened?

W: I just stubbed my toe on the coffee table.

M: Ooh. I can see the toe and the toenail are both bruised. An ice pack on your foot can prevent swelling. That'll also feel better.

W: Anything else? It really hurts!

M: Raising your leg could also be a good idea.

Q: According to the man, how can the woman feel better?

  **(A) by icing her foot**

  (B) by soaking her heels

  (C) by painting her toenails

  (D) by rubbing cream on her leg

해석 여: 아야! 아파!

남: 무슨 일이야?

여: 나는 그 탁자에 나의 발가락을 부딪혔어.

남: 오 저런. 나는 네 발가락과 발톱 둘 다 멍이 생긴 게 보여. 너의 발 위에 얼음팩을 올려두면 붓기를 예방할 수 있어. 그럼 좀 나아질 거야.

여: 다른 건 또 없어? 너무 아파!

남: 네 다리를 들고 있는 것도 좋은 방법이야.

질문: 남자의 말에 의하면, 여자의 아픔을 낫게 하는 방법은 무엇인가?

  (A) 발에 얼음찜질하기

  (B) 발 뒤꿈치를 물에 담그기

  (C) 발톱에 매니큐어 칠하기

  (D) 다리에 크림 바르기

풀이 여자가 탁자에 발을 부딪혀 "I just stubbed my toe on the coffee table."라고 했고, 이에 대해 남자가 얼음찜질 'ice pack'을 추천하고 있으므로 (A)가 정답이다. (C)는 'toenails'를, (D)는 'leg'를 다시 한 번 언급하여 혼동을 주는 오답이다.

Words and Phrases  smart 욱신[따끔]거리다, 쓰리다 | stub (~에) 발가락이 차이다 | bruise 멍[흠]이 생기다[생기게 하다] | swell 붓다, 부풀다

**20.** M: This cereal is my favorite.

W: That junk? You know it's full of sugar, right?

M: Are you kidding? It's called "Health Oats".

W: That's just a name, and it doesn't fit. Check the ingredients on the box.

M: It says it has only 1 gram of fat.

W: Fat and sugar content are not the same.

Q: What does the woman think  about the man's cereal?

  (A) It is her favorite.

  (B) It is very high in fat.

  **(C) It has too much sugar.**

  (D) It has an appropriate name.

해석 남: 이 시리얼은 내가 가장 좋아하는 시리얼이야.

여: 저 불량식품이? 너는 그것이 설탕 덩어리인 것을 알잖아, 그렇지?

남: 농담하는 거지? 그건 "Health Oats"라고 불린다고.

여: 그건 단지 이름이고 맞지도 않아. 그 상자에 있는 구성 성분을 확인해봐.

남: 오직 1g의 지방만이 포함돼 있다는데?

여: 지방과 설탕 함량은 다르지.

질문: 여자는 남자의 시리얼에 대해서 어떻게 생각하는가?

  (A) 그녀가 가장 좋아하는 시리얼이다.

  (B) 지방이 많이 포함되어 있다.

  (C) 설탕이 너무 많이 포함되어 있다.

  (D) 적절한 이름을 가지고 있다.

풀이 여자는 남자의 시리얼에 대해서 'it's full of sugar'라고 말하며 구성 성분에서 지방의 함유량이 낮다는 남자의 말에 'fat and sugar content are not the same'이라고 다시 한 번 설탕의 높은 함량을 경고하고 있으므로 (C)가 정답이다. (B)의 경우, 지방의 함량이 낮은 것을 언급했으므로 오답이다.

Words and Phrases  cereal 곡물; 시리얼[가공 곡물] | junk 쓸모없는 물건, 폐물, 쓰레기 | ingredient (특히 요리 등의) 재료[성분] | fat 지방 | sugar 설탕, 당분

**21.** W: I feel like my backside is melting into this swivel chair.

M: Get up and stretch. You're doing these 9-hour days at your desk.

W: I can't be away from my computer. I have a deadline on this report.

M: Then why are you talking to me?

W: A person has to vent sometimes.

M: Stand up and go to the water cooler for a stretch.

Q: What is the most likely relationship between the speakers?

(A) surgeon - patient

**(B) office worker - office worker**

(C) fitness instructor - gym user

(D) waterslide employee - waterslide manager

해석 여: 나는 내 엉덩이가 이 회전의자에 녹아드는 중인 것 같은 느낌이야.

남: 일어나서 기지개를 켜봐. 너 책상에서 9시간 동안 일했잖아.

여: 나는 내 컴퓨터에서 떨어질 수 없어. 나는 이 보고서 마감기한을 지켜야 하거든.

남: 그럼 너는 왜 나랑 얘기하고 있는 중이니?

여: 사람은 가끔 숨통을 터야 하거든.

남: 일어나서 스트레칭 하면서 음료수 마시는 곳 좀 갔다 와.

질문: 화자의 관계로 가장 적절한 것은 무엇인가?

(A) 외과 의사 – 환자

**(B) 직장 동료 – 직장 동료**

(C) 체육관 지도사 – 체육관 고객

(D) 물놀이 미끄럼틀 직원 – 물놀이 미끄럼틀 관리자

풀이 여자는 컴퓨터 앞에서 9시간 동안 보고서를 작성하는 직장인이라는 것을 알 수 있고 남자는 여자에게 가벼운 운동을 권해주면서 걱정하는 태도를 보이고 있다. 이는 직장 동료 사이의 대화라고 할 수 있으므로 (B)가 정답이다. (C)의 경우, 남자가 'stretch'를 권하는 상황을 통해, 'gym'을 연상하도록 유도한 오답이다.

Words and Phrases  melt 녹다[녹이다] | swivel chair 회전의자 | deadline 기한, 마감 시간 | vent (감정분통을) 터뜨리다

**22.** M: I'm doing a wash. Got anything to go in the laundry?

W: Yeah, my pink blouse for work.

M: Can that go in with the towels?

W: No, I guess you'd better do towels separately.

M: Okay, I'll start with the towels and then do the work clothes later when the towels are in the dryer.

W: Sounds good.

Q: What will the man do next?

(A) dry towels

**(B) wash towels**

(C) dry work clothes

(D) wash work clothes

해석 남: 나는 빨래를 할 거야. 빨래 할 것 있어?

여: 어, 내 직장용 분홍색 블라우스.

남: 저거 수건들이랑 같이 넣어도 되는 거지?

여: 아니, 내 생각엔 수건이랑 따로 넣는 게 좋을 거 같은데.

남: 알았어, 나는 수건을 먼저 돌리고 나서 그 수건들이 건조기에 들어갈 때, 작업복을 돌릴게.

여: 좋아.

질문: 남자가 다음 할 행동은 무엇인가?

(A) 수건 말리기

**(B) 수건 세탁하기**

(C) 작업복 말리기

(D) 작업복 세탁하기

풀이 여자가 수건과 옷을 따로 세탁할 것을 부탁하고, 이에 대해 남자가 'I'll start with the towels and then do the work clothes later'라고 말하고 있는 것으로 보아 수건을 먼저 세탁할 것을 알 수 있으므로 (B)가 정답이다. (A)의 경우, 수건 세탁 이후, 수건 건조를 진행하며 의복을 세탁한다고 말하고 있으므로 오답이다.

Words and Phrases  laundry 세탁(물), 세탁소 | towel 수건 | separately 따로따로, 별도로

**23.** W: Dr. Krowski's office. How can I help you?

M: Hello, I'm scheduled for a dental check-up on Friday at 10 but was hoping I could make it an hour later.

W: The name was…

M: Watterson. With two 't's.

W: Aha, I see it. I don't have space at 11, but could squeeze you in at 10:30.

M: That would help. Thanks very much.

Q: What is the man's purpose in the conversation?

(A) to select a new test date

(B) to cancel a visit to his dentist

(C) to check the spelling on a form

**(D) to change an appointment time**

해석 여: Krowski 의사 사무실입니다. 무엇을 도와드릴까요?

남: 안녕하세요, 제가 금요일 10시에 구강 검진 예약을 했었는데, 한 시간 늦추고 싶어서 연락드렸습니다.

여: 성함이…

남: Watterson이요. 't'를 두 번 써요.

여: 아, 알겠습니다. 11시에는 예약이 가득 찼지만, 10시 반에는 넣어드릴 수 있을 것 같습니다.

남: 그럼 그렇게 해주세요. 감사합니다.

질문: 대화에서 남자의 목적은 무엇인가?

(A) 새로운 시험 날짜를 선택하기 위해

(B) 치과 의사 방문을 취소하기 위해

(C) 서식의 맞춤법을 확인하기 위해

**(D) 약속 시간을 변경하기 위해**

풀이 남자가 'I'm scheduled for a dental check-up on Friday at 10'이라고 말한 이후 'was hoping I could make it an hour later'라고 말하며 치과 예약 시간을 변경하기 위해 전화를 한 것이므로 (D)가 정답이다. (B)의 경우, 여자가 'I don't have space at 11'이라고 말했지만, 뒤에 'but could squeeze you in at 10:30'이라고 답했으므로 오답이다.

**24.** M: I can't figure out this remote control for the TV.

W: Dad, did you touch the yellow button? You're not supposed to.

M: I didn't mean to.

W: Here, give me the remote. I'll find your channel again.

M: Can you take the yellow button off so I won't accidentally
press it?

W: Maybe that's a good idea. Let me try.

Q: What does the man ask the woman to do?

  (A) press a button on the TV

  (B) find a lost remote control

  **(C) remove a remote control button**

  (D) change the colors on a remote control

해석  남: 난 그 TV 리모컨을 어떻게 사용하는 건지 알 수가 없어.

  여: 아빠, 혹시 그 노란색 버튼을 누르셨나요? 누르면 안 돼요.

  남: 내가 의도하고 누른 것은 아니란다.

  여: 여기, 저에게 그 리모컨 주세요. 제가 아빠가 원하시는 채널을 다시
찾아 드릴게요.

  남: 내가 실수로 그 노란색 버튼을 누르지 않게 네가 그것을 리모콘에서
떼어 줄 수 있니?

  여: 좋은 생각일 거예요. 제가 시도해볼게요.

  질문: 남자가 여자에게 부탁한 일은 무엇인가?

  (A) 그 TV에 있는 버튼 누르기

  (B) 잃어버린 리모컨 찾기

  (C) 리모컨 버튼을 제거하기

  (D) 리모컨의 색상을 바꾸기

풀이  리모컨을 잘 다루지 못하는 남자가 'Can you take the yellow button
off'라며 리모컨에 있는 버튼을 제거해 주기를 부탁하고 있으므로 (C)가 정
답이다. (A)의 경우 TV에 있는 버튼을 언급하고 있으며, 남자는 버튼을 누
르지 않기를 원하고 있으므로 오답이다.

Words and Phrases  figure out ~을 이해하다[알아내다]; 해결하다 |
remote control 리모콘 | mean to ...할 셈이다 |
accidentally 우연히, 뜻하지 않게; 잘못하여

**25.** W: Let's cut the story about the zoo's baby elephant.

M: But our viewers love light-hearted stories.

W: We need more time to talk about economics and the recent
floods.

M: We can use the weather segment to talk about the floods.

W: Let's do at least a more in-depth look at the economy.

M: Okay, we'll do the zoo story in tomorrow's broadcast.

Q: Where does this conversation most likely take place?

  (A) at a political rally

  (B) at a weather station

  (C) in a zookeeper's office

  **(D) in a news writers' room**

해석  여: 동물원의 아기 코끼리에 관한 이야기의 분량을 줄이자.

  남: 하지만 우리 시청자들은 밝고 가슴 따뜻한 이야기를 좋아하는 걸요.

  여: 우리는 경제와 최근의 홍수와 관련하여 더 많은 얘기를 해야 해.

남: 우리는 그 홍수와 관련된 얘기를 위해서 기상정보 시간 때를 활용할 수
있어요.

여: 경제에 대해서 적어도 더 깊게 다뤄 보도록 하자.

남: 좋아요, 우리는 내일 방송에서 그 동물원 이야기를 할게요.

질문: 대화가 이루어지고 있는 가장 적절한 장소는 어디인가?

  (A) 정치 집회에서

  (B) 기상 관측소에서

  (C) 사육사 사무실에서

  (D) 뉴스 작가 사무실에서

풀이  다양한 주제에 대해서 토의를 하고 있는 상황에서 남자가 'viewers'와
'broadcast'를 언급하고 있고 뉴스 방송을 위한 분량을 조절하고 있다고
할 수 있으므로 (D)가 정답이다. (C)의 경우, 'zoo's baby elephant'를 이
용해 혼동을 유도한 오답이다.

Words and Phrases  viewer 시청자 | flood 홍수; 물에 잠기다, 침수되다 |
economy 경기, 경제 | broadcast 방송하다, 방송;
광고하다 | rally 집회[대회]; 경주

**26.** M: Has the dog gone out for a walk?

W: Not yet. I thought I'd wait until it was less sunny.

M: Why? The dog likes the sun.

W: Yeah, but his paws can get burnt on the pavement.

M: You won't be there long. It's just a couple blocks to the grass
in the park.

W: Well, maybe I could carry him to the grass.

Q: What does "there" mean when the man says, "You won't be
there long"?

  (A) on the grass

  (B) on the blanket

  (C) on the doorstep

  **(D) on the pavement**

해석  남: 그 개가 산책하러 나갔니?

  여: 아니 아직. 나는 햇빛이 약해질 때까지 기다리려고 생각했어.

  남: 왜? 그 강아지는 햇빛을 좋아하잖아.

  여: 맞아, 하지만 발이 보도에서 데일 수 있거든.

  남: 거기서 오래 있지 않을 거잖아. 공원의 잔디까지 두 블록밖에 안돼.

  여: 음, 내가 그를 잔디밭까지 들고 갈 수 있을 것 같아.

  질문: "거기서 오래 있지 않을 거잖아"라고 말한 부분에서 "거기"는
어디인가?

  (A) 잔디 위

  (B) 담요 위

  (C) 문간 위

  (D) 보도 위

풀이  여자가 강아지의 발바닥이 보도 위에서 데일 수 있다는 말에 남자가 'You
won't be there long'이라고 말하고 있다. 따라서 'there'는 강아지의 발
바닥이 데일 수 있는 'pavement'를 의미한다고 할 수 있으므로 (D)가 정
답이다.

Words and Phrases  paw (동물의 발톱이 달린) 발 | burn 화상, 덴 상처;
(불이) 타오르다 | pavement 보도, 인도, 포장 지역 |
grass 풀, 잔디

**[27-28]**

W: Our guest speaker tonight needs no introduction. Ever since her scene-stealing performance as "Carla" in the movie "Carla's Big Adventure", she has delighted audiences with her hilarious characters. But her contribution to the world of humor also extends to being a celebrated joke-writer for others. For over 30 years, her clever jokes have been delivered by actors in the funniest shows on TV. And now, I'm thrilled to bring to the stage, Mariana Sanchez!

**27.** Whom is the speaker most likely introducing?
   (A) a producer
   **(B) a comedian**
   (C) a film director
   (D) a dramatic actor

**28.** What does the speaker mention about Mariana Sanchez?
   (A) She has attended clown school.
   **(B) She has written for other people.**
   (C) She has worked in postal delivery.
   (D) She has performed on thirty stages.

해석  여: 오늘 밤의 초청 연사는 소개가 필요 없는 분입니다. 영화 "Carla's Big Adventure"의 매우 인상적인 "Carla" 배역 이후, 그녀는 익살스러운 등장인물을 연기해오며 관객들을 즐겁게 해주었습니다. 하지만 유머의 세계에 대한 그녀의 공헌은 다른 사람들을 위한 저명한 농담 작가가 되는 것으로 이어집니다. 지난 30년 동안, 그녀의 영리한 농담은 가장 재미있는 TV 쇼의 배우들에 의해 전달되어왔습니다. 그리고 지금, Mariana Sanchez를 무대에 불러오면서 몹시 흥분됩니다!

27. 연사가 소개하는 가장 적절한 사람은 누구인가?
   (A) 방송 제작자
   (B) 코미디언
   (C) 영화 감독
   (D) 드라마 배우

28. 화자가 Mariana Sanchez에 대해서 언급한 것은 무엇인가?
   (A) 그녀는 광대 학교에 다녔다.
   (B) 그녀는 다른 사람들을 위해 글을 써왔다.
   (C) 그녀는 우편 배달업에 종사해왔다.
   (D) 그녀는 30개의 무대에서 공연해왔다.

풀이  초청 연사에 대해서 화자는 'delighted audiences with her hilarious characters', 'contribution of humor', 'joke-writer' 등으로 표현하고 있다. 위 표현을 모두 담아낼 수 있는 직업을 골라야 하므로 27번의 정답은 (B)이다. (D)의 경우, 초청 연사가 배우로 활동한 적이 있으나, 드라마 출연에 대한 언급은 없으므로 오답이다.

'But her contribution to the world of humor also extends to being a celebrated joke-writer for others'에서 Mariana Sanchez는 영화에 출연하는 것 이외에도 유명한 농담 작가로서 활동하며 다른 사람들을 위해 글을 써왔다는 것을 알 수 있으므로 28번의 정답은 (B)이다. (D)의 경우, 'For over 30 years, ~'에서 그녀의 농담이 30년 넘게 전해졌다는 언급만이 있을 뿐, 30개의 무대에서 공연했다는 사실은 확인할 수 없으므로 오답이다.

Words and Phrases  introduction (사람) 소개; 도입, 전래 | delight 기쁨 [즐거움], 기쁨을 주다 | hilarious 아주 우스운 [재미있는] | contribution 공헌, 기여; 기부금

**[29-30]**

M: Here is today's weather report for Oslo. This morning's weather: clear overall, with periodic clouds and a high of 12 degrees Celsius. This afternoon, expect temperatures in the high tens, up to 20 degrees by three o'clock, but with an 80% chance of rain. Clear skies and sunshine again this evening starting around eight in the evening until sunset, which will be at ten after nine today. Sadly for star-gazers, we're expecting cloud cover all across Norway after sunset.

**29.** According to the speaker, what will the weather be like in the morning?
   (A) mainly rainy, with a chance of hail
   (B) mostly cloudy, with patches of rain
   **(C) generally clear, with occasional clouds**
   (D) sunny overall, with one thundershower

**30.** According to the speaker, what time will the sun set?
   (A) 8:00 PM
   (B) 8:09 PM
   **(C) 9:10 PM**
   (D) 10:09 PM

해석  남: Oslo의 오늘의 날씨 안내해 드리겠습니다. 오늘 아침은 전반적으로 맑은 가운데, 간헐적으로 구름이 동반하며 기온은 섭씨 12도까지 오르겠습니다. 오늘 오후에는 기온이 10도 후반에서, 3시에는 20도까지 오르겠지만, 강수 확률은 80%일 것으로 예상하고 있습니다. 오늘 저녁 8시부터 9시 10분경 일몰까지 맑은 하늘과 햇빛이 다시 보일 것으로 예상합니다. 별을 구경하러 오는 사람들에게는 아쉽게도, 일몰 이후 Norway 전역이 구름으로 덮일 것으로 예상합니다.

29. 화자에 따르면, 아침에 날씨가 어떨 것인가?
   (A) 주로 비가 오면서, 우박의 가능성이 있다.
   (B) 주로 흐린 가운데, 조금씩 비가 온다.
   (C) 주로 맑은 가운데, 때때로 흐리다.
   (D) 주로 맑은 가운데, 뇌우가 한 번 온다.

30. 화자에 따르면, 일몰 시간은 언제인가?
   (A) 8:00 PM
   (B) 8:09 PM
   (C) 9:10 PM
   (D) 10: 09 PM

풀이 화자가 아침에 맑은 가운데, 간헐적인 구름이 동반할 'This morning's weather: clear overall, with periodic clouds'라고 말하고 있으므로 29번의 정답은 (C)이다. (B)의 경우 오후에 비가 오고, 밤에 흐린 날씨가 될 것으로 예상하고 있으므로 오답이다.

일몰 시간에 대해서 화자는 'until sunset, which will be at ten after nine today'라고 말하고 있으므로 30번의 정답은 (C)이다. (A)의 경우, 단순히 저녁 시간 8시를 표현하고 있으므로 오답이다.

Words and Phrases overall 대부분, 전체의 | periodic 주기적인 | Celsius 섭씨의 | gazer 응시[주시]하는 사람

## SECTION II READING AND WRITING

**Part 5.** Picture Description (p.56)

**31.** Carrie and Ben played a prank on their dad, and now they're in ___________.

   (A) case
   (B) matter
   **(C) trouble**
   (D) question

해석 Carrie와 Ben은 아빠에게 장난을 쳤다, 그리고 그들은 이제 곤경에 처해 있다.
   (A) 경우
   (B) 사안
   (C) 곤경
   (D) 질문

풀이 아빠에게 장난을 치고 나서, 아이들이 곤란에 처할 수 있다는 의미를 완성하기 위해서 '곤란에 처하다'라는 뜻을 가진 'be in trouble'이라는 표현을 사용할 수 있으므로 (C)가 정답이다.

Words and Phrases prank (농담으로 하는) 장난 | be in trouble 난경에 처하다

**32.** Why does everybody only mess up the house all the time and never help __________?

   **(A) tidy up**
   (B) throw up
   (C) hang out
   (D) weed out

해석 왜 모두 항상 집을 더럽히기만 하고 절대로 치우는 것을 도와주지 않는 거야?
   (A) 정리하다
   (B) 토하다
   (C) 많은 시간을 보내다
   (D) 잡초를 뽑다

풀이 집을 더럽히기만 하고 치우는 것을 도와주지 않느냐고 질책하고 있다. 이때 '정리하다'라는 영어 표현인 'tidy up'을 사용할 수 있으므로 (A)가 정답이다.

Words and Phrases mess up (~을) 엉망으로 만들다 | tidy up 정리하다

**33.** Don't bother going to that town. It's not __________ the trip.

   (A) price
   (B) merit
   (C) value
   **(D) worth**

해석 저 마을에 굳이 가지 마라. 여행할 가치가 없다.
   (A) 가격을 매기다
   (B) (칭찬, 관심 등을) 받을 만하다
   (C) 소중하게 생각하다
   **(D) ~할 가치가 있는**

풀이 마을에 가지 말라는 말을 하고 있다. 마을에 가 볼 필요가 없다는 뜻을 완성하기 위해서 '~할 가치가 있는'이라는 뜻인 'worth'을 사용할 수 있으므로 (D)가 정답이다.

Words and Phrases don't bother 신경 쓰지 마, 수고할 것 없다 | merit (칭찬, 관심 등을) 받을 만하다; 장점 | value 소중하게 생각하다; 가치 | worth ~의 가치가 있는

**34.** I only see my ______________ family, including my aunts and uncles, on special occasions.

   (A) passed
   (B) nuclear
   **(C) extended**
   (D) magnified

해석 나는 특별한 날에만 나의 고모와 삼촌을 포함한 대가족들을 본다.
   (A) 지나간
   (B) 핵(가족)
   (C) 확대된
   (D) 과장된

풀이 고모와 삼촌을 포함한 대가족이라는 뜻을 가진 영어 표현 'extended family'를 사용할 수 있으므로 (C)가 정답이다.

Words and Phrases occasion (어떤 일이 일어나는 특정한) 때[기회/경우]; 행사 | magnify (렌즈, 현미경 등으로) (크기, 소리를) 확대하다; (중요성을) 과장하다

**35.** We're going to ______________ bowling this weekend. Do you want to come?

   **(A) go**
   (B) ride
   (C) take
   (D) throw

해석 우리는 이번 주말에 볼링 치러 갈 거야. 너도 같이 갈래?
   (A) 가다
   (B) 타다
   (C) 가지고 가다
   (D) 던지다

풀이 친구와 함께 이번 주말에 '볼링을 하러 간다'라는 의미를 완성하기 위해서 '활동을 하러 가다'라는 의미의 'go'를 사용할 수 있으므로 (A)가 정답이다.

Words and Phrases bowling 볼링

**36.** Alexei usually hides his emotions, but then he'll suddenly
___________________ angry.

    **(A) get**
    (B) roll
    (C) pick
    (D) bear

**해석** Alexei는 보통 그의 감정을 숨기다가도 갑자기 화를 낸다.

    **(A) 되다**
    (B) 구르다
    (C) 고르다
    (D) 참다

**풀이** 평소에 감정을 숨기다가 갑자기 화를 낸다는 의미를 완성하기 위해서 '화를 내다'라는 뜻을 가진 'get angry'라는 표현을 사용할 수 있으므로 (A)가 정답이다.

**Words and Phrases**  hide 감추다[숨기다] | emotion 감정, 정서



**37.** This is without a doubt _______________ cutting-edge application of our company's technology.

    (A) most
    (B) most of
    **(C) the most**
    (D) more than

**해석** 이건 의심의 여지 없이 우리 회사 기술 중에서 가장 최첨단 기술로 만든 응용 프로그램이야.

    (A) 최고의
    (B) ~의 대부분
    **(C) (~중에서) 가장 최고의**
    (D) ~보다 더

**풀이** 빈칸에 형용사 'cutting-edge'를 수식할 수 있는 최상급 부사가 와야 하며, 'the most + 형용시' 형태의 표현이 필요하므로 (C)가 정답이다. (B)의 경우 '~의 대부분'이라는 뜻으로 빈칸에 들어가기에는 어색하므로 오답이다.

**Words and Phrases**  cutting-edge 최첨단의 |
application 응용 프로그램; 지원[신청]; 적용, 응용

**38.** Ray and Judy, ___________ met at a party, have been married fifty years.

    **(A) who**
    (B) which
    (C) whom
    (D) of whom

**해석** 파티에서 만났던 Ray와 Judy는 결혼한 지 50년이 되었다.

    **(A) 관계대명사 who**
    (B) 관계대명사 which
    (C) 관계대명사 whom
    (D) 관계대명사 of whom

**풀이** 빈칸에는 'Ray와 Judy'와 '파티에서 만났던' 두 구절을 이어줄 수 있는 적절한 관계 대명사가 들어갈 수 있다. 주어가 사람일 때 적절한 주격 관계대명사는 'who'이므로 (A)가 정답이다. (C)의 경우 목적격 선행 명사를 취할 수 있으므로 오답이다.

**Words and Phrases**  marry (…와) 결혼하다; 주례하다; (~에게) 결혼시키다

**39.** Your glasses are somewhere _______________ that pile of papers.

    (A) lower
    (B) of lower
    **(C) beneath**
    (D) of beneath

**해석** 너의 안경은 서류더미 아래 어딘가에 있다.

    (A) 낮은
    (B) 하등의
    **(C) 아래에**
    (D) 하위의

**풀이** 안경이 위치적으로 서류 더미 아래에 놓여 있다는 의미를 완성하기 위해서 빈칸에는 '~아래에'라는 의미가 있는 'beneath'를 사용할 수 있으므로 (C)가 정답이다. (A)의 경우, 형용사로서 '(무엇의) 아래쪽의'라는 의미로 쓰일 수 있지만, 'lower' 바로 뒤에 수식을 받는 명사가 존재해야 하므로 오답이다. (D)의 경우, 앞에 있는 'of'는 특정 명사 뒤에만 올 수 있고, 'some-where'와 같은 부사 뒤에 올 수 없으므로 오답이다.

**Words and Phrases**  pile 포개(쌓아)놓은 것, 더미; 무더기 |
beneath 아래에; (수준 등이) …보다 못한

**40.** Don't blame _______________ for one small mistake. You'll know better for next time.

    (A) you
    (B) your
    (C) you're
    **(D) yourself**

**해석** 실수 하나로 너 자신을 비난하지 마. 다음에는 더 잘할 수 있다는 것을 알게 될 거야.

    (A) 너
    (B) 너의
    (C) 너는
    **(D) 너 자신**

**풀이** 실수에 대해서 자책하지 말라는 의미를 완성하기 위해서 빈칸에 재귀대명사인 'yourself'를 사용할 수 있으므로 (D)가 정답이다.

**Words and Phrases**  blame …을 탓하다[책임으로 보다] |
mistake 실수, 잘못; 오해하다

**41.** I found the art show _______________ from beginning to end. I highly recommend it.

    (A) fascinate
    **(B) fascinating**
    (C) be fascinating
    (D) to be fascinated

**해석** 나는 미술 전시회가 처음부터 끝까지 대단히 흥미로웠다. 강력히 추천한다.

(A) 매혹하다

(B) 대단히 흥미로운, 매력적인

(C) 매혹적이다

(D) 매료되다

**풀이** 빈칸에는 'found + 명사 + 형용사'의 형태로 '...가 ~한 것을 알았다'라는 의미를 완성하기 위해서 형용사 역할을 할 수 있는 'fascinating'이라는 표현이 와야 하므로 (B)가 정답이다. (D)의 경우 형용사적 역할보다는 적절한 동사와 결합하여 동사적 역할을 수행하는 것이 타당하므로 오답이다.

**Words and Phrases**  fascinate 마음을 사로잡다, 매혹하다 |
recommend 추천하다; 권고하다

**42.** The turnout for the events last weekend ______________ quite low, so the organizers are rethinking next year's plans.

(A) is

(B) are

(C) was

(D) were

**해석** 지난 주말 행사 참가자의 수가 꽤 적어서, 관리자들이 내년 계획에 대해 다시 생각 중이다.

(A) be동사 3인칭 현재

(B) be동사 2인칭 현재

(C) be동사 3인칭 과거

(D) be동사 2인칭 과거

**풀이** 빈칸이 있는 종속절에서 주어는 참가자의 수 'The turnout'이다. 이는 특정 수치를 나타내는 단수 개념이므로, 단수를 받을 수 있는 be동사와 과거 시제를 나타내는 (C)가 정답이다.

**Words and Phrases**  turnout 참가자의 수; 투표율 | quite 꽤, 상당히

**43.** I don't know whether ______________ or not, but I've decided to go to South America.

(A) approve

(B) you approve

(C) approve you

(D) do you approve

**해석** 네가 찬성하는지 안 하는지는 모르겠지만, 나는 남미로 가기로 결정했다.

(A) 찬성하다

(B) 네가 찬성하다

(C) 너를 찬성하다

(D) 너는 찬성하니

**풀이** 빈칸에는 접속사 'whether'의 의미를 완성하기 위해서 주어와 동사가 필요하므로 (B)가 정답이다. (A)와 (C)의 경우 적절한 주어가 없으므로 오답이다.

**Words and Phrases**  whether ...인지(아닌지); ...이든(아니든) |
approve 찬성하다; 승인하다; 인가하다

**44.** Once she sets her mind to something, there's no stopping her ______________ her goal.

(A) achieve

(B) to achieve

(C) from achieving

(D) that she achieves

**해석** 일단 그녀가 무엇인가에 대해 마음을 먹으면, 그녀가 목적을 성취하는 것을 멈출 수 없다.

(A) 성취하다

(B) 성취하기 위해

(C) 성취하는 것으로부터

(D) 그녀가 성취한 것

**풀이** 빈칸에는 '누군가 ~하는 것으로부터 멈출 수 없다'라는 의미를 가진 'stop + 목적어 + from + ~ing' 표현을 완성하기 위해서 'from achieving'이라는 표현을 사용할 수 있으므로 (C)가 정답이다.

**Words and Phrases**  once 한 번[일단]...하면; ...하자마자; ...할 때 |
stop A from B A가 B하는 것을 멈추게 하다

**45.** Ten years ago, he ______________ as a cook in the biggest hotel in town.

(A) works

(B) was working

(C) has been working

(D) was started his work

**해석** 10년 전에, 그는 마을에 있는 가장 큰 호텔에서 요리사로서 일하는 중이었다.

(A) 일하다

(B) 일하는 중이었다

(C) 일해왔다

(D) 그의 일이 시작되었다

**풀이** 10년 전에 그가 요리사로서 일하는 중이었다는 의미를 완성하기 위해서 빈칸에는 과거진행형 표현으로 'was working'이라는 표현을 사용할 수 있으므로 (B)가 정답이다. (C)의 경우, 현재완료 형태로 과거의 특정 시점을 나타낼 수 없으므로 오답이다.

**Words and Phrases**  cook 요리사

**46.** While ______________ up the mountain, some rocks broke loose.

(A) is climbing

(B) was climbing

(C) it was a climb

(D) I was climbing

**해석** 내가 산을 오르고 있었던 동안에, 몇몇 바위들이 부서졌다.

(A) 오르고 있다

(B) 오르고 있었다

(C) 등산이었다

(D) 내가 오르고 있었다

**풀이** 빈칸에는 'while'접속절을 이끌 주어와 동사가 필요하고, 주절의 동사 'broke'를 통해 과거 시제를 표현할 수 있는 단어가 필요하므로 (D)가 정답이다.

**Words and Phrases**  while ...하는 동안[사이]; 잠깐, 잠시 | loose 마음대로 돌아다니는; (조직, 통제가) 느슨한; 헐렁한

**[47–48]**

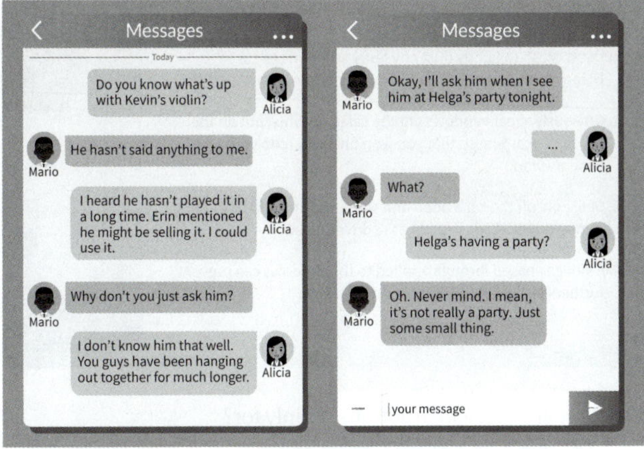


**47.** Why does Alicia write to Mario?

    (A) to ask where Kevin bought something

    (B) to find out why Kevin is quitting music

    (C) to find out why Mario has Kevin's music

    **(D) to ask whether Kevin is selling something**

**48.** Which of the following can be inferred about Alicia?

    (A) She is going to Kevin's house tonight.

    (B) She refuses to see Helga after a fight.

    (C) She does not like Kevin's violin playing.

    **(D) She has not been invited to Helga's party.**

**해석**

> Alicia: Kevin의 바이올린에 무슨 문제 있는지 아니?
>
> Mario: 그는 나한테 아무 말도 안 했어.
>
> Alicia: 내가 듣기로는 그가 오랫동안 바이올린을 연주하지 않았다고 들었어. Erin이 그가 아마 팔 것 같다고 말했는데. 내가 쓸 수 있을 거 같은데.
>
> Mario: 그한테 직접 물어보는 게 어때?
>
> Alicia: 난 그를 잘 모르거든. 너희들은 오랫동안 같이 친하게 지내 왔잖아.
>
> Mario: 알았어, 오늘 밤 Helga의 파티에서 그를 보면 말해줄게.
>
> Alicia: ...
>
> Mario: 왜?
>
> Alicia: Helga가 오늘 파티를 열어?
>
> Mario: 오. 신경 쓰지 마. 내 말은, 진짜 파티가 아니고. 그냥 별 거 아니야.

**47.** Alicia는 왜 Mario에게 문자를 보냈는가?

    (A) Kevin이 무언가를 어디서 샀는지 물어보기 위해

    (B) 왜 Kevin이 음악을 그만두는지 알기 위해

    (C) 왜 Mario가 Kevin의 음악을 가지고 있는지 알기 위해

    **(D) Kevin이 무언가를 파는지 물어보기 위해**

**48.** 다음 중 Alicia에 대해 추론할 수 있는 것은 무엇인가?

    (A) 그녀는 오늘 밤 Kevin의 집에 방문할 것이다.

    (B) 그녀는 Helga와 싸운 이후 그녀와 볼 것을 거부한다.

    (C) 그녀는 Kevin의 바이올린 연주를 좋아하지 않는다.

    **(D) 그녀는 Helga의 파티에 초대받지 못했다.**

**풀이** 'he might be selling it. I could use it'에서 Alicia는 Kevin의 바이올린에 관심이 있다는 사실을 알 수 있다. 하지만 'I don't know him that well'에서 Alicia와 Kevin은 친한 사이가 아니라는 것을 알 수 있다. 그래서 Mario가 'I'll ask him'이라고 말하며 Kevin에게 바이올린을 팔 생각인지 사실 여부를 확인하기로 했으므로 47번의 정답은 (D)이다.

Mario가 오늘 밤 Helga의 파티에 간다고 말하자 Alicia는 '...' 그리고 'Helga's having a party?'라고 되물어보며 Helga의 파티에 대해서 처음 들어 본 듯한 모습을 보인다. 이는 곧 Alicia는 Helga의 파티에 초대받지 못했다는 의미이므로 48번의 정답은 (D)이다.

**Words and Phrases**   mention 말하다, 언급하다 | hang out 많은 시간을 보내다 | tonight 오늘 밤에 | never mind 신경 쓰지 마; 걱정하지 마

**[49–51]**

### Crazy Chem Chemistry Set

- Fun, safe educational product for young chemists
- 110 different experiments to do at home
- Appropriate for teenagers aged 13 and up (adult supervision required at all times)

8 new available for as low as $35.99 (free shipping for Yangtze Optimum members)
15 used available for as low as $24.25 (plus $6.00 shipping)

**Customer reviews**

Sandra:
Be aware: Not everything to conduct all the experiments is included. You still need stuff like filter papers.

Maiko:
This is 400 times better than those silly cheap sets that just contain colored water. It's hardcore: the chemicals here are real and some are toxic.

**49.** What is the minimum price of a new set for Yangtze Optimum members?

    (A) $24.25

    (B) $30.25

    **(C) $35.99**

    (D) $41.99

**50.** What is true about the set?

    (A) Users must be legally adults.

    **(B) Filter papers are sold separately.**

    (C) It is designed to be used in schools.

    (D) It allows users to do up to 100 experiments.

**51.** What does Maiko mean by "It's hardcore"?

    (A) The set comes in a hard case.

    **(B) The set contains toxic chemicals.**

    (C) The set lacks the 400 promised chemicals.

    (D) The set's chemicals are only colored water.

Crazy Chem 화학실험 용품
– 어린 화학자들을 위한 재밌고, 안전한 교육적인 제품
– 집에서 할 수 있는 110가지의 다양한 실험
– 13세 이상의 십 대 청소년들에게 적절함 (항상 성인 보호자의 관리,
  감독이 요구됨)

$35.99의 저렴한 가격으로 8개의 신규 제품 구매 가능(Yangtze Opti-
mum 회원에게는 무료배송)
$24.25의 저렴한 가격으로 15개의 중고 제품 구매 가능(배송비 6$ 별도)

고객 후기
Sandra: 주의하세요: 실험에 필요한 모든 것이 포함된 것은 아니에요.
당신은 여과지 같은 물건이 여전히 필요할 거예요.

Maiko: 이 제품은 색깔 있는 물만 들어 있는 바보 같은 싸구려 제품보다
400배 더 좋아요. 그것은 진짜 화학물질이에요: 여기 있는 화학 물질은
진짜고 일부는 독성이 있어요.

49. Yangtze Optimum 회원에게 새로운 용품의 최저 가격은 얼마인가?
    (A) $24.25
    (B) $30.25
    (C) $35.99
    (D) $41.99

50. 실험 용품에 대해서 사실인 것은 무엇인가?
    (A) 사용자들은 법률상 성인이어야만 한다.
    (B) 여과지는 별도로 판매한다.
    (C) 학교에서 사용할 수 있도록 설계되었다.
    (D) 100가지의 실험을 할 수 있게 한다.

51. Maiko가 말한 "It's hardcore"는 무슨 의미인가?
    (A) 실험 용품이 단단한 상자에 담겨 온다.
    (B) 실험 용품이 유독 물질을 포함한다.
    (C) 실험 용품에 약속된 400가지의 물질이 부족하다.
    (D) 실험 용품의 물질은 오직 색을 탄 물뿐이다.

풀이   '8 new available for as low as $35.99 (free shipping for Yangtze
Optimum members)'에서 Optimum 회원에게는 최저 $35.99에 제공
하므로 49번의 정답은 (C)이다.

고객 후기에서 ' Not everything to conduct all the experiments is
included'에서 몇몇 별도의 제품이 존재한다는 것을 알 수 있고, 'You still
need stuff like filter papers'에서 특히, 여과지는 해당 제품에 포함되어
있지 않다는 것을 알 수 있으므로 50번의 정답은 (B)이다.

"It's hardcore: the chemicals here are real and some are toxic."에
서 'hardcore'의 부연 설명으로 'real'이라는 표현과 'toxic'이라는 표현을
사용하고 있다. 따라서 위 실험 제품은 진정한 의미의 화학물질이고 이는
유독물질을 포함하고 있다고 전하고 있으므로 51번의 정답은 (B)이다.

Words and Phrases  chemistry set 화학실험 용품 | available 구할[이용할]
수 있는; 시간[여유]이 있는 | ship 수송하다; 출하하다;
선적하다 | be aware ~을 알다, 인지하다 | conduct
(특정한 활동을)하다; 지휘하다; 안내하다 |
silly 어리석은, 바보 같은

---



Is it your job to scrape snow off the family car in the morning?
Follow these tips:

1. Use a brush to lightly dust any fluffy snow off the car
   before you take out the ice scraper for harder bits.

2. Obviously, clear windows are the safety priority, but do the
   top of the car first so that you won't have to redo your
   window work.

3. Get snow off the car's hood and sides, too. It could blow off
   during the drive, obstructing the driver's view.

4. A vinegar-based formula applied to the windows can prevent
   further frost build-up. And of course, so can _____________.

52. What are these instructions mainly for?
    (A) removing snow from a car
    (B) driving in snowy conditions
    (C) cleaning a dirty vehicle in winter
    (D) preparing a car for winter storage

53. Which instruction is mentioned?
    (A) Stand on the vehicle's roof.
    (B) Use a scraper for hard parts.
    (C) Lift up the windshield wipers.
    (D) Wash the car's undercarriage.

54. Which of the following would most likely go in the blank?
    (A) a large pile of snow
    (B) a stiff sweeping brush
    (C) a plastic ice-scraping tool
    (D) a blanket covering the car

55. The underlined "obstructing" is closest in meaning to:
    (A) showing
    (B) blocking
    (C) legalizing
    (D) facilitating



아침에 가족 자동차 위의 눈을 긁어서 치우는 것이 당신의 일입니까?
이 조언을 따르세요.

1. 단단한 결정들을 위한 성에 제거기를 사용하기 이전에 솔을 사용해서
가벼운 먼지와 솜털 같은 눈을 제거하세요.

2. 확실히, 투명한 창문은 안전을 위한 우선순위이지만, 차 위의 눈을 먼저 제
거하여 창문 작업을 두 번 하지 않도록 하십시오.

3. 또한, 차의 덮개와 옆면의 눈을 제거하세요. 차를 운전하는 동안 불어서 날
아가 운전자의 시야를 방해할 수 있습니다.

4. 창문에 식초를 바르는 것은 차후에 성에가 생기는 것을 방지할 수
있습니다. 그리고 물론, 이는 차를 덮는 담요도 그 역할을 할 수도 있습니다.

52. 이러한 지시사항들은 주로 무엇을 위한 것인가?

    (A) 차에서 눈을 제거하기

    (B) 눈이 오는 상황에서 운전하기

    (C) 겨울에 더러운 차량을 청소하기

    (D) 겨울 차량 보관을 위해 준비하기

53. 어떤 지시사항이 언급되었는가?

    (A) 차량 지붕 위에 서있기

    (B) 단단한 결정을 위한 성에 제거기 사용하기

    (C) 차량 와이퍼를 올려두기

    (D) 차량 하부 구조를 청소하기

54. 빈칸에 들어갈 가장 적절한 말은 무엇인가?

    (A) 거대한 눈더미

    (B) 뻣뻣한 청소용 솔

    (C) 플라스틱으로 된 성에 제거 도구

    (D) 차량을 덮는 담요

55. 밑줄 친 "obstructing"과 가장 유사한 뜻을 가진 단어는:

    (A) 보여주는

    (B) 방해하는

    (C) 합법화하는

    (D) 가능하게 하는

**풀이** 'Is it your job to scrape snow off the family car in the morning? Follow these tips'에서 윗글은 겨울 차량에 쌓여 있는 눈을 치우기 위한 정보를 주려고 하는 것을 알 수 있으므로 52번의 정답은 (A)이다. (C)의 경우, 윗글은 'dirty'를 치우는 것을 포함하여 'snow'를 제거하는 것이 목적이므로 오답이다.

'~ before you take out the ice scraper for harder bits'에서 단단한 결정들을 제거할 때에는 성에 제거기를 사용해야 한다는 사실이 지문에서 언급되었으므로 53번의 정답은 (B)이다.

빈칸 앞에서 'A vinegar-based formula applied to the windows can prevent further frost build up'에서 차후 성에가 생기는 것을 예방하기 위한 방안을 제시하고 있다. 이어지는 빈칸에는 위의 내용과 일맥상통할 수 있는 내용이 필요하므로 54번의 정답은 (D)이다.

'obstructing'은 '방해하는'이라는 뜻을 가진 단어로 55번의 정답은 (B)이다.

**Words and Phrases** scrape (무엇을 떼어 내기 위해) 긁다 | fluffy 솜털 같은 | ice scraper 성에 제거기 | priority 우선순위 | redo 다시 하다 | car hood 자동차 덮개 | obstruct 막다, 방해하다 | vinegar 식초 | build-up 증가

[56-59]

**Program October 8-14**

| | Show 1 | | | Show 2 | | |
|---|---|---|---|---|---|---|
| | Time | Country | Performance | Time | Country | Performance |
| Mon, 8th | 8 PM | Finland | "Heartless" Ballet | | | |
| Tues, 9th | 4 PM | China | "Dreaming Fields" Contemporary | 8 PM | Argentina | "Nowhere" Tango |
| Wed, 10th | 8 PM | Finland | "Marriage" Contemporary | 8 PM | Japan | "Come from Afar" Ballet |
| Thurs, 11th | 4 PM | Russia | "Be Mine" Jazz | | | |
| Fri, 12th | 8 PM | USA | "Cities Reborn" Tap | 8 PM | Malaysia | "Seeing Waves" Ballet |
| Sat, 13th | 5 PM/ 8 PM | Mexico | "Seeing Stars" Ballet | 8 PM | Zimbabwe | "Post Everything" Contemporary |
| Sun, 14th | 5 PM/ 8 PM | Albania-UK | "Mending Fabric" Ballet | 8 PM | Guatemala | "Stay Near" Contemporary |

Performances are 90 minutes.
Ballet performances are in the Memorial Theater.
All other performances are in the Main Hall (10-minute walk to Memorial Theater).

56. Where would this schedule most likely be published?

    (A) on an advertisement for tap shoes

    **(B) on an international dance festival's website**

    (C) on a subway platform highlighting train times

    (D) on a poster board for a theater's summer workshops

57. What is mentioned about Finland?

    (A) It performs on a weekend.

    (B) It performs both jazz and ballet.

    **(C) It has two different performances.**

    (D) It performs before Japan on Wednesday.

58. According to the schedule, what is the maximum number of different performances one viewer could see?

    (A) 7

    **(B) 10**

    (C) 12

    (D) 14

59. Which of the following is true?

    (A) Mexico has three different shows.

    (B) The USA has two tap performances.

    (C) The UK's show is a collaboration with Guatemala.

    **(D) Russia's performance takes place in the Main Hall.**

**해석**

## 10월 8-14일 프로그램

|  | 월, 8일 | 화, 9일 | 수, 10일 | 목, 11일 | 금, 12일 | 토, 13일 | 일, 14일 |
|---|---|---|---|---|---|---|---|
| 쇼 1 | 8 PM 핀란드 "Heartless" 발레 | 4 PM 중국 "Dreaming Fields" 현대무용 | 8 PM 핀란드 "Marriage" 현대무용 | 4 PM 러시아 "Be Mine" 재즈 | 8 PM 미국 "Cities Reborn" 탭댄스 | 5 PM/8 PM 멕시코 "Seeing Stars" 발레 | 5 PM/8 PM 알바니아- 영국 "Mending Fabric" 발레 |
| 쇼 2 |  | 8 PM 아르헨티나 "Nowhere" 탱고 | 8 PM 일본 "Come from Afar" 발레 |  | 8 PM 말레이시아 "Seeing Waves" 발레 | 8 PM 짐바브웨 "Post Everything" 현대무용 | 8 PM 과테말라 "Stay Near" 현대무용 |

공연은 90분 동안 진행됩니다.

발레 공연은 기념 극장에서 진행됩니다.

다른 모든 공연은 본관에서 진행됩니다. (기념 극장에서 걸어서 10분 거리)

56. 다음 일정표는 어디서 가장 발간된 것 같은가?

    (A) 탭슈즈 신발 광고에서

    (B) 국제 춤 행사의 웹사이트에서

    (C) 열차 시간을 강조하는 지하철 플랫폼에서

    (D) 극장의 여름 직무교육을 위한 게시판에서

57. 핀란드에 대해서 언급된 것은?

    (A) 주말에 공연한다.

    (B) 재즈와 발레 모두 공연한다.

    (C) 두 가지의 다른 공연을 진행한다.

    (D) 수요일에는 일본 공연 이전에 공연한다.

58. 일정표에 따르면, 한 사람이 최대 몇 개의 다른 공연을 볼 수 있는가?

    (A) 7

    (B) 10

    (C) 12

    (D) 14

59. 다음 중 사실인 것은 무엇인가?

    (A) 멕시코는 서로 다른 3개의 공연을 진행한다.

    (B) 미국은 두 개의 탭댄스 공연을 진행한다.

    (C) 영국의 공연은 과테말라와 합동 공연으로 진행한다.

    (D) 러시아의 공연은 본관에서 진행한다.

**풀이** 표에서 시간별로 여러 나라의 다양한 장르의 춤 공연에 관한 내용을 확인할 수 있으므로 56번의 정답은 (B)이다. (A), (C), (D)는 각각 'tap shoes', 'train times', 'workshop'을 강조하고 있지만, 이는 제시된 표에서 확인할 수 없는 내용이므로 오답이다.

표에서 핀란드의 공연은 월요일과 수요일 각각 발레와 현대무용 공연을 진행하므로 57번의 정답은 (C)이다. (D)의 경우, 수요일에는 일본 공연과 동시간대에 진행하기 때문에, 일본 공연 이전에 진행한다는 내용은 틀린 내용이므로 오답이다.

제시된 정보에 따르면, 동시간대에 공연하는 경우를 제외하고는 다른 모든 공연을 관람할 수 있다. 그러므로 한 사람이 최대한 많은 공연을 관람하는 경우 월요일 1개, 화요일 2개, 수요일 1개, 목요일 1개, 금요일 1개, 토요일 2개, 일요일 2개로 총 10개의 서로 다른 공연을 관람할 수 있으므로 58번의 정답은 (B)이다.

표 아래에 제시된 정보 'All other performances are in the Main Hall'에 따르면, 발레를 제외한 다른 모든 공연은 본관에서 진행된다는 사실을 알 수 있다. 러시아의 공연은 목요일 4시 재즈 공연으로 이 역시 본관에서 진행할 것을 추론할 수 있으므로 59번의 정답은 (D)이다.

Words and Phrases   contemporary 현대의; 동시대의 | performance 공연, 연주회; (개인의) 연기[연주]; 실적, 성과 | memorial 기념비(적인 것); (죽은 사람을) 기념하기 위한, 추도[추모]의

## Part 8. General Reading Comprehension (p.63)

[60–61]

Rip currents are narrow yet strong water flows from the shore to the open sea. They form in shallow spots near shorelines and around human-made structures in water, such as docks. They can range from 15 meters to 90 meters long. Rip currents are surprisingly fast. Most rip currents flow at around 60 centimeters per second. However, they can flow as fast as 2 meters per second. Because of the potentially deadly strength of rip currents, swimmers should not try to swim against them. Instead, swimmers who feel they are being pulled out to sea should first swim in alignment with the shore. When they get out of the rip current, they can then swim diagonally towards the shore.

Summary:

Rip currents are powerful water flows that occur in shallow parts of the ocean near the shore or near   [A]   structures. Ranging in length from 15 to 90 meters, they flow at speeds of up to 2 meters per second. To escape a rip current, swimmers should swim   [B]   to the shore at first, and then at a diagonal towards the shore.

**60.** Choose the most suitable word for blank [A], connecting the summary to the passage.

    (A) coral

    (B) natural

    (C) tropical

    (D) artificial

**61.** Choose the most suitable word for blank [B], connecting the summary to the passage.

    (A) parallel

    (B) squarely

    (C) diagonally

    (D) perpendicularly

**해석** Rip 해류는 좁지만, 해안가에서 바다로 흐르는 강한 물줄기이다. 해류는 물가 얕은 지역에서 형성되어 부두와 같은 인공 구조물 근처를 흐른다. 해류는 15m에서 90m의 물 길이를 가지고 있다. Rip 해류는 놀랄 만큼 빠르다. 대부분의 Rip 해류는 초속 60cm의 흐름을 보이지만, 초속 2m 속도로 빠르게 흐를 수도 있다. 잠재적으로 극도로 빠른 Rip 해류 때문에, 수영하는 사람들에게 이 해류를 거스르는 것은 권고되지 않는다. 대신에, 바다를 향해 끌려나가고 있다고 느끼는 사람들은 먼저 해안가와 일직선으로 맞추어 수영해야 한다. 그들이 Rip 해류에서 벗어났을 때, 그제야 그들은 해안가를 향해 사선으로 수영할 수 있다.

요약:
Rip 해류는 해안가 근처 혹은 인공 구조물 근처 바다의 얕은 부분에서 발생하는 강력한 해류이다. 물 길이는 15에서 90m에 이르고, 초속 2m까지의 속도로 흐른다. Rip 해류에서 벗어나기 위해서, 수영하는 사람들은 먼저 해안가와 평행하게, 그리고 해안가를 향해 사선으로 수영해야 한다.

60. 본문과 요약본을 연결할 수 있는, 빈칸 [A]에 들어갈 가장 적절한 단어를 고르시오.
   (A) 산호
   (B) 자연
   (C) 열대지방의
   **(D) 인공적인**

61. 본문과 요약본을 연결할 수 있는, 빈칸 [B]에 들어갈 가장 적절한 단어를 고르시오.
   **(A) 평행하게**
   (B) 정면으로
   (C) 사선으로
   (D) 수직으로

**풀이** 빈칸 앞의 문맥은 Rip 해류가 어디에서 형성되고 있는지를 나타낸다. 그리고 "They form in shallow spots near shorelines and around human-made structures in water, such as docks."에서 해류는 해안가 얕은 지역과 인공 구조물 근처에서 형성된다는 것을 알 수 있으므로, 60번의 정답은 (D)이다.

빈칸 앞의 문맥은 Rip 해류에서 벗어나기 위한 지침을 설명하고 있다. 그리고 "Instead, swimmers who feel they are being pulled out to sea should first swim in alignment with the shore."에서 해류를 벗어나기 위해서 처음에는 해안가에 일직선으로 맞추어 수영을 해야 한다는 것을 알 수 있으므로 61번의 정답은 (A)이다. (C)의 경우, 먼저 평행하게 수영한 이후, 흐름에서 빠져나와 해안가를 향해 사선으로 수영하라고 제시되어 있으므로 오답이다.

**Words and Phrases** current (물, 공기의) 흐름, 해류, 기류; 현재의 | shore (바다호수 따위) 기슭, 해안[해변] | shallow 얕은, 피상적인 | dock 부두, 선창, 독 | range from A to B (범위가) A에서 B 사이이다 | alignment 가지런함, (정치적) 지지 | diagonally 대각선으로, 비스듬하게

[62-65]

[1] While they may not be commonly needed for residents of many modern cities, the abilities to chop wood, saw logs, and climb trees are still important for lumberjacks—that is, people who work in the logging industry.

[2] Held each year since 1960 in the state of Wisconsin, USA, the Lumberjack World Championships test competitors in traditional lumberjack skills. Contestants show their ability to saw, chop, and climb. There's even an event for logrolling in which competitors run on logs that are floating in water. In each <u>round</u>, the competitors must stay on a log for a certain amount of time. They are then given smaller and smaller logs to stand on. In the end, the winner survives the best three out of five rounds.

[3] Meanwhile, in the 90-foot speed climb, contestants win by being the fastest person to go all the way up and down a cedar pole. In the single buck event, competitors saw through a pine log, and in the block chop event they use an ax to chop down a vertical standing log.

[4] The races are more than just entertainment for urban spectators. Rather, they are a reminder of the skills involved in the work of lumberjacks.

62. What is the passage mainly about?
   (A) a discontinued contest
   (B) lumberjack skills of the 1960s
   (C) the people in a sporting championship
   **(D) proceedings in a competition for lumberjacks**

63. Which of the following is mentioned about the Lumberjack World Championships?
   **(A) its frequency**
   (B) which town hosts it
   (C) how judges are selected
   (D) how many people compete

64. The underlined "round" is closest in meaning to:
   (A) disk
   **(B) match**
   (C) cylinder
   (D) inspection

65. According to the passage, what can be inferred?
   **(A) The single buck event requires a saw.**
   (B) The logrolling event requires rubber boots.
   (C) The 90-foot speed climb requires teamwork.
   (D) The block chop event requires climbing skills.

 [1] 많은 현대 도시에 거주하고 있는 사람들에게는 보통 필요하지 않지만, 나무를 자르고, 통나무를 톱으로 자르고, 나무에 오르는 능력은 벌목꾼들 — 즉, 벌목 산업에 종사하고 있는 사람들에게 여전히 중요하다.

[2] 1960년 미국 위스콘신주에서 개최된 이후, 매년 개최된 세계 벌목 선수권 대회는 경쟁자들의 전통적인 벌목 기술을 시험한다. 참가자들은 그들의 톱질하고, 자르고, 오르는 능력을 보여준다. 심지어 경쟁자들이 물 위에 떠 있는 통나무를 타고 달리는 통나무 달리기 행사도 있다. 각 <u>회차</u>에서 경쟁자들은 일정 시간 동안 통나무에 있어야 한다. 그들은 서 있기 위한 점점 더 작은 통나무를 받는다. 결국, 승자는 5라운드 동안 가장 잘한 3명에게 돌아간다.

[3] 한편, 90m 나무 오르기 경연에서는, 참가자들은 가장 빠르게 삼나무 기둥을 오르고 내리는 사람이 됨으로써 승리한다. 단일 톱질 경기에서는 솔통나무를 톱으로 자르고, 나무 덩어리 패기 경기에서는 도끼를 이용하여 통나무를 수직으로 자른다.

[4] 그 대회는 도시 관중들에게 단순한 오락 이상이다. 오히려, 그것들은 벌목꾼의 작업과 관련된 기술을 상기시켜준다.

62. 이 지문의 요지는 무엇인가?
　　(A) 중단된 대회
　　(B) 1960년대의 벌목 기술
　　(C) 운동 대회에 종사하는 사람들
　　(D) 벌목 대회의 진행 과정

63. 세계 벌목 선수권 대회에 대해 다음 중 언급한 사실은 무엇인가?
　　(A) 대회의 빈도
　　(B) 개최 마을
　　(C) 평가단 선발 과정
　　(D) 참가자의 수

64. 밑줄 친 "round"와 가장 유사한 뜻을 가진 단어는:
　　(A) 원판
　　(B) 경기
　　(C) 원기둥
　　(D) 점검

65. 지문에 따르면, 무엇을 추론할 수 있는가?
　　(A) 단일 톱질 경기에는 톱이 필요하다.
　　(B) 통나무 달리기 경기에는 고무장화가 필요하다.
　　(C) 90m 나무 오르기 경기에는 협동이 필요하다.
　　(D) 나무 덩어리 패기 경기에는 나무 타기 기술이 필요하다.

 [1] 문단에서 벌목 기술의 필요성을 언급하였고, 이후 세계 벌목 선수권 대회를 소개하며 각 종목의 진행 과정을 설명하고 있다. 그리고 마지막으로 대회는 벌목 기술을 상기시켜준다는 의의를 제시하며 글을 마무리하고 있다. 그러므로 지문의 중심 소재는 벌목 대회의 진행 과정이라 할 수 있으므로 62번의 정답은 (D)이다.

[2] 문단의 'Held each year since 1960 in the state of Wisconsin, USA ~'에서 세계 벌목 선수권 대회는 매년 개최된다는 사실을 알 수 있으므로 63번의 정답은 (A)이다. (B)의 경우, 1960년에 개최한 마을은 'the state of Wisconsin, USA'이지만, 이후 개최 마을에 대해서는 언급하지 않았으므로 오답이다.

지문에서 'In each round'는 '각 경기의 회차'를 의미하고 있으므로 'round'는 '경기'의 의미를 가지고 있다. 따라서 64번의 정답은 (B)이다.

[3] 문단의 'In the single buck event, competitors saw through a pine log'에서 참가자들은 솔통나무를 톱으로 잘라야 한다는 사실을 알 수 있다. 그러므로 단일 톱질 경기에는 톱이 필요하다는 사실을 추론할 수 있으므로 65번의 정답은 (A)이다.

Words and Phrases　commonly 흔히, 보통 | resident 거주자 | saw 톱, 톱질하다 | lumberjack 벌목꾼 | log 통나무 | cedar 삼나무, 향나무 | vertical 수직의, 세로의 | reminder 상기시키는[생각나게 하는] 것

# TOSEL High Junior

## 실전 4회

### Section I  Listening and Speaking

1 (C)  2 (A)  3 (B)  4 (B)  5 (B)
6 (C)  7 (A)  8 (B)  9 (D) 10 (A)
11 (B) 12 (A) 13 (D) 14 (D) 15 (C)
16 (B) 17 (A) 18 (A) 19 (B) 20 (C)
21 (B) 22 (B) 23 (C) 24 (A) 25 (B)
26 (C) 27 (D) 28 (D) 29 (A) 30 (A)

### Section II  Reading and Writing

31 (D) 32 (A) 33 (C) 34 (A) 35 (C)
36 (C) 37 (A) 38 (B) 39 (A) 40 (B)
41 (B) 42 (A) 43 (C) 44 (B) 45 (C)
46 (B) 47 (A) 48 (D) 49 (C) 50 (A)
51 (B) 52 (C) 53 (A) 54 (C) 55 (C)
56 (A) 57 (B) 58 (D) 59 (D) 60 (A)
61 (C) 62 (C) 63 (C) 64 (A) 65 (C)

---

## SECTION I  LISTENING AND SPEAKING

**Part 1.** Listen and Recognize (p.68)

**1.** W: So you decided to go as a pirate in the end.
　M: Yeah, I had the eye patch, and it wasn't hard to cut up a
　　shirt.
정답 (C)
해석 여: 결국은 해적으로 하기로 결정했구나.
　　남: 응, 안대를 가지고 있었고, 셔츠를 자르는 것도 어렵지도 않았어.
풀이 여자가 남자가 해적 복장을 한 것에 대해 언급하고 있으므로 (C)가
　　정답이다.
Words and Phrases  eye patch 안대

**2.** M: My sister's coding skills are unbelievable.
　W: Good for her! Is she hoping to become a site developer?
정답 (A)
해석 남: 내 여동생 코딩 실력은 믿기지 않을 정도야.
　　여: 잘됐네! 그녀는 웹 개발자가 되는 것을 희망하고 있니?
풀이 여자가 남자의 여동생을 칭찬하며 그녀가 웹 개발자로서 진로희망을 하는
　　지 물어보고 있으므로 (A)가 정답이다.

**3.** W: Part of the window's been brushed off, but it's tough work.
　M: The snow sure came down last night.
정답 (B)
해석 여: 창문 일부를 솔질로 털어냈는데 너무 고된 일이야.
　　남: 어젯밤 눈이 확실히 많이 오기는 했어.
풀이 여자가 창문을 솔질했다고 하였으므로 (B)가 정답이다. (A)는 'brush'를 빗
　　과 혼동하여 유도한 오답이다.
Words and Phrases  brush off (솔질로) 털다

**4.** M: How's Helena liking her work in the lab? Is it still fun?
　W: She's been staring into a microscope for hours on end,
　　but she likes it.
정답 (B)
해석 남: Helena는 실험실 일이 어떻대? 아직도 재미있대?
　　여: 몇 시간 동안 계속 현미경만 들여다보고 있었다는데, 그래도
　　　좋아하는 거 같아.
풀이 여자는 Helena가 오랫동안 현미경만 보고 있음에도 만족한다고 했으므로
　　(B)가 정답이다.
Words and Phrases  stare 빤히 쳐다보다, 응시하다

**5.** W: That dog's surfing! And in sunglasses, no less.
　M: My dog wouldn't set foot on one of those. He's not even
　　into the beach.
정답 (B)
해석 여: 저 개가 서핑하는 것 좀 봐! 선글라스도 쓰고 있어, 역시.
　　남: 나의 개는 절대로 보드 위에 올라가지 않을 거야. 바다에 관심조차
　　　없어.
풀이 개가 선글라스를 쓰고 서핑하는 모습을 언급했으므로 (B)가 정답이다.
　　(A)와 (C)는 개가 선글라스를 쓴 것은 맞지만 서핑은 하지 않고 있기
　　때문에 오답이다.
Words and Phrases  no less (놀람,감탄을 나타냄) 역시

**6.** M: What on earth is that racket?
　W: Ugh. It's the neighbors' kid. He got a drum kit for his
　　birthday.
정답 (C)
해석 남: 세상에 이게 무슨 시끄러운 소리야?
　　여: 에휴, 이웃집에 사는 애야. 그는 그의 생일로 드럼 세트를 선물로
　　　받았어.
풀이 남자가 소음에 대해 물어보자 여자는 이웃에 사는 아이가 생일선물로 드럼
　　세트를 받았다고 했으므로 (C)가 정답이다. (B) 같은 경우 'racket'을
　　(테니스 등의) 라켓이라고 잘못 해석했을 때 고를수 있는 오답이다.
Words and Phrases  racket 시끄러운 소리, 소음; (테니스 등의) 라켓

**7.** W: My thumb really hurts these days.

　M: ________________

　　　**(A) Does it hurt from texting?**

　　　(B) Where is my thumb drive?

　　　(C) Is there another pair of glasses?

　　　(D) When does your leg cast come off?

해석　여: 요즘 들어서 내 엄지손가락이 아파.

　　　남: ________________

　　　**(A) 문자해서 아픈 거 아니야?**

　　　(B) 내 플래시 드라이브가 어딨지?

　　　(C) 또 다른 안경 있어?

　　　(D) 네 다리 깁스는 언제 풀어?

풀이　여자가 자신의 엄지손가락이 요즘 들어서 아프다고 하자, 남자는 문자를 해서 그런 것이 아니냐는 이유를 드는 (A)가 정답이다.

Words and Phrases　thumb drive 플래시 드라이브 (컴퓨터의 휴대용 저장 장치)

**8.** M: Are you selling your old desk? I could buy it from you.

　W: ________________

　　　(A) This stool fits that old desk.

　　　**(B) You can just have it for free.**

　　　(C) I'll take the large one, please.

　　　(D) You'll see it in the bottom drawer.

해석　남: 오래된 네 책상 팔 거야? 내가 너한테서 사도 돼.

　　　여: ________________

　　　(A) 이 의자랑 오래된 책상이랑 잘 어울린다.

　　　**(B) 그냥 공짜로 가져도 돼.**

　　　(C) 내가 큰 거 가져갈게.

　　　(D) 맨 아래 서랍에서 찾을 수 있을 거야.

풀이　남자가 여자에게 오래된 책상을 팔 것인지 물어보고 구매의사를 밝히고 있다. 그러므로 여자가 그냥 무료로 가져가라는 (B)가 정답이다. (A)의 'stool'이나 (D)의 'drawer'는 책상과 연관시켜 연상하도록 유도한 오답이다.

Words and Phrases　stool (등받이와 팔걸이가 없는) 의자 | drawer 서랍

**9.** W: Why are you still on the computer, young man? It's past midnight.

　M: ________________

　　　(A) Could I go next time?

　　　(B) Is the computer working?

　　　(C) Are you ready for school?

　　　**(D) Can I have five more minutes?**

해석　여: 얘야, 왜 아직도 컴퓨터를 하는 거니? 자정이 넘었어.

　　　남: ________________

　　　(A) 다음 번에 가도 돼요?

　　　(B) 컴퓨터가 작동하나요?

　　　(C) 학교 갈 준비는 됐나요?

　　　**(D) 5분만 더하면 안 돼요?**

풀이　여자는 밤 12시가 넘었는데도 왜 남자가 아직도 컴퓨터를 하는지 궁금해하는 상황이다. 이에 남자는 5분만 더 하겠다는 (D)가 정답이다.

**10.** M: How do you think these sandals suit me?

　W: ________________

　　　**(A) They look pretty good.**

　　　(B) Sure, that suit looks nice.

　　　(C) Yes, I have some sandals.

　　　(D) We had a great time there.

해석　남: 이 샌들 나한테 어울리는 것 같아?

　　　여: ________________

　　　**(A) 정말 잘 어울리는 것 같아.**

　　　(B) 당연하지, 정장 멋지다.

　　　(C) 응, 나도 샌들 있어.

　　　(D) 거기서 좋은 시간을 보냈어.

풀이　남자가 샌들이 본인한테 잘 어울리는지에 대한 여자의 답변으로 (A)가 정답이다. (B)의 경우 'suit'를 명사인 정장으로 해석하여 선택하게 되는 오답이다.

Words and Phrases　suit 신사복[숙녀복] 정장; 어울리다

**11.** W: Where is the wedding going to be held?

　M: ________________

　　　(A) That kind of weather is perfect.

　　　**(B) The venue hasn't been decided yet.**

　　　(C) They are getting married in October.

　　　(D) This January is their third anniversary.

해석　여: 결혼식은 어디에서 하는 거야?

　　　남: ________________

　　　(A) 그런 날씨면 완벽하지.

　　　**(B) 아직 장소는 미정이야.**

　　　(C) 그들은 10월달에 결혼한대.

　　　(D) 이번 1월이 그들의 결혼 3주년이래.

풀이　결혼식을 어디서 하는지 묻는 여자의 말에 남자의 아직 정해지지 않았다는 답변 (B)가 정답이다.

Words and Phrases　venue 장소

**12.** M: Do you happen to have a pen on you?

　W: ________________

　　　**(A) Sure do. Here you go.**

　　　(B) Pardon me. That's my pen.

　　　(C) Never. You should pin it up.

　　　(D) Certainly. It's much appreciated.

해석　남: 혹시 펜 가지고 계신가요?

　　　여: ________________

　　　**(A) 그럼요. 여기요.**

　　　(B) 실례지만 그건 제 펜이에요.

　　　(C) 절대로요. 핀으로 고정시키세요.

　　　(D) 물론이죠, 감사합니다.

풀이　남자가 펜이 있냐고 여자에게 물어보자 흔쾌히 건네주는 (A)가 정답이다. (C)는 지문의 'pen'과 혼동할 수 있는 'pin'을 언급하여 유도하는 오답이다.

**13.** W: Why is your dog sitting right by me with those big eyes?

    M: _________________

      (A) They do not get along with cats.

      (B) She sensed he was quite hungry.

      (C) We often walk in the rain together.

      **(D) He thinks you're going to feed him.**

해석 여: 왜 너의 개는 그렇게 큰 눈으로 내 옆에 앉아있는 거야?

    남: _________________

      (A) 그들은 고양이들이랑 사이가 별로 안 좋아.

      (B) 그녀는 그가 상당히 배가 고픈 것을 감지했어.

      (C) 우리는 자주 빗길을 같이 걸어.

      **(D) 그는 네가 먹이를 주려는 줄 아는 거 같아.**

풀이 여자가 개의 행동에 대해 묻자 남자가 왜 개가 그러한 행동을 하는지 언급하고 있는 (D)가 정답이다.

Words and Phrases  feed 먹이다

**14.** M: Have you seen this show? I love it. It's hilarious.

    W: _________________

      (A) I'll take you to see my show.

      (B) I can, and you're invited, too.

      (C) I have, and I didn't like it either.

      **(D) I've seen it and agree it's funny.**

해석 남: 너 이 공연 본 적 있어? 난 정말 좋았어. 진짜 웃겨.

    여: _________________

      (A) 내가 널 내 공연에 데려갈게.

      (B) 나도 할 수 있지, 너도 초대됐어.

      (C) 나도 봤어, 근데 나도 별로였어.

      **(D) 나도 봤어, 정말 재미있다는 것에 동의해.**

풀이 남자가 공연이 재미있었다고 하자 여자도 봤고 남자와 같은 의견이라는 (D)가 정답이다. (C)는 남성의 질문에 답하기는 하지만 재미있게 봤던 남성의 의견과 상충되므로 오답이다.

Words and Phrases  hilarious 아주 우스운, 재미있는

**15.** W: I can't believe how rude that clerk was to you just now.

    M: _________________

      (A) Can I get a refund on that item?

      (B) Were the employees there polite?

      **(C) Should I complain to his manager?**

      (D) Did you check at the information kiosk?

해석 여: 가게의 점원이 너한테 그렇게 무례하게 행동하다니 믿어지지 않아.

    남: _________________

      (A) 해당 품목에 대해 환불 받을 수 있나요?

      (B) 그쪽 직원들은 친절했어?

      **(C) 내가 그의 관리자한테 항의할까?**

      (D) 안내 부스에 가서 확인해 봤어?

풀이 여자가 점원의 무례한 행동에 대해 언급하고 이에 항의하는 것을 고려하는 남자의 답변 (C)가 정답이다.

Words and Phrases  information kiosk 안내소, 안내 부스

**16.** M: Do you still need help with that report for school?

    W: _________________

      (A) No one. I did it all myself.

      **(B) Not anymore. It's all done.**

      (C) Never again. I hate presentations.

      (D) No way. You should complain to her.

해석 남: 아직도 보고서 작성하는 데 도움이 필요해?

    여: _________________

      (A) 아무도. 나 혼자 했어.

      **(B) 이젠 아니야. 끝냈어.**

      (C) 두 번 다시는. 난 발표가 정말 싫어.

      (D) 안 돼. 넌 그녀한테 항의해야 해.

풀이 남자는 여자가 리포트 작성하는 데 도움이 필요하냐는 질문에 적절한 여자의 답변 (B)가 정답이다. (B)를 제외한 나머지 선지들은 남자의 질문에 대한 답을 전혀 하지 않고 관련 없는 말만 나열하고 있다.

## Part 3. Short Conversations (p.71)

**17.** W: Excuse me!

    M: Um, yeah?

    W: Don't you think your group is being awfully loud? This is a residential neighborhood.

    M: Well, it's a free country, and it's four in the afternoon.

    W: There are laws in this country, you know. This is noise pollution.

    M: Well, have you ever thought of moving?

    Q: What is the woman's purpose in the conversation?

      **(A) to ask a group to be quieter**

      (B) to make a complaint to the police

      (C) to get someone to help her move

      (D) to find directions to a neighborhood

해석 여: 저기요!

    남: 음, 네?

    여: 일행 분들이 너무 시끄러운 거 같지 않으세요? 여긴 주택가예요.

    남: 글쎄요, 이곳은 자유 국가고 오후 4시밖에 안 됐는데요.

    여: 아시다시피, 이 나라에는 법이 있어요. 이것은 소음 공해에요.

    남: 저, 그럼 이사 가실 생각은 안 해보셨나요?

    질문: 대화에서 여자의 목적은 무엇인가?

      **(A) 일행에게 좀 조용히 해달라고 하기 위해**

      (B) 경찰에게 항의를 제기하기 위해

      (C) 그녀의 이사를 도와줄 사람을 구하기 위해

      (D) 인근 지역으로 가는 길을 찾기 위해

풀이 여자가 남자의 일행이 주택가에서 소란스럽게 하여 조금만 정숙해달라는 요청을 하는 대화이므로 (A)가 정답이다. (B)의 경우 항의를 하는 것은 맞으나 그 대상이 경찰이기 때문에 혼동을 유도한 오답이다.

Words and Phrases  residential neighborhood 주택가

18. M: Want to make some popcorn?

W: Absolutely. Do we use the microwave, or…

M: No, we can just make it right here on the stove.

W: How does that work?

M: You just heat up some oil in a pan and dump some kernels in.

W: Doesn't that make the popcorn too oily?

Q: Where does this conversation most likely take place?

(A) in a kitchen

(B) in a living room

(C) at a movie theater

(D) at a home goods store

해석 남: 팝콘 같이 만들래?

여: 물론이지. 전자레인지 쓰면 돼? 아니면…

남: 아니, 그냥 여기 가스레인지 사용해서 만들면 돼.

여: 어떻게 하는 거야?

남: 프라이팬에 기름을 조금 데우고 옥수수 낟알들을 넣으면 돼.

여: 그렇게 하면 팝콘이 너무 기름지지 않아?

질문: 이 대화가 일어나는 장소로 가장 적절한 곳은 어디인가?

(A) 부엌에서

(B) 거실에서

(C) 영화관에서

(D) 가정용품점에서

풀이 남자가 여자에게 팝콘을 같이 만들자는 제안을 하고 어떻게 만들지에 대해서 논하고 있다. 조리법에 대해 대화를 나누고 있으므로 (A)가 정답이다.

Words and Phrases goods 상품, 제품


19. W: Are you coming to my play next week?

M: Oh, I didn't realize you were in a play. How great!

W: Yeah, I'm in a musical. I'm the lead!

M: Oh, how wonderful for you! Is the show on every night?

W: Thursday, Friday, and two shows each on Saturday and Sunday.

M: Wonderful. I'll definitely be there.

Q: What does the woman mean by "I'm the lead"?

(A) She talks first in the play.

(B) She plays the main character.

(C) She is becoming class president.

(D) She is on the cover of a newspaper.

해석 여: 다음주 내 공연에 오는 거지?

남: 아, 네가 공연에 출연하는 줄 몰랐어. 정말 잘 됐다!

여: 어, 뮤지컬 공연에 나와. 내가 주인공이야.

남: 오, 너 정말 멋지다! 매일 밤마다 공연하는 거야?

여: 목요일, 금요일에 하고 토요일, 일요일은 하루에 2회씩 해.

남: 멋지다. 반드시 갈 거야.

질문: 여자가 "내가 주인공이야"라고 말한 의도는 무엇인가?

(A) 그녀가 공연에서 첫 번째로 말을 한다.

(B) 그녀가 주연 배우를 연기한다.

(C) 그녀는 학급회장을 한다.

(D) 그녀가 신문 표지를 장식했다.

풀이 여자는 남자에게 자신이 다음주에 주연 배우로 뮤지컬 공연을 한다는 것을 언급하고 있는 상황이므로 (B)가 정답이다.

Words and Phrases lead (연극/영화 등의) 주인공, 주연


20. M: Hey Marnie.

W: Oh, hey Daniel. You're looking dressed up today.

M: We're going to a photo studio today for family photos. It's going to be a gift for my great-grandma's birthday.

W: Oh, that'll be nice. So is that after school?

M: No, during lunch. It's the only time my parents can get off.

W: Have a great time!

Q: When will the man go to a photo studio?

(A) in the evening

(B) on the weekend

(C) during lunchtime

(D) right after school

해석 남: 안녕 Marnie.

여: 어, 안녕 Daniel. 오늘 옷을 갖춰 입었네.

남: 오늘 사진관 가서 가족 사진을 찍을 거야. 증조할머니 생신 선물로 드릴 거야.

여: 와, 멋지다. 학교 끝나고 가는 거야?

남: 아니, 점심시간에. 부모님이 그때밖에 시간이 안되신다고 해서.

여: 좋은 시간 보내!

질문: 남자는 언제 사진관에 갈 것인가?

(A) 저녁에

(B) 주말에

(C) 점심시간에

(D) 학교 끝나고 바로

풀이 남자가 옷을 갖춰 입은 것을 여자가 언급하였고 이에 남자는 증조할머니 생신 선물로 가족사진을 드리기 위해 점심시간에 사진관을 간다고 했으므로 (C)가 정답이다. 여자가 학교 끝나고 사진관에 가는 것이냐고 물었으나 남성의 부모님이 점심시간밖에 안 된다고 언급했으므로 (D)는 혼동할 수 있는 오답이다.

Words and Phrases dress up 옷을 갖춰 입다, 격식을 차려 입다


21. W: So that comes to thirty-five fifty.

M: Here's my debit card.

W: And do you already have a membership? It gets you ten percent off all our books and stationery supplies.

M: I don't think I do.

W: It only takes 5 minutes to sign up over at customer service.

M: Maybe next time.

Q: What most likely is the woman's job?

(A) banker

(B) cashier

(C) librarian

(D) accountant

해석 여: 35달러 50센트입니다.

  남: 여기 제 체크카드요.

  여: 혹시 멤버십 있으세요? 도서와 문구류에서 10% 할인 받으실 수
    있으세요.

  남: 없는 거 같아요.

  여: 고객센터에서 5분 안에 가입 가능하세요.

  남: 다음에 할게요.

  질문: 가장 예상되는 여자의 직업은?

  (A) 은행원

  **(B) 계산원**

  (C) 사서

  (D) 회계사

**풀이** 여자가 남자에게 지불가격을 언급하면서 추가 할인 혜택을 받을 수 있는 멤
  버십 가입을 권유하고 있으므로 (B)가 정답이다.

**Words and Phrases** accountant 회계사

**22.** M: Darn. I forgot my wallet at home.

  W: Do you need some money for today?

  M: No, I think I can get by.

  W: Do you have your card for the subway?

  M: Ah, man. I guess not.

  W: Here. Take this. It's ten bucks to tide you over.

  Q: What is the man's problem?

  (A) He lost his money.

  **(B) He forgot his wallet.**

  (C) He missed the subway.

  (D) He left money on the subway.

**해석** 남: 이런. 집에 내 지갑을 놓고 왔네.

  여: 오늘 쓸 돈 필요해?

  남: 아니야, 그럭저럭 괜찮을 거 같아.

  여: 지하철에서 쓸 카드는 있어?

  남: 아 맞다, 없네.

  여: 여기, 가져가, 10달러면 해결될 거야.

  질문: 남자의 문제는 무엇인가?

  (A) 돈을 잃어버렸다.

  **(B) 지갑을 깜빡하고 가져오지 않았다.**

  (C) 지하철을 놓쳤다.

  (D) 지하철에 돈을 놓고 내렸다.

**풀이** 남자가 깜빡하고 자신의 지갑을 집에 놓고 왔다고 하자 여자는 오늘과 지하
  철에 쓸 돈은 있는지 물어보고 있는 상황이므로 (B)가 정답이다. 대화에서
  'subway'를 언급했기 때문에 남자의 문제를 지하철과 연관지어서 생각할
  수 있는 (C)와 (D)는 혼동을 유도한 오답이다.

**23.** W: I'm trying to get into the comics business. Any ideas about
  how to make money?

  M: Do you write your own comics?

  W: Kind of. I take old stories and reimagine them with different endings.

  M: So you need a business partner?

  W: You like marketing. I thought you'd be interested.

  M: I'd love to help you with that. Let's see your work.

  Q: What will the woman most likely do next?

  (A) look at the man's drawings

  (B) write a new ending for a story

  **(C) show some comics to the man**

  (D) go to a market to look for comics

**해석** 여: 만화 사업에 뛰어들려고 하는데 혹시 돈 벌 수 있는 아이디어 없어?

  남: 직접 만화 만드는 거야?

  여: 어느 정도. 옛날 얘기를 가져다 다른 결말을 생각해 내.

  남: 사업 파트너 필요하겠네?

  여: 너 마케팅 좋아하지 않아? 나는 네가 관심있어 할 것 같았는데.

  남: 기꺼이 도와줄게. 네 작품 좀 보자.

  질문: 여자가 다음으로 가장 할 행동은 무엇인가?

  (A) 남자가 그린 그림을 본다

  (B) 이야기의 새로운 결말을 쓴다

  **(C) 남자에게 몇 개의 만화를 보여준다**

  (D) 시장에 가서 만화를 찾아본다

**풀이** 여자가 만화 사업을 시작하려고 하는데 남자에게 조언 및 동업을 제안하는
  상황이다. 남자가 동업을 수락하면서 여자의 작업물을 보자고 하므로 (C)가
  정답이다. (D)는 'marketing'과 'market'의 혼동을 유도한 오답이다.

**Words and Phrases** marketing 마케팅 | market 시장

**24.** M: I'm really looking forward to the school dance tomorrow.

  W: I don't know if I want to go.

  M: How come? I thought you loved dancing.

  W: Yeah, I do, but… Ben said he's not going. And dance music
  is always so silly anyway.

  M: Aha! So you like Ben, then.

  W: Hey, I didn't say that.

  Q: What is true about the woman?

  **(A) She may not go to a dance.**

  (B) She cannot dance anymore.

  (C) She does not want to see Ben.

  (D) She generally enjoys dance music.

**해석** 남: 내일 있을 학교 무도회 정말 기대된다.

  여: 난 가고 싶은 건시 잘 모르겠어.

  남: 왜? 난 너 춤추는 거 좋아하는 줄 알았는데.

  여: 응, 맞아, 근데… Ben이 그러는데 걔는 안 간대. 어차피
    무도곡(댄스음악)은 항상 유치했어.

  남: 아하! 그럼 너 Ben 좋아하는구나.

  여: 야, 내가 언제 그랬어.

  질문: 여자에 대해서 사실인 것은 무엇인가?

  **(A) 여자는 무도회에 안 갈 수도 있다.**

  (B) 여자는 더 이상 춤을 출 수 없다.

  (C) 여자는 Ben을 보고 싶지 않다.

  (D) 여자는 기본적으로 무도곡을 좋아한다.

**풀이** 춤추는 것을 좋아하는 여자가 Ben때문에 학교 무도회에 가는 것을 망설인
  다고 했으므로 (A)가 정답이다.

**Words and Phrases** silly 어리석은, 바보 같은; 우스꽝스러운, 유치한

**25.** W: Hey, look! It's the first few flakes of the year.

M: Ah, it's only a light dusting.

W: Nah, I think it's enough to make a snowball.

M: Should we have a snowball fight?

W: What are we, five?

M: Hey fifteen-year-olds can have fun, too. Shouldn't we at least go out and see it?

Q: What is the main topic of the conversation?

  (A) fine dust

  **(B) first snow**

  (C) slushy streets

  (D) snowman outside

해석 여: 야, 저기 좀 봐! 올해 첫 눈송이야.

남: 에이, 그냥 가볍게 흩날리는 정도네.

여: 아니야, 충분히 눈뭉치는 만들 정도야.

남: 우리 눈싸움 할까?

여: 우리가 무슨 다섯 살이야?

남: 야 열다섯짜리도 즐길 수 있지. 적어도 나가서 보기라도 하자.

질문: 대화의 요지는 무엇인가?

  (A) 미세먼지

  **(B) 첫 눈**

  (C) 눈 녹은 질퍽한 거리

  (D) 밖에 있는 눈사람

풀이 여자가 올해 첫 눈송이를 언급했으므로 (B)가 정답이다. (A)는 대화에서 'light dusting'을 가볍게 흩날리는 눈으로 해석하지 않고 'fine dust' 미세 먼지로 해석했을 때 고를 수 있는 오답이다.

Words and Phrases  flake 눈송이 (=snowflakes) | dust (고운 가루를) 뿌리다 | fine dust 미세먼지 | slushy 눈 녹은, 진흙탕의, 진창의

**26.** M: Minji, are you a whitewater rafting guide?

W: Well, just since last summer.

M: I was hoping to try out whitewater rafting.

W: Is this about discounts? I work for my uncle, so I have no control over that.

M: Oh, no. Not that. I was just hoping you could show me how to do it.

W: Oh, that? Yeah, that I could do.

Q: What does the man ask the woman to do?

  (A) help him to build a raft

  (B) ask her uncle for a discount

  **(C) teach him whitewater rafting**

  (D) get tickets for whitewater rafting

해석 남: 민지야, 네가 급류 래프팅 안내 요원이야?

여: 응, 저번 여름부터.

남: 나도 급류 래프팅 해보고 싶었는데.

여: 할인해 달라는 거 아니지? 나는 삼촌 밑에서 일하는 거라 아무 권한도 없어.

남: 아니, 그런 거 아니야. 난 단지 네가 하는 방법을 알려줬으면 해서 그랬어.

여: 아, 그럼, 당연히 알려주지.

질문: 남자가 여자에게 하도록 제안한 것은 무엇인가?

  (A) 뗏목을 만드는 것 돕기

  (B) 삼촌에게 할인 부탁하기

  **(C) 급류 래프팅 강습하기**

  (D) 급류 래프팅 티켓 받기

풀이 대화에서 남자가 여자가 급류 래프팅 안내 요원인 것을 알고 강습을 부탁 했으므로 (C)가 정답이다. (A)는 'rafting' 과 'raft'를 혼동하여 고를 수 있 는 오답이다.

Words and Phrases  whitewater 급류 | rafting 래프팅 | raft 뗏목

**Part 4.** Talks (p.72)

**[27-28]**

W: Here is today's weather for Luzon Island. Temperatures will remain in the mid-twenties to low-thirties on the island, with heavy rainfall all throughout the day. Luzon is still under a tropical storm warning. If you live in an area susceptible to flooding, please take appropriate action. Sea travel is not advised today, so those residents visiting outer islands should rearrange their plans. Residents should also rearrange important household goods to the highest location possible.

**27.** What is the main topic of the announcement?

  (A) cloudy skies

  (B) high temperatures

  (C) the aftermath of a flood

  **(D) a tropical storm warning**

**28.** According to the speaker, what should residents do?

  (A) go to underground shelters

  (B) swim only at marked beaches

  (C) wear sunscreen before going out

  **(D) move valuable items in their homes**

해석 여: Luzon섬의 오늘의 날씨입니다. 온도는 20도 중반에서 30도 초반을 유 지하며, 하루 종일 폭우가 쏟아질 거 같습니다. Luzon에는 아직도 열대 폭 풍우 주의보가 내려져 있습니다. 홍수에 취약한 지역에 거주하시면, 필요한 조치를 취해주십시오. 선박 여행은 오늘은 권고하지 않으며 외곽에 있는 섬 을 방문하시는 주민분들은 계획 변경 바랍니다. 또한 주민분들께서는 중요 한 가정용품들을 높은 곳으로 재위치 시켜주시길 바랍니다.

27. 안내 방송의 요지는 무엇인가?

  (A) 구름 낀 하늘

  (B) 높은 온도

  (C) 홍수의 여파

  **(D) 열대 폭풍우 주의보**

28. 화자에 의하면, 주민들이 해야 할 일은?

  (A) 지하 대피소로 피신

  (B) 표지된 해변에서만 수영

  (C) 외출 시 자외선 차단제 바르기

  **(D) 집에서 귀중품 재위치시키기**

**풀이** 안내 방송의 요지는 Luzon 섬의 열대 폭풍우 주의보 발령과 주민들의 안전을 위한 행동수칙이므로 27번의 정답은 (D)이다.

발표에서 홍수에 대비하여 가정용품들을 높은곳으로 재위치시키는것을 권고하였으므로 28번의 정답은 (D)이다.

**Words and Phrases**  susceptible ~에 민감한, 걸리기 쉬운 | advise 조언하다,권고하다 | aftermath 여파, 후유증 | underground shelter 지하 대피소 | mark 위치를 표시하다

**[29-30]**
M: For an easy frittata, all you need is six eggs, a quarter cup of heavy cream, 1 cup of grated cheese, and 2 cups of raw vegetables or meat. Cook your meat and hardest vegetables for about 8 minutes. Then, add the other vegetables, topped with a layer of grated cheese. Beat the eggs with the cream, and pour them over the vegetables. Note: It helps to use a cast iron or nonstick pan instead of stainless steel.

**29.** Which is NOT a listed ingredient?
   **(A) boiled eggs**
   (B) heavy cream
   (C) grated cheese
   (D) raw vegetables

**30.** Which is an instruction?
   **(A) Use a nonstick pan.**
   (B) Stuff the eggs with cheese.
   (C) Add pepper and salt to taste.
   (D) Wait for the vegetables to harden.

**해석** 남: 간편한 프리타타를 만들기 위해선, 단, 달걀 6개, 유지분이 많은 크림 1/4컵, 갈은 치즈 1컵 그리고 생야채 또는 육류 2컵이 필요합니다. 육류와 딱딱한 채소를 8분 정도 요리해주세요. 다음, 나머지 야채를 추가해주시고, 위에다가 갈은 치즈를 한 겹으로 뿌려주세요. 크림과 함께 달걀을 섞이주시고 야채 위에 뿌려주시면 됩니다.
참고: 스테인리스 강 대신 무쇠 또는 눌어 붙지 않는 팬을 사용하시면 편리합니다.

29. 열거된 재료 중 언급되지 않은 것은 무엇인가?
   (A) 삶은 계란
   (B) 유지분이 많은 크림
   (C) 갈은 치즈
   (D) 생 야채

30. 다음 중 지시사항은 어떤 것인가?
   (A) 눌어 붙지 않는 팬 사용하기
   (B) 치즈로 계란 채워 넣기
   (C) 맛을 내기 위해 후추와 소금 넣기
   (D) 야채들이 딱딱하게 굳을 때까지 기다리기

**풀이** 남자가 프리타타 재료로 달걀 6개를 언급했지만 삶은 계란이라고는 하지 않았으므로 29번의 정답은 (A)이다.

남자가 마지막에 참고사항으로 눌어붙지 않는 팬을 사용할 것을 권고했으므로 30번의 정답은 (A)이다. (D)는 딱딱한 채소를 육류와 함께 요리하라는 지시를 혼돈한 오답이다.

**Words and Phrases**  frittata 채소,치즈 등을 달걀에 섞어 만든 오믈렛 | heavy cream 유지분이 많은 크림 | grated 갈은 | beat 휘저어 섞다 | cast iron 무쇠

---

## SECTION II  READING AND WRITING

**Part 5.** Picture Description (p.74)

**31.** This region of the country is ___________ for its apples. People come from all over to taste them.
   (A) happy
   (B) tender
   (C) abrupt
   **(D) famous**

**해석** 이 나라의 지역은 사과로 유명합니다. 여러 곳에서 사람들이 맛보기 위해 옵니다.
   (A) 행복한
   (B) 부드러운
   (C) 갑작스러운
   **(D) 유명한**

**풀이** 특정 지역이 사과로 유명해서 사람들이 맛보러 온다는 의미를 완성하기 위해서는 (D)가 정답이다.

**Words and Phrases**  tender (고기 등이) 부드러운 | abrupt 갑작스러운

**32.** My amazing dad raised three kids on his own. I will always _________ him as a role model.
   **(A) look up to**
   (B) catch sight of
   (C) come out with
   (D) stay away from

**해석** 나의 멋진 아버지는 혼자서 자식 셋을 키웠어. 나는 항상 그를 우러러볼 거야.
   (A) 우러러보다
   (B) 언뜻 보다
   (C) 보여주다
   (D) 가까이하지 않다

**풀이** 아버지 혼자서 자식을 양육한 것에 대해 존경한다라는 의미를 완성해야 하므로 (A)가 정답이다.

**Words and Phrases**  catch sight of 흘끗 보다 | come out with ~을 사람들에게 선보이다

**33.** For my graduation exam, I have to _________ over 400 terms. It's too much to remember!
   (A) run by heart
   (B) run by clock
   **(C) learn by heart**
   (D) learn by clock

해석 나의 졸업 시험을 위해, 400 용어나 **외워야 돼**. 외울 게 너무 많아!

    (A) 틀린 표현

    (B) 틀린 표현

    **(C) 외다, 암기하다**

    (D) 틀린 표현

풀이 기말고사를 위해 외워야 하게 너무 많다는 의미를 완성하기 위해서는 '암기하다'라는 의미를 가진 ' learn by heart'를 쓸 수 있으므로 (C)가 정답이다.

Words and Phrases  learn by heart 외우다


**34.** She promised to be there at noon, and she arrived

_______________ on time—12 o'clock sharp.

    **(A) right**

    (B) stuck

    (C) raced

    (D) straight

해석 그녀는 정오에 거기 있겠다고 약속했고, 그녀는 12시 **정각**에 도착했어.

    **(A) 딱 제시간에**

    (B) 빠져

    (C) 쏜살같이 가다

    (D) 곧장

풀이 그녀가 정시에 도착했다는 의미를 완성하는 (A)가 정답이다.

Words and Phrases  stuck on ~에 빠져 [미쳐, 반해]


**35.** I need to run to the washroom. Can you _______________ my

seat? I'll be back in a minute.

    (A) free

    (B) give

    **(C) save**

    (D) make

해석 제가 화장실에 가야 돼서요. 제 자리 좀 **맡아주시겠어요?** 1분 안에 돌아올게요.

    (A) 석방시키다, 풀어주다

    (B) 주다

    **(C) 남겨두다**

    (D) 만들다

풀이 화장실에 다녀오는 동안 자리를 맡아달라는 의미를 완성하기 위해선 '나중에 쓰려고 남겨 두라'라는 의미를 가지는 'save'를 사용할 수 있으므로 (C)가 정답이다.

Words and Phrases  free 석방시키다, 풀어주다


**36.** Kathy's feeling a bit under _______________, so she's not

going to school today.

    (A) the cloud

    (B) the thunder

    **(C) the weather**

    (D) the lightning

해석 Kathy가 **몸이 안 좋은**가 봐, 그래서 오늘은 학교에 가지 않을 거야.

    (A) 틀린 표현

    (B) 틀린 표현

    **(C) 몸이 좀 안 좋은**

    (D) 틀린 표현

풀이 Kathy가 등교하지 않는 이유는 몸이 아파서인데 '몸이 좀 안 좋은'이라는 뜻의 숙어인 'under the weather' (C)가 정답이다.

Words and Phrases  washroom 화장실


**Part 6.** Sentence Completion (p.76)

**37.** What _______________ the reason for the school to change its

policy on soda?

    **(A) was**

    (B) were

    (C) could

    (D) might

해석 그 학교가 탄산음료에 대한 정책을 바꾼 이유가 뭐**였어?**

    **(A) Be동사 3인칭 과거형 단수**

    (B) Be동사 3인칭 과거형 복수

    (C) ~할 수 있었다

    (D) ~할 것 같다

풀이 탄산음료에 대한 정책이 이미 바뀐 상태이다. 과거에 있었던 일이고 '정책'이라는 뜻을 가진 'policy'가 단수이므로 (A)가 정답이다.

Words and Phrases  policy 정책


**38.** That's the best movie _______________ ever seen.

    (A) that I

    **(B) I have**

    (C) have I

    (D) when that

해석 그것은 **내가 본** 영화 중에 최고였어.

    (A) 저 내가

    **(B) 나는 있다**

    (C) 있다 나는

    (D) 언제 저

풀이 내가 본 영화 중 최고였다는 의미로 'I have ever seen'이라는 표현을 사용해야 하므로 (B)가 정답이다.


**39.** I met her when I _______________ to Taiwan last year.

    **(A) went**

    (B) visited

    (C) were been

    (D) have been

해석 나는 작년에 대만 **갔을** 때 그녀를 만났다.

    **(A) 가다**

    (B) 방문하다

    (C) 틀린 표현

    (D) ~해 왔다

풀이 나는 그녀를 대만에 갔을 때 만났다는 것을 말하기 위해 'went to'라는 표현을 사용할 수 있으므로 (A)가 정답이다. 'Visited'도 'went'와 비슷한 의미이지만 'visited' 뒤에 'to'라는 전치사가 나올 수 없어서 오답이다.

**40.** Martin went home sick. He _______________ feeling
very well.

    (A) been

    **(B) wasn't**

    (C) weren't

    (D) not been

**해석** Martin은 아파서 집에 갔어. 그는 몸이 좋지 **않다고** 말했어.

    (A) Be동사 과거분사형

    (B) Be동사 3인칭 과거형 단수 부정형

    (C) Be동사 3인칭 과거형 복수 부정형

    (D) Be동사 과거분사 부정형

**풀이** 'Martin은 몸이 안 좋아서 이미 집에 갔다.'의 시제는 과거형이고 Martin은
한 명이기 때문에 (B)가 정답이다.

**41.** You'll be _______________ with a thicker pillow. I'll get you
one.

    (A) nearly so comfortable

    **(B) much more comfortable**

    (C) more much comfortable

    (D) nearly much comfortable

**해석** 너는 두꺼운 베개를 사용하면 **훨씬 더 편할 거야.** 내가 하나 가져다 줄게.

    (A) 거의 편안한

    (B) 훨씬 더 편한

    (C) 더 훨씬 편한

    (D) 거의 더 편한

**풀이** 두꺼운 베개가 있으면 훨씬 더 편할 거라는 문장이다. '훨씬 더 편한'이라
는 뜻을 가진 'much more comfortable'을 사용해야 하므로 (B)가 정답
이다.

Words and Phrases  comfortable 편한

**42.** All the kids _______________ town enjoy playing in that park.

    **(A) in**

    (B) to

    (C) on

    (D) for

**해석** 도시에 있는 모든 아이들은 저 공원에서 노는 것을 즐긴다.

    (A) ~안에, ~에서

    (B) ~쪽에, ~로

    (C) ~위에

    (D) ~위해

**풀이** 도시에 살고 있는 아이들에 대해 이야기 하고 있는 중이다. 도시 안에 살
고 있는 아이들이라는 뜻을 가진 'in'이라는 단어를 사용하면 되므로 (A)
가 정답이다.

**43.** He was _______________ disappointed that he did not win
the prize.

    (A) bitter

    (B) bitters

    **(C) bitterly**

    (D) bittering

**해석** 그는 자신이 상을 타지 못해서 **몹시** 서운했다.

    (A) 쓰다

    (B) 틀린 표현

    (C) 몹시

    (D) 틀린 표현

**풀이** 그는 자신이 상을 타지 못해서 아쉬워 하고 있다. '서운하다' 앞에는 부사를
사용해야 하므로 (C)가 정답이다.

Words and Phrases  bitterly 몹시

**44.** I wonder whether _______________ his driving test or not.

    (A) passed Jim

    **(B) Jim passed**

    (C) did Jim pass

    (D) Jim had pass

**해석** 나는 Jim이 운전면허 시험을 **통과했는지** 못했는지 궁금하다.

    (A) 통과했다 Jim

    (B) Jim이 통과했다

    (C) Jim이 통과했나

    (D) 틀린 표현

**풀이** Jim이 운전면허 시험을 통과했는지 못했는지에 대해 묻는 질문이다. 주어
가 먼저 와야 하므로 (B)가 정답이다.

Words and Phrases  pass 통과하다, 합격하다

**45.** I am completely _______________ by this artwork. I'd like to
learn more about it.

    (A) intrigue

    (B) intrigues

    **(C) intrigued**

    (D) intriguing

**해석** 나는 그 미술작품이 아주 **흥미롭다고 생각한다.** 나는 그것에 대해 더
배우고 싶다.

    (A) 흥미를 불러일으키다

    (B) 흥미를 불러일으키다 (3인칭 단수)

    (C) 흥미롭다 생각하다

    (D) 흥미로운

**풀이** 수동태 문장이며, 어떤 것이 흥미롭다고 생각한다는 의미로 'intrigued by'
라는 표현을 사용해야 하므로 (C)가 정답이다.

Words and Phrases  intrigue 흥미를 불러일으키다

**46.** If _______________ it would be raining, we never would have
started this hike.

    (A) had we known

    **(B) we had known**

    (C) known we had

    (D) had known we

**해석** **우리가** 만약 비가 온다는 것을 **알았더라면,** 이 등산을 시작하지 않았을 것
이다.

    (A) 우리가 알았더라면 (If가 생략된 경우)

    (B) 우리가 알았더라면

    (C) 틀린 표현

    (D) 틀린 표현

**풀이** 가정법 과거완료형 문장이며, '우리가 만약에 알았더라면'이라는 의미를 가
진 'If we had known'을 사용할 수 있으므로 (B)가 정답이다.

**[47–48]**

**47.** What is the main purpose of the sign?

(A) to clarify visitors' rights

**(B) to outline rules for visitors**

(C) to explain how to register for a visit

(D) to notify visitors of new park features

**48.** According to the sign, which of the following is true?

(A) Snacks are sold at the park.

(B) Pet rabbits are permitted entry.

(C) Vaccinations are conducted at the site.

**(D) Up to 15 dogs can enter simultaneously.**

**해석**

> Cadron 공원에 오신 걸 환영합니다!
>
> 1) 접종 및 등록된 반려견 및 보호자만 입장 가능합니다.
> 2) 한번에 최대 15마리의 개만 수용할 수 있습니다.
> 3) 반려견들은 항상 보호자의 시야에 있어야 합니다.
> 4) 보호자들은 쓰레기를 즉시 처리해야 합니다.
> 5) 음식물 섭취 (사람과 개 모두)를 금합니다.

47. 안내판의 주목적은 무엇인가?

(A) 방문객의 권리를 명확하게 하기 위해

(B) 규정을 서술하기 위해

(C) 방문 등록 하는 법을 설명하기 위해

(D) 방문객들에게 공원의 새로운 특징을 알리기 위해

48. 표지판에 따르면 다음 중 사실인 것은 무엇인가?

(A) 공원에서 간식을 판매한다.

(B) 반려토끼의 출입을 허가한다.

(C) 공원에서 백신 접종을 한다.

(D) 동시에 15마리의 개가 입장할 수 있다.

**풀이** 안내판의 목적은 공원 내 지켜야할 수칙을 알리는 것으로 47번의 정답은 (B)이다.

안내판의 두 번째 규칙에 의하면 한 번에 15마리의 개를 수용할 수 있다고 했으므로 48번의 정답은 (D)이다.



Words and Phrases  canine 개, 개의 | at the site 현장의, 현지의 | simultaneously 동시에

**[49–51]**

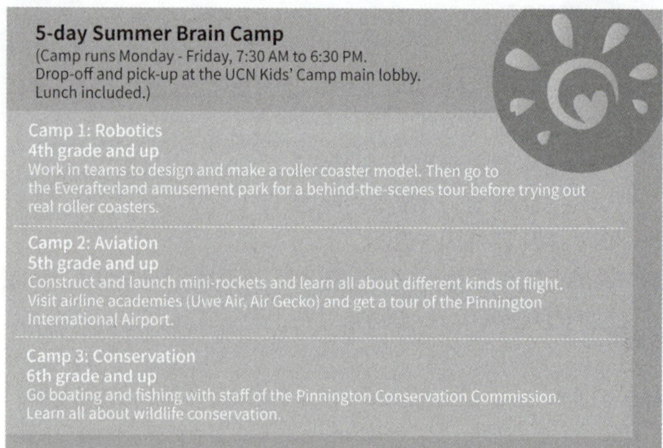


**49.** How many hours do kids spend in each camp in total?

(A) 40

(B) 45

**(C) 55**

(D) 60

**50.** Which experience is NOT offered at the camps?

**(A) sitting in a rocket**

(B) taking a boat ride

(C) touring an airport

(D) riding a roller coaster

**51.** Who would most likely benefit from Camp 3?

(A) a fifth grade student

**(B) a student who likes nature**

(C) someone wanting to windsurf

(D) someone interested in art history

**해석**

> 5일 여름 뇌 캠프
>
> (월요일부터 금요일까지 오전 7:30부터 오후 6:30까지
> UCN 어린이 캠프 메인 로비에서 자녀를 내려주시고 데려가시면 됩니다.
> 점심 포함.)
>
> 캠프 1: 로봇 공학
> 4학년 이상
> 조별로 롤러코스터 모델을 설계 및 제조. 그런 다음, Everafterland 놀이 공원에 방문하여 무대 뒤를 투어 후 실제 롤러코스터 탑승.
>
> 캠프 2: 항공
> 5학년 이상
> 미니 로켓 조립과 발사 그리고 여러 종류의 비행에 대해 공부.
> 항공사 연수원 (Uwe항공, Gecko 항공) 방문과 Pinnington 국제공항 투어.
>
> 캠프 3: 보존
> 6학년 이상
> Pinnington 보존위원회 관계자와 뱃놀이 그리고 낚시.
> 야생동물 보호에 대해 공부.

49. 아이들이 캠프에서 참여하는 총 시간은?
    (A) 40
    (B) 45
    (C) 55
    (D) 60

50. 캠프에서 제공하지 않는 경험은 무엇인가?
    (A) 로켓 타기
    (B) 배 타기
    (C) 공항 투어
    (D) 롤러코스터 타기

51. 캠프 3에 의해 가장 많은 혜택을 볼 사람은 누구인가?
    (A) 5학년 학생
    (B) 자연을 좋아하는 학생
    (C) 윈드서핑을 하고 싶은 사람
    (D) 미술사에 관심있는 사람

**풀이** 5일짜리 캠프이고 하루에 오전 7:30부터 오후 6:30까지라고 했으므로 49번의 정답은 (C)이다.

(B), (C), (D)는 홍보물에 언급되는 내용이지만 로켓 타기는 캠프에서 제공하지 않는 프로그램이므로 50번의 정답은 (A)이다.

캠프3은 뱃놀이, 낚시 그리고 야생동물 보호와 관련된 프로그램으로 가장 혜택을 많이 볼 사람은 자연을 좋아하는 학생이므로 51번의 정답은 (B)이다.

[52-55]

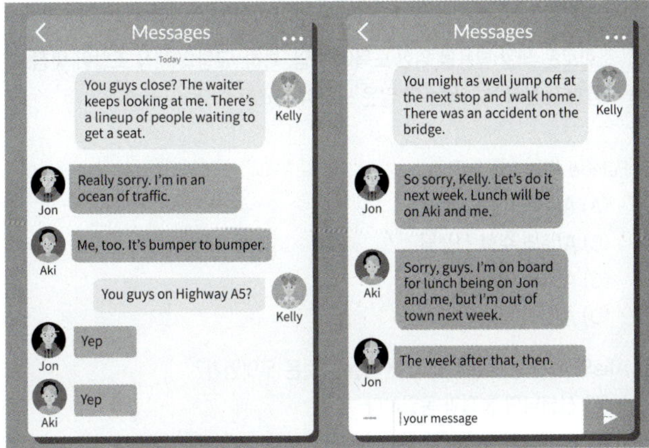


52. Where is Kelly most likely writing from?
    (A) a car
    (B) a bus
    (C) a cafe
    (D) a bookstore

53. What does Kelly suggest Jon and Aki do?
    (A) go home
    (B) go by the sea
    (C) take Highway A5
    (D) walk to the bridge

54. When does Jon first suggest meeting?
    (A) this afternoon
    (B) tonight
    (C) next week
    (D) in two weeks

55. What does Aki mean by "I'm on board for lunch being on Jon and me"?
    (A) He and Jon will make a new plan.
    (B) He and Jon are enjoying their day.
    (C) He and Jon will pay for Kelly's lunch.
    (D) He and Jon are committed to meeting.

**해석**

메세지
Kelly: 너희들 근처야? 종업원이 계속 나 쳐봐. 사람들이 자리에 앉으려고 줄 서서 기다리고 있어.
Jon: 진짜 미안해. 난 교통 체증 속에 있어.
Aki: 나도야. 차가 꽉 들어차 있어.
Kelly: 너희들 지금 A5 고속도로야?
Jon: 응
Aki: 응

메세지
Kelly: 다음 정류장에서 내려서 걸어서 집에 가는 게 좋을 것 같아. 다리에서 사고가 있었대.
Jon: 정말 미안해, Kelly. 다음주에 보자. 나랑 Aki가 점심 살게.
Aki: 미안해, 얘들아. 나도, 나랑 Jon이 점심 산다는 것에 동의해, 그런데 나 다음주에 교외로 나가.
Jon: 그럼 다다음주에.

52. Kelly가 문자를 보낼만한 가장 적절한 장소는 어디인가?
    (A) 차에서
    (B) 버스에서
    (C) 카페에서
    (D) 서점에서

53. Kelly는 Jon과 Aki에게 무엇을 하기를 추천하는가?
    (A) 집에 가기
    (B) 바닷가에 가기
    (C) A5 고속도로를 타기
    (D) 대교로 걸어가기

54. Jon은 처음에 다음 약속을 언제로 제안하는가?
    (A) 오늘 오후
    (B) 오늘 밤
    (C) 다음주
    (D) 2주 후

55. Aki가 "나도 나랑 Jon이 점심 산다는 것에 동의해"라고 말했는데 그 의미가
무엇인가?
    (A) 그와 Jon은 새로운 계획을 구성할 것이다.
    (B) 그와 Jon은 그들의 하루를 즐기고 있다.
    (C) 그와 Jon은 Kelly의 점심을 대신 지불해줄 것이다.
    (D) 그와 Jon은 만나는 것에 전념한다.

**풀이** 첫 문자메시지에서 Kelly가 종업원이 자신을 쳐다본다는 사실과 사람들이
앉기 위해 기다린다는 것을 미루어 볼 때 52번의 정답은 (C)이다.

Jon과 Aki가 길이 막혀 약속에 오지 못하자 Kelly는 다음 정류장에 내려 집
에 걸어갈 것을 권유하고 있으므로 53번의 정답은 (A)이다.

Kelly가 약속을 취소하자 Jon이 다음주로 모임을 미루자고 했으므로
54번의 정답은 (C)이다. 최초가 최종적으로는 2주 후에 만날 것을 약속했
기 때문에 (D)는 오답이다.

"I'm on board for lunch being on Jon and me"에서 'on board'는 '동
의한다'라고 해석할 수 있다. Aki는 Jon과 같이 Kelly의 점심값을 대신 내
줄 거라는 의미가 되므로 55번의 정답은 (C)이다.

**Words and Phrases** bumper to bumper 차가 꽉 들어찬 |
on board 동의하다 | committed to ~에 전념하는

**[56-59]**

| | Criterion | Student's Self Assessment | Teacher's Assessment |
|---|---|---|---|
| | **Name: Afia Olowe**    **Teacher: Mrs. Falade** | | |
| | **Project: Impressionism**    **Date Submitted: Dec 5, 2019** | | |
| 1 | Produced high-quality, original work. | 8 | 9 |
| 2 | Demonstrated knowledge of core principles. | 8 | 8.5 |
| 3 | Showed technical skill and craftsmanship in the medium used for this project. | 9 | 8.5 |
| 4 | Made an effort. Used time well during class to do the project. | 9 | 9 |

Rating 1 (lowest) to 10 (highest)
Projects with total teacher's scores of 38 and above will be displayed at the festival.

Overall impressions: Nice effort in using complementary colors. In particular, the bridge
has a nice color blend. Note that more work is needed on using various types of brushstrokes.

56. Who most likely, is Mrs. Falade?
    **(A) Afia's art teacher**
    (B) Afia's math teacher
    (C) Afia's history teacher
    (D) Afia's social studies teacher

57. What is true about Afia's total self-assessment score?
    (A) It is the same as that given by the teacher.
    **(B) It is 1 point lower than that given by the teacher.**
    (C) It is 1 point higher than that given by the teacher.
    (D) It means that Afia's project will be displayed at the
festival.

58. Which of the following is NOT included in the criteria?
    (A) originality
    (B) use of time
    (C) technical skill
    **(D) ability to collaborate**

59. The underlined "complementary" is most similar to:
    (A) whimsical
    (B) affordable
    (C) soft-hearted
    **(D) harmonizing**

**해석**

이름: Afia Olowe      선생님: Mrs. Falade
프로젝트: 인상주의      제출일: 2019년 12월 5일

| | 평가 항목 | 학생 자체 평가 | 선생님 평가 |
|---|---|---|---|
| 1 | 최상의 독창적인 작품을 창작해냄. | 8 | 9 |
| 2 | 핵심적인 원리들에 대한 이해도를 보임. | 8 | 8.5 |
| 3 | 해당 작품을 표현하기 위한 수단에 대한 기교 및 솜씨를 보임. | 9 | 8.5 |
| 4 | 노력을 함. 프로젝트를 위해 수업시간을 잘 활용. | 9 | 9 |

1 (최저)부터 10 (최고)까지 부여
선생님의 총점이 38 또는 그 이상인 작품들의 경우 축제 때 전시됨.

총평: 조화로운 색깔 활용을 위한 노력이 보임. 특히, 교량의 색상 조합이 멋짐.
여러 다양한 붓질에 대해서는 더 많은 노력이 필요함.

56. Falade 씨는 누구인가?
    **(A) Afia의 미술 선생님**
    (B) Afia의 수학 선생님
    (C) Afia의 역사 선생님
    (D) Afia의 사회 선생님

57. Afia의 자체 평가 총점에 대해 사실인 것은 무엇인가?
    (A) 선생님의 총점과 동일하다.
    **(B) 선생님의 총점보다 1점 더 낮다.**
    (C) 선생님의 총점보다 1점 더 높다.
    (D) Afia의 작품이 축제 때 전시 될 것이다.

58. 다음 중 평가항목에 포함되지 않는 것은 무엇인가?
    (A) 독창성
    (B) 시간 활용
    (C) 기술적인 능력
    **(D) 협업하는 능력**

59. 밑줄 친 단어 "complementary"와 가장 유사한 뜻을 가진 단어는:
    (A) 엉뚱한
    (B) (가격 등이) 적당한
    (C) 마음씨가 상냥한
    **(D) 조화를 이루는**

풀이 인상주의는 주로 미술 또는 음악계에서 쓰이는 용어이며 총평에서 다양한 종류의 붓질에 대한 노력이 필요하다는 것을 미루어 볼 때 Falade 씨는 Afia의 미술 선생님일 가능성이 높으므로 56번의 정답은 (A)이다.

학생 자체 평가의 총점은 34인 반면 선생님의 평가 총점은 35이므로 57번의 정답은 (B)이다. Afia의 작품은 선생님 평가 총점이 38점 또는 그 이상이 아니므로 (D)는 오답이다.

협업하는 능력을 제외하고는 평가지에 있는 평가항목이므로 58번의 정답은 (D)이다.

'상호보완적'이라는 뜻인 complementary는 '조화로운'이라는 의미도 갖고 있으므로 59번의 정답은 (D)이다.

Words and Phrases  whimsical 변덕스러운; 별난, 기발한 ┃ soft-hearted 마음씨 고운, 인정 많은 ┃ harmonizing 조화되는 ┃ complementary 상호보완적인

## Part 8. General Reading Comprehension (p.81)

[60-61]

Look in the lunchbox of an innocent school child and you may find within it a sandwich. Yet sandwiches themselves may not have such innocent origins. Named after John Montagu, the 4th Earl of Sandwich, one story about the sandwich is that it got its start due to gambling. As legend has it, Lord Sandwich was constantly at the card table. An addicted gambler, he would play night and day without taking a break to eat. He was looking for a way to eat meat without getting his hands dirty while he was playing cards. The solution his servants came up with was two pieces of toasted bread with salted beef in the middle.

Summary:

The sandwich may have been invented due to the gambling problem of the Earl of Sandwich. Lord Sandwich played cards for long hours with no   [A]  . breaks. He wanted to be able to eat without   [B]   the game. The solution was to put beef in between slices of bread.

**60.** Choose the most suitable word for blank [A], connecting the summary to the passage.

    **(A) dining**
    (B) music
    (C) school
    (D) looking

**61.** Choose the most suitable word for blank [B], connecting the summary to the passage.

    (A) losing
    (B) playing
    **(C) pausing**
    (D) legalizing

해석 순수한 학생의 도시락통을 보게 된다면 당신은 그 안에 샌드위치를 찾을 수도 있을 겁니다. 하지만 샌드위치 그것들은 순수한 유래를 가지지 않고 있을 수도 있습니다. 제4대 샌드위치 백작 존 몬태규의 이름을 딴 샌드위치의 한 이야기에 따르면 도박에 의해 시작됐다고 알려져 있습니다. 전설에 의하면 샌드위치 백작은 끊임없이 카드 게임 테이블에 앉았다고 알려졌습니다. 중독된 도박꾼으로서 식사도 하지 않고 밤낮 게임을 했다고 합니다. 그는 손을 더럽히지 않은 채 게임을 하면서 육류를 먹을 수 있는 방법을 찾고 있었습니다. 그의 하인들이 생각해낸 해결책은 바로 두 쪽의 구운 식빵 사이에 소금에 절인 쇠고기를 중간에 넣는 것이었습니다.

요약:
샌드위치는 샌드위치 백작의 도박문제 때문에 발명된 것일 수도 있습니다. 샌드위치 경은 수 시간 동안 <u>식사시간</u> 없이 카드놀이를 했습니다. 그는 게임을 <u>멈추지</u> 않고 먹기를 원했습니다. 해결책은 바로 쇠고기를 빵 조각 사이에 넣는 것이었습니다.

60. 본문과 요약본을 연결할 수 있는, 빈칸 [A]에 들어갈 가장 적절한 단어를 고르시오.

    (A) 식사
    (B) 음악
    (C) 학교
    (D) ~으로 보이는

61. 본문과 요약본을 연결할 수 있는, 빈칸 [B]에 들어갈 가장 적절한 단어를 고르시오.

    (A) 지다
    (B) 하다
    (C) 멈추다
    (D) 합법화 하다

풀이 본 지문에서 식사를 하지 않고 카드게임을 한다고 했으므로 60번의 정답은 (A)이다.

본 지문에서 샌드위치 백작은 식사도 하지 않고 밤낮 카드게임을 한다고 했<u>으므로</u>, 이로부터 그는 식사를 하면서도 카드를 끊임없이 하고 싶었을 거라는 추론을 할 수 있으므로 61번의 정답은 (C)이다.

Words and Phrases  legalizing 합법화하는

[1] Jaguars are large cats found in the Americas, from the Southern United States, to Mexico, Central America, and South America. The third largest species of cat after lions and tigers, jaguars range in length from 90 to 190 centimeters and in weight from 28 to 90 kilograms. These large <u>felines</u> roam the dense tropical rainforests and grasslands that comprise their main habitat.

[2] Jaguars behave much like tigers, but most closely resemble African leopards due to their spots. Jaguars are larger, however, and their spots differ from those of a leopard. While leopards have spots shaped like rings, the spots on jaguars are filled with dots in the middle.

[3] Skilled hunters, jaguars possess a bite more powerful than a lion's. The bite of a jaguar is so strong, in fact, that it can crush the prey's skull. A jaguar's prey includes any kind of animal found in its habitat. Because jaguars are powerful swimmers, they can hunt anything in the rivers of their habitat, from fish to turtles, and even a type of small alligators called caimans. And on land, their prey includes everything from tiny mice to large domestic cows and deer.

**62.** Which is the best title for the passage?
(A) Spotted Cats of the Plains
(B) The Cat with the Strongest Bite
**(C) Jaguars: Habitat, Appearance, Hunt**
(D) Wild Cats: Jaguars versus Leopards

**63.** Which of the following is mentioned about jaguars?
(A) Most are found in Mexico.
(B) They are hunted by alligators.
**(C) Their spots are filled with dots.**
(D) Many have golden brown coats.

**64.** The underlined "felines" is closest in meaning to:
**(A) cats**
(B) animals
(C) hunters
(D) mammals

**65.** According to the passage, which of the following can be inferred about jaguars?
(A) They cannot get fully wet.
(B) They very rarely climb trees.
**(C) They sometimes eat farm animals.**
(D) They can thrive on the plains of Africa.

해석 [1] 재규어는 아메리카 대륙, 미국 남부에서부터 멕시코, 중앙아메리카 그리고 남아메리카에서 발견되는 큰 고양이들입니다. 사자들과 호랑이들 다음으로 세 번째로 큰 고양이 종으로, 재규어는 길이로는 90에서 190cm 그리고 무게로는 28에서 90kg의 범주에 있습니다. 그들의 주요 서식지인 우거진 열대 우림과 초원에서 이런 큰 <u>고양잇과들이</u> 돌아다닙니다.

[2] 재규어들은 호랑이들과 비슷하게 행동하지만, 그들의 반점들 때문에 아프리카 표범들과 굉장히 유사합니다. 비록, 재규어들이 더 크지만, 그들의 반점들은 표범의 것과는 다릅니다. 표범들은 반지 모양의 반점들을 가지고 있으나, 재규어의 반점들은 중간이 꽉 찬 점들입니다.

[3] 능숙한 사냥꾼으로서, 재규어들은 사자에 비해 더 강력한 저작력을 가지고 있습니다. 재규어의 씹는 힘은 워낙 강해, 먹잇감의 두개골을 으스러뜨릴 정도입니다. 재규어의 먹잇감으로는 서식처에서 발견되는 모든 종류의 동물입니다. 재규어들은 강력한 수영꾼들이기 때문에 그들의 서식처의 강가에서도 생선부터 거북이까지, 심지어 카이만이라고 불리우는 작은 악어들까지 사냥합니다. 그리고 지상에서는 작은 쥐들부터 가축으로 사육되는 큰 젖소들과 사슴 또한 그들의 먹잇감에 포함됩니다.

62. 이 지문에 가장 적절한 제목은 무엇인가?
(A) 평지의 반점 있는 고양이들
(B) 가장 강력한 씹는 힘을 가진 고양이
(C) 재규어: 서식지, 생김새, 사냥
(D) 야생 고양이: 재규어 대 표범

63. 다음 중 재규어들에 대해서 언급된 것은 무엇인가?
(A) 대부분이 멕시코에서 발견된다.
(B) 악어들에 의해서 사냥된다.
(C) 그들의 반점들은 채워진 점들이다.
(D) 많은 이들이 금빛의 갈색 외피를 가진다.

64. 밑줄 친 단어 "felines"와 가장 유사한 뜻을 가진 단어는:
(A) 고양이들
(B) 동물들
(C) 사냥꾼들
(D) 포유류들

65. 다음 중 이 지문으로부터 재규어들에 대해 추론할 수 있는 것은 무엇인가?
(A) 그들은 완전히 젖을 수 없다.
(B) 그들은 매우 드물게 나무를 오른다.
(C) 그들은 때때로 농장 동물들을 먹는다.
(D) 그들은 아프리카 평지에서 살 수 있다.

**풀이** [1] 문단에서 재규어들의 서식지를 언급, 두 번째 단락에서는 그들의 외형에 대해 서술, 그리고 마지막 단락에서 그들의 먹잇감에 대해 언급하고 있으므로 62번의 정답은 (C)이다.

[2] 문단의 마지막 줄에 보면 표범들과는 달리 재규어들의 반점은 꽉 찬 점들이라고 서술하고 있으므로 63번의 정답은 (C)이다. 첫 번째 단락에서 재규어들의 서식지로 멕시코를 언급하고 있으나 대부분이 멕시코에서 발견된다는 서술은 하고 있지 않으므로 (A)는 유도된 오답이다.

첫 번째 단락 첫 번째 줄에서 재규어들은 큰 고양이라는 문장으로부터 추론 가능하므로 64번의 정답은 (A)이다.

[3] 문단의 마지막 줄에서 재규어들은 지상에서 가축으로 사육되는 젖소 또한 먹잇감으로 사냥한다고 언급한 것으로 보아 농장동물들을 먹는다고 추론할 수 있으므로 65번의 정답은 (C)이다.

**Words and Phrases**  plain 평원, 평지 | bite 무는 행위 | thrive 번성하다; 성공하다; 무럭무럭 자라다 | feline 고양잇과 동물

# MEMO

# MEMO

# MEMO

ITC 국제토셀위원회

# TOSEL
## 실전문제집 2

### HIGH JUNIOR